Books by Mike McAlary

Buddy Boys
Cop Shot
Good Cop, Bad Cop

GOOD COP, BAD COP

MIKE McALARY

POCKET **STAR** BOOKS

New York   London   Toronto   Sydney   Tokyo   Singapore

PHOTO INSERT CREDITS:

1. Courtesy of Joe Trimboli; 2. ©1993 Mitsu Yasukawa, *New York Newsday;* 3. ©1992 Dick Kraus, *New York Newsday;* 4. ©1993 Courtesy of *New York Newsday;* 5. *Daily News;* 6. *Daily News;* 7. *Daily News;* 8. ©1993 Dan Sheehan, *New York Newsday;* 9. AP/Wide World Photos; 10. *Daily News;* 11. AP/Wide World Photos; 12. AP/Wide World Photos; 13. *Daily News;* 14. ©1993 Jon Naso, *New York Newsday;* 15. ©1989 Fay Ellman, *N.Y. Law Journal*

A Pocket Star Book published by
POCKET BOOKS, a division of Simon & Schuster Inc.
1230 Avenue of the Americas, New York, NY 10020

ISBN: 978-1-4767-9207-1

First Pocket Books paperback printing December 1996

10 9 8 7 6 5 4 3 2 1

POCKET STAR BOOKS and colophon are registered trademarks of Simon & Schuster Inc.

Front cover photo credits: top, Betsy Herzog, *The New York Post*; bottom, Gigi Cohen, *Los Angeles Times*

Printed in the U.S.A.

For Kevin,
the brother even my dearest friends
call ''The Good McAlary''

ACKNOWLEDGMENTS

Alice, now more than ever. As I kind of died in a car accident in the middle of this story, this book could not have been written without the help of the incredible life-support system at Bellevue Hospital. Specifically, thank you Dr. Paul Glatt, head of the emergency room trauma team, for not going home early on September 18, 1993.

Unfortunately, this is a true story that did not need to happen. When police corruption is allowed to happen, every badge in the country is diminished. Joseph Trimboli would have preferred a simple, anonymous arrest at the end of the chase. Instead, he got an outrage and the formation of the first commission to investigate police corruption since Knapp. None of that would have transpired absent the fundamental bravery and dogged determination of one good cop. None of this would have ensued, unless Trimboli had the courage to step out of the shadows.

The support and love of my friends was instrumental in surviving to write this story. Dan Klores, Mark Kriegel, and Edward Hayes are great and grand friends. Bob Drury and J. Moses have been there every step of the way. Michael Daly, Jim Dwyer, and Denis Hamill taught me friendship is deeper than bar room camaraderie. No matter what my newspaper, Bill Boyle has remained a reliable, polished thinker. Denise Housman has always been a majestic buddy. Ken Moran taught me to walk, again. Abbie Goldman, Joanna Molloy, Karen Hunter, Rob Gearty, Juan Gonzalez, Ed Fay, Delores, and Hap Hairston were there even before I knew I needed them. Greg Lasak, Joe Hall, Sundance, and Richie Sica too. At the end, Ray Kelly.

Mort Zuckerman was more of a friend and ally than I

deserved or understood. Fred Drasner banged me over the head with decency.

You are nothing in the newspaper business without a generous, noble editor. So, as ever, thank you Don Forst and Jim Willse. Then Lou Colasuonno, and Martin Dunn. My late inventor, John Cotter, is always with me. So is Andrew Cuomo. Jim Catterson will not be forgotten. It is wonderful, too, to have found a new friend, Dona Chernoff. Thanks again, Flip and Jim Gucciardo. Of course to Ryan, Carla, and Mickey.

Joe Trimboli almost died in March 1993. Dr. Mitchell Lipton saved the hero cop for Nicole Perkins, and his story for the rest of us. We are all grateful.

GOOD COP, BAD COP

PROLOGUE

The Watcher is actually afraid of bad guys, especially when the bad guys are supposed to be the good guys. But fear, the Watcher knows, is good. It keeps you from making the last mistake. The Watcher is what the other Internal Affairs cops called Detective Sergeant Joseph Trimboli.

The Watcher's suspects attended his old school. They have drilled holes through the hearts of the same targets at the same shooting range. They mouthed the same oath. They have even stood beside him, with angry, white-knuckled hands crossed in ceremonial white gloves and grim faces reflected in polished black dress shoes at a dozen cop funerals.

They are carrying the same badge.

The Watcher is out there looking for bad cops. How scary can that be? But when rogue cops are abusing their position, their antennae are up. They are suspicious of people who are interested in them. They are wary of the Watcher.

So the Watcher is smart to be afraid. Tailing bad guys, especially cops, is not easy. It's not like on television. Let's say—for example—you see a guy leave his job, get in his car, and pull away. You just ease in behind and follow. Right? *Bullshit.* You can't do a simple-minded tail with real New York City rogues. You can't just follow him home from the station. He's going to blow traffic lights and see in his rearview mirror that you are following him.

If you're sniffing at a dirty cop you have to get his routine down a little piece every day and begin anticipating his moves. How does your suspect get home? Does he stop at a girlfriend's house? Where does she live? The Watcher wants to be waiting along that route. But you're not falling in behind him; that would be suicidal.

Long before Joseph Trimboli started looking at cops he had to learn some basic rules about ordinary criminals. He started walking a beat along some forsaken stretch of cracked inner-city sidewalk. He graduated to marriage, shoot-outs, medals, promotions, family problems, and loneliness. In the beginning Officer Trimboli would spot some creep in the street, tail the guy, and maybe catch the mutt robbing somebody at knifepoint. Sometimes Trimboli would even tell himself that the crook actually smelled bad. He'd study the suspect for a second and think, This guy doesn't smell right.

But the criminals also seemed to be able to smell the good guys around them. Cops say that when a good cop spots a crook, the cop gets pins and needles in his arms and legs. They have even nicknamed this wholly imagined allergy: Perp Fever.

When some creep breaks the law, you jump them. But if the bad guys are your colleagues, it's different. The same experts who coached you in how to spot slime, also taught them how to look out for you.

Each of you has a gun. He may be in uniform, you're always in plainclothes. If some trapped cop gets the chance, he's going to shoot his way out of the snare and kill you to cover his ass.

They will even make their own opportunities. That happened to two guys who worked in the Field Internal

Affairs Unit who got made during a surveillance. It was just luck that those watchers weren't shot to death. Two guys from Trimboli's office, following cops they suspected of dealing coke, were sitting in an unmarked automobile, a generic sedan that everybody knows is a cop car. The car's engine was running; cups of coffee were on the dashboard.

The bad guys, uniformed cops, spotted them. They've been made. Now these two geniuses from Internal Affairs didn't even have a portable police radio. One of the bad cops walked to a pay phone and dialed 911. He proceeds to report Man with a Gun and describes the Internal Affairs cops and their Plymouth Fury. Five marked patrol cop cars suddenly surrounded the car, and at least ten uniformed sweat-faced rookies were pointing .38 special revolvers in their surprised faces. No shots were fired but the battle was lost. It was a psych job done to send them a message: We know you are out there, watching. And we can kill you anytime we want.

Those bad cops never lost a day's pay. The department tried to get them for phoning in a bogus 911 radio run but failed. The Man with a Gun call sure sounded legitimate to those young cops who showed up, guns drawn, expecting to get shot themselves. But when they realized that the scared cops in the unmarked car actually worked for dreaded Internal Affairs, no one even bothered to apologize.

So now everyone knows the rules. Fear works. And if you're going to follow a cop out of his precinct be aware, he's looking for you. The first thing he's going to do is blow lights that other people stop for. And when the rogue blows through the steady red light, he's going to check his rearview mirror. And if somebody blows that red light behind him, that somebody better be someone who just left the police station. Because if the car doesn't belong to a co-worker, he ain't no civilian. No average Joe is gonna have the balls or reckless stupidity to blow the traffic light outside a police precinct in New York

City. It's IAD, pal—the watchers. That's why you have to know the route.

So this is what Sergeant Trimboli thinks about. He envisions tough situations and how to survive them.

One day Trimboli is driving through the toughest neighborhood in the country's toughest city—East New York, in Brooklyn, New York. Known as the Murder Capital of Democracy, East New York has more murders committed in and around the grounds of the local high school than in most average American towns. The school—Thomas Jefferson High—has a shop, gym, and the city school system's first grieving room. So many kids have lost family members and friends that most school days start with a publicly encouraged crying session. The precinct number is 75. At headquarters the frustrated football bettors used to say the over/under number for homicides in the precinct is seventy-five a year. But that's an old joke, Trimboli knows. Last year the murder total hit three digits.

One cop is killed in the precinct every year. Except for the easy commute, none of the cops like working there. An infected pimple on the Brooklyn rump, East New York serves as a kind of dilapidated front porch to the suburban Long Island home. The internal police news report on this spring day in 1986 is that a confidential informant said that two cops from the 75th are ripping off prisoners, drug dealers, and DOAs. It is one thing to rip off crooks and junkies, but cops stealing money from dead bodies? Holy shit, Trimboli thought. What kind of lowlife would rip off a corpse?

The commanding officer of the command, Deputy Inspector Kevin Farrell, wrote on February 27, 1986, "P.O. Michael Dowd. P.O. Gerald DuBois. Information received from a confidential source that the two above-named officers are known to take money from prisoners, DOAs, and drug dealers. He further claims that four months ago on a gun run, the two officers split a large amount of money taken from a person who was arrested for possession of a gun. Other officers were possibly involved in the split of the cash.''

The information was on target and just the tip of the iceberg. But it would take the better part of a decade and the biggest police investigation since Frank Serpico and the Knapp Commission to prove it. The Watcher had never seen a complaint like this one before. Stealing from the dead went against accepted police lore. City firemen stole from the dead, but cops didn't; at least that was the cops' version.

Anyway, one of the first things that Trimboli did was look at the officers' records of arrests. If the charge was that the cops were ripping off prisoners, then the arrest records seemed like a good place to start. Michael Dowd and Gerald DuBois were not what their supervisors would call Big Collar Men. Most cops, especially in the city's most murderous precinct, would have averaged one decent arrest every two weeks. Active cops would have grabbed guns and drugs. They would have busted people carrying knives and stolen goods. Yet these two rarely arrested anyone—seven people over a two-year period. They didn't even write traffic tickets. There's something to this, the Watcher thought. If a cop is arresting people, you can understand drug dealers getting angry with him. But if a cop isn't making arrests in a tough precinct, he's either lazy or down with the bad guys.

Interested, Trimboli called a friend who worked in the precinct. Unofficially, the sergeant inquired about the reputations of the two inactive cops.

"Dowd is a world-class dirtbag,'' the cop said. "His partner, DuBois, is just a lazy piece of shit. Why do you ask?''

So, the Watcher had lots of allegations, but unfortunately there is nothing illegal or unusual about being either a dirtbag or a lazy piece of shit. The Watcher didn't expect to find much. He got into his car and drove out to the 75th precinct, a three-story brick-faced fortress on

Sutter Avenue in East New York. At the time, the neighborhood surrounding the station house was burned out and gutted for two blocks in every direction. The suburban cops seemed to like that. They joked that they could see the city coming.

They saw Trimboli coming too. He was a white man walking in a black neighborhood. That meant cop. But hey, the precinct cops said, this cop doesn't work here, why are they letting him look at our roll call? Oh God—he must be with Internal Affairs. A silent alarm went off in the squad room. The Watcher felt the eyes of the precinct on him.

Trimboli walked into the parking lot with the photographs of the cops in his hands, and there right in front of him was one of the real cops—Michael Dowd. The patrolman was getting out of his radio car. He was athletic and handsome, maybe twenty-five years old, five foot ten, with jet black hair and a big dark mustache.

As Trimboli stepped off the sidewalk to let the young cop pass, Michael Dowd looked sideways and sneered. Their eyes met, and Trimboli was back in uniform again walking an anticrime detail on Nostrand Avenue. The detective felt something flip in his stomach. His old mentor, long since dead, had taught Trimboli about perps. There's always recognition between a perp and a cop on the street, insisted the old-timer. In the presence of Michael Dowd, Trimboli felt that tingling sensation on his neck. In the next instant, Perp Fever washed over him.

By now Trimboli had a good idea the cop was slime, but he was surprised by the sensation. The cop in Trimboli was confused by his conflicting instincts: The detective was feeling perp but staring at a man in a blue uniform. With all that would transpire during the ensuing years of chase and escape, failure and triumph, Joseph Trimboli would never forget the feeling that consumed him upon being in the presence of Police Officer Michael Dowd for the first time.

It was pure evil.

1

THE GOOD COP

The thought of being a cop never crossed his mind. He was a Brooklyn kid, and at least in those days, Brooklyn kids didn't think that way. People who tell you different are either full of shit, politicians, or police union reps. Kids grow up wanting to hit home runs and jump shots. Especially city kids. Joe Trimboli was ten years old in 1961, and he wanted to be Mickey Mantle. Only nitwits wanted to be Roger Maris, who hit sixty-one home runs that summer. Only the brain-dead wanted to wear cop blue when they could be wearing pinstripes. When a city kid dreamed that summer, it was about being in the Yankee clubhouse getting dressed in Mantle's stall—not about guarding the famous clubhouse door.

Joe Trimboli was young in a neighborhood the gentrification people have since renamed Sunset Park. Joe never knew the landscape as anything but South Brooklyn. It didn't need or even want a pretty name. Joe was the older of two boys living in a two-family house on Twenty-Third Street near Fourth Avenue. His widowed grandmother lived downstairs. The Trimboli boys—Joe and his younger brother, Jerry—attended a nearby Catholic grammar school. Their father was a pipe fitter in the Brooklyn Navy Yard. As long as America was fighting a war and building ships, there was plenty of work. When the Navy Yard finally shut down, the old man found work at the U.S. Customs office on Varrick Street in Manhattan.

It was a mostly Irish, Italian, German, and Puerto Rican working-class neighborhood at the end of an era, beginning to witness the end of the traditional New York family. The well-muscled men went off to work, showered, and shaved in the morning, returning home to dinner on the table and a sweaty glass of beer. No one knew criminals on Twenty-Third Street, and no one was ever murdered in the neighborhood. Only once when Joe was growing up did he confront violence. When he was twelve, a teenager arguing over a girl got stabbed to death at a subway stop two blocks from Trimboli's home. Later, Joe rushed to the murder scene to stare in disbelief. Like all kids, he had to go and see for himself. Somebody actually got killed here; that seemed impossible. Later in life, Detective Trimboli would step over dead bodies every day without even bothering to look at the faces.

Kids grew up playing stickball and not thinking about swinging a nightstick. A neighborhood girl was dating a cop named Vinnie. Knowing Vinnie became an act of self-preservation for kids on the block. Nobody would talk bad to the girl or hit on her because Vinnie worked in the 72nd precinct and he would come around and do a number on you, or so they assumed. No one blamed the guy. You screwed around with a cop's girlfriend, kids said, and you deserved what you got. Back then there was nothing politically incorrect about dating a girl in your own precinct. So Vinnie drove up to the girl's house while on duty. Kids respected the cop but not as much as they respected the beat cop's girlfriend. Beyond that there wasn't much attention given or respect paid the men in blue.

The neighborhood of old European working-class stock was poor but working poor. This was before welfare—it was the last generation of American inner-city poor to believe you were stigmatized by handouts. It was a world before drugs, a world where everybody knew the local resident drunk.

The neighborhood was fairly close to the docks and filled with longshoremen who would get half-whacked. The kids never actually thought of rolling the drunks, but the beat cops were there anyway. This was the first incarnation of what is now called Community Policing.

The streets were the kids' playground—there were no video arcades or take-out movies. Kids had to entertain themselves. Once Trimboli joined a karate club that turned into a de facto gang. If a kid wanted to earn a colored belt he had to go out into the street and beat somebody out of one. It wasn't long before Twenty-Third Street was the first belt-free society. A sudden outbreak of suspenders killed the karate gang completely.

On those rare occasions when Joe actually had pocket money, he used to plunk down fifty cents for a bamboo pole and go fishing in the park pond. Back then you rarely caught anything. As an adult, Detective Trimboli would help fish bodies out of the same pond. Times sure change.

At some point, Trimboli began to realize that he wasn't going to replace Mickey Mantle, or Roger Maris, for that matter. After grammar school he enrolled in Bishop Ford High School. He was policed by a faculty of Franciscan monks that dry-shaved his sideburns before gym class and said he was smart enough to think about college and a career in medicine. Trimboli graduated from high school in a focal American year, 1968.

A war was going on, and the draft became a monstrous neighborhood worry. How do you survive long enough to be even able to imagine a future? Trimboli began classes at Brooklyn College, and one chemistry course cured him of any ideas about a career in medicine. He marched in some peace demonstrations and smoked a joint or two. He drew a fine number in the draft lottery:

156, good enough to stay home. Trimboli felt guilty about not going to war because a lot of his friends were going. So he did your basic South Brooklyn gung-ho thing. He joined the reserves. But about a week before going into the reserves he had this, well, incident.

Joe was driving through Bay Ridge with a friend, and they were smoking a joint. The friend, feeling no pain, was driving with his headlights off. A cop car fell in behind them, and the kids panicked. Joe rolled down the window and threw the roach-size joint out, which the cop retrieved. The car stop at the corner of Fifth Avenue and Eighty-Second Street shifted from routine to raucous.

"You forgot something, greaseball," said the bigger cop, an Italian. The cop waved the soggy roach at them. Trimboli was pulled from the car and rear cuffed. Fair enough. Then things got out of hand. The cop grabbed Joe by the back of the neck and slammed his head onto the hood of the car. Joe offered no protest. But the cop banged him again and again. Each of the kids was beaten and then locked up.

"You Guinea bastard," the Italian cop told Trimboli as they drove to the lockup. "You are a disgrace to your people."

This was the first time he had ever really been spoken to by a New York City cop. Yes, he had been caught with a roach. But hell, that was all he had on him, and he was no long-haired hippie. So the beating and the insults seemed extreme. All this for a roach in Brooklyn? Trimboli had a good-size lump on his head, and he would never forget, as his head was being slammed into the car hood, the heat of the car engine against his bare cheek. He had never been in trouble before, and he didn't necessarily dislike cops. But now that he had been beaten and humiliated, he was filled with an overwhelming and lasting sense of disorder.

Being involved with the law made Joe an instant two-time loser. After being smacked by the cops, he knew his father was going to beat him even harder. Heading home, he now faced the real test: How to tell the old man he was an accused pothead? It did not go well. They got a lawyer and headed to court the next day. The lawyer stood up and said, "Your Honor, my client is going into the service next week. Can we do something about this?" The judge was severely unimpressed.

"Yeah, Vietnam," the judge said. "Well, maybe that's where he belongs. I mean if he wants to smoke this horseshit." Having thus dismissed defendant Trimboli, the judge adjourned the case pending dismissal.

A week later Trimboli's father wordlessly packed his son's bag and drove him to La Guardia Airport. The old man stepped out of the car, dumped the bag, and walked away. To the old man's way of thinking, the kid was history. The parting bothered Joe for a long time. Italians do nothing so well, Trimboli thought, as show you their disapproval.

The next thing Joe knew he was standing in a Fort Knox, Kentucky, parking lot with a few dozen other young men. The drill instructor looked as if he would hate them all equally. He stood at the podium and eyed them with distaste.

"All right," he barked. "I want to know how many of you guys are from New York. Stand forward."

About half the guys took a proud step forward. Now the DI said, evenly, "And now I know every one of you bastards has been collared." Trimboli thought, Oh shit I've been arrested. But it was also true that most of the guys standing next to him had been recently busted. That week's deal with judges had been the army. They put off all the cases by entering defendants in the service. The New York recruits were told, "Put all your guns and knives in this here box. You won't be needing them."

Joe Trimboli spent six months learning Morse code and did his six months of advanced infantry training. When the United States invaded Cambodia, the DI rushed in and shouted, "Pack your bags, you're not coming back." Joe said, "Wait a minute, this isn't part of my contract." But they backed up a truck and filled it with everyone's gear, only to unload it two hours later. Some sense of humor these guys had.

Joe came home and lived the life of the weekend warrior. He spent the week in college and his weekends at Fort Hamilton army base. Mostly Trimboli worried about his future, though he knew what he wasn't going to be. Joe was not going to be a Mickey Mantle, Doctor Kildare, or Major Hogan. But he didn't have a clue about what he was going to be.

In Joe's neighborhood people looked up to people with city jobs, which meant a secure future. In 1973 the newspapers were filled with reports on corrupt cops. Frank Serpico had finished sitting for the Knapp Commission. The police department, people were saying, would never be the same.

Still, being a cop was a steady, secure job and could even become a career. They were pigs in certain circles, true. But not in a working-class neighborhood like Joe's. Hell, there was still even some mystique. Joe took the test but only scored a seventy—the bare minimum—to pass the written test. So Joe was placed on the list. He waited while working as a bank teller. Then the call finally came.

"Report to the academy tomorrow," they said. And just like that Joseph Trimboli gave up his claim to the ordinary life. Initially they didn't even want him. An investigator asked Joe if he had ever been arrested. Joe said no, but an alarm went off. The roach problem again. The city doesn't like and shouldn't like police recruits with arrest records. The judge had promised to make the record of Joe's arrest go away. But no one had ever erased the arrest record. The judge simply forgot to see his order through. Joe was told to go home.

"What are you, a fucking wise guy?" the investigator said. "You've been arrested for drugs. Good-bye, dirtbag."

A month passed. The examiner that turned Trimboli

down was promoted. His replacement in applicant processing, a fellow named Lopez, later said he wanted to see Joe. The candidate's arrest record, which this examiner learned a judge had ordered expunged, did not scare Lopez. He told Joe, "I went over your record. You're a good kid; I saw what happened. The police department is not looking for angels and you're no angel. But I think you will be a good cop."

Joe loved everything about the academy except the dopey powder blue khaki uniforms the recruits wore. You called yourself a cop from the time you were sworn in even though you didn't have a gun or badge. But people would look at a group of mostly white young guys in the powder blue and figure they were some friggin' private Catholic college on an outing. This was still the old police academy, where you could bench-press your way to a badge. Mostly you jogged and sweated. There was some academic work, but for a college graduate like Trimboli, the thinking part was an easy lift. There was no reading list at the academy. No one wanted them to read what should have been the police primer—Peter Maas's matchless biography of Frank Serpico—or even see the movie. Still, this was the first police class to have to pass an academic test before receiving their badges, and you didn't get the gun until you left the academy. Previously, they had given you the tin and pistol as soon as you were sworn in. A recruit picked out his own service revolver, notwithstanding, in his first hour at the academy. They even made you select a variety that day: Colt or Smith & Wesson? Even though Joe had never fired a pistol before, he picked a Smith & Wesson .36 caliber. Everybody said it was the easier gun and the cylinder went clockwise. Then they made you read the serial number off the gun, write it down on a voucher, and place the gun back in a box, not to be seen again for four months.

There isn't much more to remember about the police academy. Once he knew a guy named Angel who got in trouble. Whenever an instructor gave Angel a situation where a suspect had to be held or let go, Angel would say, "Me, I'd just jack the guy." People laughed the first ten times they heard this answer. Then the teacher grew silent and Angel was finally told to get out. But that was about the only time Joe saw a problem. He never saw guys getting high. Coke was ten years away. Crack was twenty years down the line.

You never forget the day they give you the shield. Joe Trimboli was given badge number 7443 in an auditorium. After five months recruits were called to the stage one at a time and handed their tin shields. Joe clutched his to his chest and walked back to his seat. Only then did he open his hand and look. By then, everyone even had their own black leather carrying case and safety pin. They let him take the badge and case home that night. He placed it on a nightstand in his bedroom and stared at it most of the night. He couldn't believe the thing was still there in the morning. Once a recruit had his badge even instructors began to act differently toward them. They weren't dirtbags anymore but were more like comrades. Joe liked his badge number; he even began playing combinations of the digits.

It was a good life: He was getting about $200 a week before taxes, and the girls suddenly seemed interested in him. Neighbors saw him coming home carrying a duffel bag and made way for him the same way he had made room for longshoremen as a kid. People nodded and smiled. They treated you with respect. Then graduation day came. The city was already talking about a fiscal crisis. So layoffs were all but certain. And the cops were scared. Still, this was your job, this was your career. You weren't just stopping here. This wasn't just for a cup of coffee. This was your way, Joe told his new frightened friends, your livelihood. Only the graduates were invited to that year's graduation ceremony in a local church. It was the first time anyone could remember seeing so many guns in a house of worship without a hostage being taken.

* * *

One of Joe's first assignments as a rookie was in Manhattan's 28th precinct. He was on loan to the Harlem precinct. He walked into the squad room, saw a familiar cop's face, and stopped dead in his tracks. It was almost four years to the day since an Italian cop had arrested Trimboli in Bay Ridge, Brooklyn. And here they were face-to-face again, now cop to cop. The older man walked up to Trimboli and said, "Do I know you?" The cop really wasn't sure.

Trimboli moved closer. He was no longer afraid of cops who beat and humiliate innocent citizens.

"Yeah, you know me," Trimboli said. "Or don't you remember me, Mr. Big. Take a good look. Four years ago, you collared me in Brooklyn. Beat the shit out of me while I was in handcuffs, dirtbag."

A bunch of cops were in the room, and they all quickly backed away. Trimboli wanted to smack the other cop. But apparently the brave cop wanted no part of a man who wasn't in handcuffs. In the presence of Police Officer Joe Trimboli again, the cop chose to back out of the room. Joe stood there for a long time, staring. The other cops liked what they had just seen. Trimboli didn't realize it at the time, but no one in the precinct liked Mr. Big. But until now, no police officer had ever stood up to him. Suddenly, a couple of the cops started to clap. Then the whole room was applauding Officer Joseph Trimboli.

2

THE BAD COP

The old man was a fireman. It was nice work for a patriarch. The family had lived in Queens when he was working for the city, but John Dowd always had an eye for the country. The old guy was brawny and Irish, a walking—make that stumbling—stereotype. He drank too much and had a house full of snot-nosed kids—six boys and a girl. (No Irish-American fireman could ever complain.) When Dowd had saved enough money, he kept a promise to himself to quit the city for suburban Suffolk County. But as dreams go, the suburban town of Brentwood, Long Island, left a lot to be desired. Old Man Dowd's side of the tracks (literally the south side of the Long Island Railroad) was a mix of neon and white trash. It was filled with the sons and daughters of New York City cops and firemen who believed themselves too good to live alongside inner-city blacks and Hispanics. So most of them quit the bodega world of Brooklyn and the Bronx for the banal 7-Eleven world of strip malls and weedy lawns.

The Dowd family was not uncommon in the suburban world, where most fathers' prejudices become their sons' passions. The city not only provided jobs for young men as firemen, cops, and sanitation workers, it also gave young men a present and a future. It provided work today and a pension tomorrow. "Twenty years and out" was the rallying cry at the Dowd dinner table. The city was there to be taken for everything, by everyone.

Many of the young men grew up hating the city and hating work. There was no overwhelming sense of good. Firemen didn't risk their lives to save people and get medals. Large, raging fires only meant overtime. You didn't admire people who saved a building full of welfare people. You loved guys who beat the system for a dollar. Sanitation workers could sell the things they picked up on the route. And police officers? Cops were the jackpot. You drove into the jungle and actually got paid big money to arrest those animals. You could carry the gun and badge home to Suffolk County. Then you could do pretty much anything you wanted. Or imagined.

The oldest Dowd boy, John Jr., didn't have the heart for either the commute or the battle. He worked as a porter on Long Island. Edward, the second oldest, was every inch his old man. And when he came of age, drinking age that is, he joined the portable saloon his old man called the New York City Fire Department. The next two boys in line wanted to wear badges. Again, they were not consumed by any resolution to do good works. It was a job, but not the way it had been a job for Joseph Trimboli. The job was a chance, Michael Dowd used to say, for him to go into the city and get paid to party big-time—no questions asked—instead of working in a pool hall. The next kid, Robert, idolized his brother Michael and wanted to follow in his footsteps. You're not talking about a lot of family ambition here.

Michael Dowd was born the year Maris hit sixty-one. That was about all he had in common with Joe Trimboli, Yankee fan. They should have shared more; they were both blue-collar kids looking for some kind of future. They became cops because they didn't know what else to do with their lives. But unlike Trimboli Dowd was looking for a score rather than a career. So though he was born in a magical New York season, Michael Dowd never really understood Mickey Mantle or hero worship. He was an average student with a less-than-average sense of success. The father had escaped the city, put his kids in a fairly good high school, and then stepped back to watch them blossom. Michael Dowd graduated from high school and even moved on to a college of sorts, Suffolk County Community College. He graduated but failed miserably when he tried to transfer to a real four-year school—C. W. Post. He majored in accounting but quickly saw that his own scores did not add up to a career of calculation. Michael Dowd was twenty years old by then, so he quit a job in a warehouse in 1982 to take the policeman's test. He was a white community college graduate from Suffolk County—the perfect police union candidate. Somehow they overlooked the fact that he was already using drugs. That year an investigator assigned to the application unit took a look at his record. The kid had gotten a couple of boating tickets; big deal. But he had also been arrested once. He cut off another driver on the parkway and then got into a fistfight with the guy. Curiously, Dowd claimed the guy waved a badge at him, so he cold-cocked him. Guy says he's a cop—whammo. The guy had Dowd arrested for third-degree assault but dropped the case a month later. The guy, a cop driving home from work, didn't need the hassle. Michael Dowd's father, ever the jingoistic fireman, had no problem with the arrest. A cop gives you shit, son, whack him.

The applicant's investigation was approved and signed by then Inspector Louis Raiford—who was on his way to becoming chief of the Housing Police Department. The neighbors of the prospect all said they liked him. The candidate had a good driving record and even had a job for a while fixing golf carts. He was qualified as a caddy and dispatched to work that year's PBA golf outing. Notes also show that the candidate was prompt and neat for his personal interview. So what if the guy assaulted a guy who said he was a cop? Would-be Chief Raiford couldn't see a problem with a candidate the newspapers would later nickname The Dirtiest Cop Ever. So much for cops and good judgment. By the time Michael Dowd took the police test his older brother Edward, nicknamed Buddy, was a New York City firefighter. Buddy's wife, Carol, had also wanted to work as a cop, but she partied too much on the night before her physical and flunked out of the academy. Apparently, many in the Dowd family, save the old man, did not frown on drug use.

On January 26, 1982, Michael Dowd joined the New York City Police Department. He signed a piece of paper swearing an oath, as many had done before and have done since. The document read: "I, Michael F. Dowd, do solemnly swear that I will support the Constitution of the United States and the Constitution of the State of New York, and I will faithfully discharge the duties of the office of police officer in the Police Department of the City of New York."

The fireman's son couldn't have been happier. He had a job. He had a gun. And he had a badge. What could be better? Police Officer Michael Dowd, badge number 22310, stayed up all night partying.

Dowd's girlfriend had problems from the start. She was also a graduate of the strip-mall society that is prevalent in parts of Suffolk County, Long Island. She too was interested in working as a cop, but bagged the idea. And life did not turn out much better on the home front. About six months after Michael became a cop, Bonnie had Officer Dowd arrested for assault. He came drunk to her apartment one night and smacked her. When she threatened to call the police, Michael Dowd threatened to kill her.

"Don't ever tell the cops about me," Michael Dowd said. They were words to live by.

She changed the charge to harassment before dropping it. Michael Dowd explained that the disagreement had been "a dating thing." They married a year later. By then Michael Dowd was becoming something of a precinct legend. He was drunk a lot, and he reportedly paraded down a bus aisle in his underwear during a precinct outing to Atlantic City. No disciplinary action was taken. His first progress report was filled out about nine months after he joined the police department. Dowd was then assigned to something called the Neighborhood Stabilization Unit. Basically all the rookie did was drive around and look respectable, occasionally answering calls of family disputes and burglaries. His first evaluation report, dated March 1, 1983, read: "The ratee meets all the necessary standards of this program and his work productivity is satisfactory. However ratee acts immature at times due to an inflated ego. This should abate in time and when it does the officer should be an asset to this department." They got that half right.

Michael Dowd cleared probationary status and wound up at the 75th precinct in East New York. By this time, early in 1983, Dowd was already living a secret life. Only a few cops knew that the worst guy they would see during their whole tour was getting dressed next to them in the precinct's dilapidated locker room. Michael Dowd was a criminal and became a cop for the opportunity to do bad things. He was the worst kind of criminal.

This police officer never wanted to be a neighborhood hero. Michael Dowd believed the city neighborhood sucked. Heroes were the guys who quit the city; the rest of the stuff was for do-gooders, bleeding heart assholes. Michael Dowd was definitely not that kind of cop. Hell, he didn't even much care for arresting people.

Dowd did, however, know the police union book pretty well. He was especially keen on line-of-duty injuries. Officer Dowd suffered his first phantom injury about two months after graduating from the police academy. The suburban kid was walking up the subway stairs one day when his foot slipped. This caused his knee to twist and Dowd's leg to bang ever so slightly against the step. Dowd was rushed to Elmhurst Hospital, where the doctor, without benefit of an X ray, marked him out—for a week, no less—with a "sprain."

The union hero was back later that same year suffering another drastic injury. Dowd was writing out a ticket, he claimed, when a guy became angry, reached out, and broke Dowd's index finger—well, sort of. Officer Dowd was actually giving this guy a ticket when the cop decided that he didn't like how the motorist looked and called him a dirtbag. The guy tried to grab Dowd by the throat. Dowd had the guy charged with resisting arrest. The driver never bothered to file a complaint with the Civilian Complaint Review Board. The broken finger turned out to be a scratch. Dowd beat the police department out of a week's pay. The following May, about seven months later, Dowd tried to claim he had been hit by a car while writing a ticket. "My right knee is sore and stiff," Dowd wrote in his sworn statement. "My upper middle back has some discomfort." Later that year Dowd tripped on the sidewalk, injuring his hand. He accused a perpetrator of hurting him with a handcuff and even biting him. He also claimed that he once fell through a staircase while chasing a suspect. Another time dirt blew in his eye. By his second year on the job Michael Dowd was calling in sick because of injury ten times a year. His partner, Gerald DuBois, was as entertaining as Dowd was original.

"While attempting to break up a fight, I did see Officer Dowd limp and grin in pain," Officer DuBois wrote. To the police union officials who encouraged officers to beat the department whenever possible, a "grin" was as good as a grimace.

Police work is dangerous. Even when a cop isn't being shot at, he can suffer a serious injury while chasing a suspect. Yet corruption, like all addictions, is gradual. Michael Dowd didn't start out grabbing money and drugs hand over fist. Thievery is a gradual matter, based on bravery. So in the beginning the corrupt cop only dared steal a little. And before he stole from drug dealers, he stole from the police department. A day's pay was a pretty good take. So by the time Officer Dowd was assigned to the 75th precinct, he was perfect company for the sordid collection of bigots, drug addicts, alcoholics, and malcontents already employed there.

"The first thing I learned how to do on this job was lie," Michael Dowd would later say of his formative years in the department. "And once you learn how to lie to cops, it's only a matter of time before you learn how to steal."

There was no shortage of teachers in the precinct. Only ten years earlier the station had been the site of a substantial corruption scandal. One of the officers working in the plainclothes detail turned around on all the thieves he worked with. The cops in the anticrime detail were raiding drug spots and even running away with the cash. The cop who turned against the others was a furious baseball bettor. He only agreed to wear a wire on the other cops after the Yankees beat the Dodgers in the World Series and the mob started to make noises about the cop who wouldn't pay his bookie. The scandal in the precinct scared wicked cops for all of five minutes. Then the guys got busy again ripping off bad guys. The lessons to the rotten cops were pretty simple: Know the guys you are stealing with and don't trust rat bastards who bet against the hometown team.

By the time Dowd arrived in the precinct all had been forgotten. Crack had hit East New York and hit it hard. No one in the neighborhood seemed legitimate anymore—least of all the cops. The crime wave seemed unstoppable. To walk anywhere in the precinct at night was to risk being shot to death. The largest mass murder in the history of the city occurred in the 75th on Palm Sunday, 1986. Ten people, mostly kids, were found shot to death in an apartment. In a crime scene photograph, the dead looked like they fell asleep while watching television. The shooting was about revenge and drugs—the most lethal combination known to twentieth-century man. That same year the circle of violence and betrayal in the 75th precinct seemed too perfect. The detective credited with arresting the city's most prolific killer was fired himself later that year for his reputed involvement with known gamblers at a bodega across the street from his precinct house. A cop from the same squad was actually shot by a teenager in line behind him at the bodega while waiting to buy cigarettes. The wanton kid, reckless even by East New York standards, knew he was shooting a cop.

But Michael Dowd was a bit much even by the standards of this precinct. One of the best cops in the city, a detective assigned to the precinct homicide squad, had taken one of his kids to a precinct outing at an Islanders game on Long Island. Dowd arrived at the game along with his father and brother. The Dowd family soon became quite looped. Then they started arguing and shouting. They cursed players by name and attributed the worst kinds of activity to them.

"Bossy, you motherfucker," Michael Dowd screamed.

It was the kind of language that would have been offensive even at a hockey game, but the remarks were uttered by drunken cops sitting in a section with other policemen, their wives and daughters. Joe Hall left the game early. The next day at work, he saw Michael Dowd again. The detective was sitting at his desk reading a homicide report about that day's dead Dominican drug dealer. This uniformed cop, Hall believed, was trying to read Hall's summary upside down.

"About last night," Dowd said. "Sorry." Someone at the game told Dowd he had screwed up in front of the detective and his kid.

Hall pulled a sheet of paper over a description of the precinct's freshest drug murder, hiding the name of a witness from Dowd.

"You were an asshole," Detective Hall replied. "And I'm only using that word because your family is so comfortable with foul language."

The roughness of the precinct terrified even Dowd. Unlike some drunk guy out on the Island feeling his oats and getting into a skirmish with you on the Belt Parkway, the bad guys in East New York carried guns. They would think nothing of icing a cop. Hell, some of the guys who used to shoot target practice in the basement of the precinct's worst housing project—the so-called A Team from Cypress Houses—had assassinated a city cop, Edward Byrne, while he sat in his patrol car guarding a witness in a drug case. They also shot up a mayoral press conference on gun control in the housing project. They sprayed the doorway with gunfire while Mayor David Dinkins was speaking in the open courtyard.

Dowd quickly learned that beating people up was a way to bond with cops. Brutality was, and is, the first kind of corruption. So instead of arresting drug dealers, Dowd and his friends started beating them up. They weren't punishing dealers for illegal acts but were simply hitting people in the head with nightsticks for the fun of it. Beating someone up was one way officers could start trusting one another. You kick some punk down the stairs in front of ten cops and you have ten friends, Dowd would say. Young officers were encouraged to use illegal and excessive force whenever and wherever their authority was challenged. They tested one another; how much bad could you be trusted to see, the old-timers wanted to know, before you ratted on another cop?

Frustration had little or nothing to do with police corruption. In other precincts ruined by corruption cases, cops always claimed they had been driven to bad acts by bad laws. Dealers were grabbed one day and on the street the next. It was all done out of frustration. The police department didn't want you arresting drug dealers. They frowned on the overtime. So why not just join the drug

dealers? But the argument was just so much union bullshit, invented by the PBA to look good with the public
and protect lazy, do-nothing cops. The so-called Buddy
Boys in Brooklyn's 77th precinct all claimed at one time
or another that ripping off dealers was a way of getting
back at them. But that was a rationalization by the corrupt cops. Some of those cops stole because they liked
stealing. Dowd and his crew called their thievery a
"tax" on dealers in their neighborhood. And if some of
them felt that police morale was low it was only because
the cops weren't stealing enough. So if some cop felt
resentful that bosses were frowning on paying overtime
to cops arresting small-time drug dealers, he could easily
pad his police income by taking down a stash house.

Michael Dowd had the world licked, or so it seemed.
He drove a new car, he carried a lot of cash. He was
considering buying a new home for his pregnant wife in
Suffolk County. Yet no one ever asked Michael Dowd
how a young cop could be doing so well on his dirt salary. If anyone suspected the worst about him—that he
was a thief—no one ever uttered the phrase "Stop. Police." Dowd even got high marks on his yearly cop report card. A supervisor wrote of Dowd in 1984, at the
end of his first year in the 75th precinct: "This officer
possesses qualities that are an inspiration to some of the
newer members of this command. He carries out his assignments well and shows a knowledge of department
policy." The report, written by a lowly patrol sergeant,
was even initialed by the precinct commander, with the
notation, "I concur."

By then, Michael Dowd even had his own clubhouse.
He had started hanging out with other off-duty cops at a
dank, former Chinese restaurant named Bailey's Bar,
which was in the middle of a strip mall. It was named
after the Irish cream liqueur, which might have been new
that year. The crew, lacking in deception and originality,
called itself the Crew, which tells you a little bit about
how easy they found it to hang out in a bar named after a

cream drink. The place, which couldn't have been more Americana, was located in a strip mall right next to a Pathmark supermarket.

The wicked seem to find their peers quickly. Dirty water seems to find its level especially fast. The guys Dowd hooked up with just happened to wear the same blue uniform. In Oakland, California, these guys would wear leather jackets and ride motorcycles and call themselves Hell's Angels. Dowd's guys were a sorry bunch. Their deviant behavior was constant, so appropriately enough, they called themselves the Loser's Club. A lot of cops from Brooklyn North started hanging out in Bailey's on their way home. The cops joked that they were working four-to-four tours. Instead of going home at midnight, they were hanging out at Bailey's until 4 A.M.

A wooden bar was at one end of the ruined room, surrounded by rusted metal stools with cracked and torn vinyl seats. The lighting was as weak as the character in the room. A pool table was in the middle of the room, its green felt torn and stained. There were no blue chalk cubes. At least one pool stick was usually broken. On occasion, when the guys weren't using the table to gangbang a cop groupie, either Dowd or one of his cohorts would rush into the place carrying a duffel bag and dump that night's stake on the green felt. The cops would then split up the cash and cocaine. Yet, getting high in Bailey's at the end of a tour was sloppy work. Sometimes a neighborhood junkie would be in the place. Not often though, because the bartender was an ex-cop thrown off the job for failing a drug test. But Bailey's was open for business in East New York, Brooklyn, and some bad guys could come in for a shooter or two. Sometimes the junkies would see the coke and get excited. They might even try to grab some of the drugs. Big mistake.

CREATING THE COP

They first needed to know how much you could be trusted. Experienced cops had a novel practice of measuring a green recruit's conviction. They didn't care, at first, how well a rookie cop could mix it up with an outlaw in a street fight. They didn't worry, either, how fast the new guy could go for his gun. Most cops, even in New York, come and go without ever even firing their guns in annoyance. The current police commissioner, William Bratton, became a street cop legend after he talked an armed psychopath into giving up his pistol and his hostage. The commissioner never told reporters, or even other cops for that matter, the real truth, which was that he was a notoriously lousy shot. If the cop had pegged a shot at the bad guy, he probably would have killed the hostage himself. The would-be commissioner was that bad a marksman.

So forget TV and shoot-out heroes. Safe and careful driving in a city where motorists are raised by subways is more of a test of temperament for the modern cop. If a partner can drive you in and out of a tough spot, who really cares what kind of sharpshooter the cop is. Shooting is for cops who get cornered, and shoot-outs are for amateurs. Getting in a shoot-out is the first and possibly the last gesture of a cop who just made an error in judgment.

The old hands aren't curious about a rookie cop's physical build and street knowledge but about his loyalty. The earliest questions Police Officer Joseph Trimboli had to answer centered on allegiance. Through the ages, with every cop in every police department, policy is policy. Cops need to know right off: Are you with them or us?

Trimboli quickly learned that the principal rule for surviving life in the New York City Police Department was pretty uncomplicated. What goes on here stays here, they said, and what you see with cops stays with cops. Basically you never turn in another cop no matter what.

Sure, you wanted to be a part of the group. The guys seemed more than decent, Trimboli believed. A few of them were even heroic. You wanted to be a cop just like them. That was the important thing: acceptance.

The old-timers were the teachers. Even the most sinister-looking ones were family men. The virgin cops just wanted to survive the streets. And the old-timers believed the best way to endure the experience of being a cop was camaraderie.

This lesson was carefully taught to Trimboli by the precinct masters. He could have been any rookie, though, listening to any old-timer. He was in the precinct for an hour or so when the old man asked him to step aside.

"Kid," the old man wanted to know, "did Internal Affairs come and talk to you while you were in the academy?"

The Rat Patrol, as IAD were known, did come to the academy one day. They come to every class, every year. You could almost smell the Rat Patrol coming; all the recruits seemed to hate them. It was almost instinctive. They said it was a cop's duty and responsibility to turn in crooked cops to them. Trimboli had glanced at the recruit seated next to him. The cop looked just like him—he had a family, he was going to the same place as Joe and carrying the same dream and badge. Trimboli could never conceive of this guy doing something bad or ever envision ratting on this guy.

Now the old guy was standing in front of the rookie, wanting to know directly which team Officer Trimboli was playing for. Finally Joe mouthed a version of the IAD lesson he had heard in the academy: "If you see a cop commit a bad act, it is your responsibility to call Internal Affairs."

"Oh, yeah," said the seasoned cop. "Well, rookie, just remember one fucking thing. If you are going to get into the habit of turning in cops then the rest of us are going to hear about it. One night you're going to go out into the street and you might get fucking hurt because there isn't going to be anybody there for you."

Trimboli trembled for the first time since the cop busted him for a joint and cracked his head. One cop alone, he thought. What kind of cop is that? What kind of life is that?

The physical threat worked. Every gathering of police officers is a self-absorbed community. That first day, Trimboli realized it was a fraternity that somehow works. And if you are going to listen to some jackass pencil pusher's idea of street cops, then you were going to get hurt because the guys would look at you differently. Ultimately, they wouldn't respond to your call for help, either. Hey, anything was possible. Wasn't Frank Serpico shot in the face when cops refused to help him? Or that's the way cops told the story. Forget the movie version of the police gospel, here's how the real moral of the Frank Serpico story went: Rotten things happen to rat cops.

And so, by the end of his first day as an authentic, badge-carrying New York City police officer, Joe Trimboli was ready to recite the appropriate mantra. *You are a cop. We are all cops. Everyone else is suspect.*

So, it was you against the people, rather than you serving the people. You didn't see every civilian as an enemy, but certainly you started hanging out with cops. It became a kind of out-of-control bowling league and the closer you became, the fewer and fewer contacts you had with people outside the department. That made the association that much stronger. You got to know the names of these guys' children, wives, and girlfriends. You ate with them, shared dreams with them, and even got caught cooping in the same cars with them. It didn't take long before you became genuinely reluctant to want to hurt even the most insufferable dolt in your command.

Trimboli's next character test came at the close of his first week on the job. The telephone started to ring outside the sitting room as the cops answered roll call. The cop who answered the phone said, "Trimboli, it's for you." Joe picked up the phone and heard a male caller say, "My name is Inspector Ryan, with Internal Affairs. I would like you to consider doing some fieldwork for us." Joe smiled. He knew it wasn't really Internal Affairs. It was one of the guys who worked upstairs. The cops were testing Trimboli to see if he would say, Sure, I'll be glad to rat out cops in the precinct for you. Instead Joe said, "You must have the wrong guy, sir. I'm no cheese-eating rat."

This test of devotion seemed to fit the historical time and place perfectly. Working cops were paranoid of everyone coming out of the academy back then. Serpico's testimony was still wet on the newspaper page. The remaining cops had barely outlasted Knapp. The survivors didn't know or trust any of the new guys, so the rookies were constantly being tested.

And the truth is you were happy to be seen as belonging. Acceptance is the goal of all rookies in all jobs and leagues. You wonder what you could do—and what you would be asked to do—on the way to being accepted. Joe's baptism came by way of alcohol, of all things. He wasn't asked to get drunk but rather to put up with an old drunk for a partner one night. He turned out for duty that night, but it could easily have been the middle of the day. Public drunkenness, particularly for cops, doesn't have a set time and day. One day Trimboli was sitting in the roll

call room, and his name was called. He answered, then
they called out the name of the cop who was to be Joe's
partner that night. Someone who wasn't his partner
yelled, "Here." Joe turned around, confused. Amazingly, the sergeant never looked up. Policy, you have to
remember, is policy. Joe quietly got both sets of radio
and car keys. Then he went outside to wait. He parked on
the side of the building and watched as two cops carried a
uniformed cop out and put him in Joe's recorder seat.
The officer was beyond drunk. He was passed out.

"Kid, don't worry about it," one of the senior cops
explained. "You watch him, and we'll watch your
back."

Joe spent his whole tour driving around with a dead
drunk. The cop was unconscious the entire shift. Joe was
in sector 63 Charlie car that night and was called out
on a number of jobs, including suspected burglaries and
assaults. Joe would answer on the radio and go. When he
arrived on the scene, there would routinely be three cop
cars waiting to back him up, if necessary. At the end of
the night Joe was contacted by radio to meet the cops by
the substation, a location two blocks south of the precinct. The cops came over to his car, pulled the drunk
out, and started to leave in a civilian automobile. Before
they left, one of the veteran cops paused to yell,
"Thanks, kid." Joe drove back to the precinct, smiling.
He had taken care of a brother cop and declined to rat
him out, and the other cops had taken care of him. Police
Officer Joseph Trimboli had passed his first ritual of police induction.

Then there came the real breakthrough night—the shift
when Joe did something bad himself, and the other cops
covered up for *him*. He was doing a late tour that night.
He went down to a basement about 3:30 A.M. to eat his
meal. Trimboli was a young guy; how hard could it have
been to stay awake? But he got into the basement and
saw the lights were out. No one in the precinct was out on
patrol. They were all sleeping, it seemed, in the precinct

basement. Joe was determined not to fall asleep. He had just got out of the academy, was still on probation. Sleep, he knew, was not an option. Joe's partner took off his gun belt and settled back for his meal hour. Joe was in a chair surrounded by a dozen sleeping cops in the dark.

As Officer Trimboli awakened, light was seeping through the basement window. It was 7 A.M., ten minutes to the end of his tour. The sleep-in had been a setup. Most of the guys waited until Trimboli fell out and snuck out of the basement. Joe was alone in the basement with his groggy partner. Joe shook the guy awake and into a slow-motion realization: We're dead. Joe rushed up the stairs, where he came face-to-face with the disinterested desk lieutenant. The boss knew where Joe and his partner had been all night and said nothing. The tour was over but Joe still had to return his radio car to the base. There was a radio call to meet the rest of the sector cars at a substation. When Joe got there the other guys began to razz him.

They screamed at him, jokingly: Who do you think you fucking are, kid? Sleeping all night. You have no time on the job and we gotta answer your calls. What kind of example are you? Is this what they're teaching you new guys at the academy? They gave him the business. And it was fun, actually, to be given the business. That was the first night Joe Trimboli went home thinking: Hell, I'm one of them. I'm a cop.

So Joe had his gun and his loyalty and his precinct—the 63rd in South Brooklyn. Trimboli's parents even lived in the neighborhood. He made the first arrest of his career on Christmas Eve. Some doper stole a car from a mall. Joe believed the only thing worse than spending Christmas in jail was possibly spending it in the station house trying to get back your stolen car.

He got his first medal about six months later when he rushed into a darkened apartment and rescued a toddler with open sores on his back from a bunch of drunks who were too stewed to hear the neglected baby crying.

Joe Trimboli never called in sick. He never faked injuries or beat up prisoners who looked at him cross-eyed. The police union hated his class of patrolman—out there every day, working hard arresting people, no complaints. A cop who actually believed in cops? Why would you even need a police union, anyway, with cops like Trimboli out there arresting people. Sure Trimboli was being paid—about $200 a week in 1974—but the truth is that Joe would have done the job for nothing. He mattered when he walked the streets of Brooklyn. He wasn't some mechanic trying to get over; he wasn't even some city worker trying to beat the system out of twenty years. He was a New York City cop, and that meant he had some significance both to the community and himself.

On July 1, 1975, the end came. One year and five days after Joe got his badge and gun, he was told to report to the squad room with about thirty other cops. They each sat waiting their turn, patiently. The big layoff had come.

Trimboli was called into the office by the commander. The boss asked for his gun and badge. He calmly presented both articles and watched the captain put them in a box with Joe's name on them. He was one of five thousand cops sent home in a box that day. It seemed so easy—so bloodless—for the city to lose that many cops so fast.

Members of Trimboli's precinct staged a mindless little protest. About thirty of them marched—empty holsters and all—down to the corner of Flatbush and Nostrand avenues for the public to see. But the voters felt no disgrace; ordinary citizens lost their jobs all the time. The city was in a fiscal mess and approaching bankruptcy. The mayor did the right thing, fiscally, to lay off a seventh of the New York City Police Department. But the cops didn't see it that way. They simply saw vindication for their "us versus them" mentality. The always-swollen but suddenly swaggering union representatives were screaming, "See, the people really hate you. Only

we care about you.'' Trimboli made himself a promise
that same morning. Someday Mayor Abe Beame would
die, and Trimboli would go to his grave and urinate on
it. That sordid promise made the cop, or ex-cop, happy.

The next day Joe woke up with his empty shield case,
which now had the badge imprint. They said he would
never work as a cop again. His wife was pregnant and he
had lost his health insurance two months into the layoff.
Trimboli was collecting unemployment, but unemployment felt like welfare. There was no honor in getting paid
and not working. Joe went to work in a machine shop for
two dollars an hour. He became a version of his father.

He was working in the shop for about six months when
he heard that the city's spanking-new integrated housing
complex was hiring laid-off cops as security guards. The
complex was located at the edge of East New York at
the point where Pennsylvania Avenue runs into the Belt
Parkway. After NYPD blue the guard uniform looked
like a clown's outfit. But the locker room was filled with
ex-cops. On his first day of work, Trimboli balked at
putting on the yellow striped pants.

"Do yourself a favor," said the square badge commanding the crew, a former cop himself. "Forget about
the other thing. Put your uniform on and don't look at
the color of it. That's the only way you are going to
survive."

The old guy was right. Security became Trimboli's
job, his livelihood. There were about a dozen former
cops working the detail. In their spare time the cops
would get another to tell war stories about the times that
never really happened. The guys would pull their cars up
into a deserted parking lot and dream about being a cop.
They all pined for that life. They all wanted to matter
again.

Sometimes the world is too small a place. The parking
lot where Trimboli and the other would-be cops met to
reminisce about times that never happened was located
in the 75th precinct next to a Safeway store. A Chinese

restaurant, Joe would recall years later, had just opened next door. Once or twice, Joe even went into the place to get some food. This was ten years before the take-out Chinese restaurant became Bailey's Bar, the crooked cop hangout made infamous by Michael Dowd's Crew.

One year passed, then two. By the time the third year approached, even Joe Trimboli had lost faith. Sure, he still carried around his empty shield case, but the holder was like a forgotten religious trinket found buried at an archaeological dig. It had no context, no meaning. Joe had a daughter now to go with the yellow striped pants, but what he didn't have was a career. Working security in a housing project had kind of lost its coplike fascination. The city began hiring again in 1977, but not former police officers. There was no shortage of refuse in the city. If you wanted a city job and future pension consideration you could always become a sanitation worker or correction officer. That was your choice. They were hiring guys to move garbage off street corners and through the prison system, but if you agreed to become a prison guard or garbage collector, you had to give up your spot on the policemen's rehire list. It was your choice, but you couldn't hold your place on the rehire list if the city offered you another job. Walk away from the department, even thirty-three months after a layoff, and you were giving up all chance of ever being a New York City policeman again.

Joe Trimboli was invited to become a city prison guard. He was losing touch with what he used to be and the people he used to know. The guy who invited him to become a correction officer used to work in the same precinct. Frankly, Joe was having trouble feeding his family, so he went down to become a correction officer. All you had to do was sign on a dotted line and the job was yours. Hell, they even gave you a gun and shield.

Joe sat in a room with the piece of paper for one hour. He had the correction package—gun and badge—right in his hands. The second hour passed. Then the third one started. The guy who invited Joe down came into the room and gave Trimboli a double take.

"Joe," he said. "Come on. You've been sitting there for hours. You didn't fire them, they fired you. Make up your mind. Are you going to take the job or not? This is a good money job."

Joe Trimboli never realized before just how much being a New York City police officer had meant to him. He was offered one job in Houston and another one in, of all places, Simi Valley, California (site of the first Rodney King trial). He thought he had dismissed the idea of being a cop shortly after the department dismissed him, but he couldn't, literally, sign the dream away. He left the room, handed them back their package with a sweaty hand, and went back out into the street.

Joe spent another six months unemployed, worrying if his decision not to become a prison guard had been a foolish one. And then just as suddenly as he had been told the ride was over he was told to report to One Police Plaza. The city had a new mayor, Edward I. Koch, who actually liked cops and had found the money to rehire them. The fiscal crisis, in any event, was over. Trimboli, who did not give up his place and join the correction department, got the call in March of 1978. Someone produced the sealed box containing his gun and shield. Joe Trimboli felt like a dead guy climbing out of a coffin at the wake. It was easy for Trimboli, actually, to be reborn as a police officer. In his mind he had never left. Every scratch and dent on shield number 7443 was precisely the way Joe remembered it. He put it back in the leather case he had never discarded and smiled.

4

CREATING THE WATCHER

What was the city to do, in 1978, with hundreds of former police officers like Joseph Trimboli who had been rescued from the long night of the walking dead? Just set them out in the street again, no questions asked? The returning cops presented a unique situation for the police department. Some of the guys had developed drinking problems while either waiting or looking for work. But some of the undead were worse than drunks. A couple of them were actually heroin-addicted felons. So all of the returning cops were sent back to the academy together for, ahem, some retraining. The cops quickly huddled and conspired.

The retraining lasted one week, or roughly until the moment one of the instructors tried to tell one of the undead cops what to do.

"Fuck you," said the cop.

This idea was seconded by two hundred bitter cops.

"Yeah," they said. "Fuck you and your mother."

Someone ran off to get the commanding officer of the precinct.

"Fuck you, Boss," the cops said. "You owe us three years' pay."

The commanding officer walked out of the room. Earlier in the week the instructors tried to give the old cops a refresher course in the law. The teacher stood up and said, "In this scenario the law says do this . . ." And a guy in the back of the room stood up and said, "No, that's not what we do. That's what you told us we do. What we actually do is hit the guy in the fucking head and then drag him into the station. Fuck that law shit." The instructors didn't try to teach the cops for the rest of that week. These cops were not to be trifled with. Most of them had been cops for one or two years prior to being laid off. What were they going to teach these guys now? They had lost three years' pay and three years' seniority. Guys got divorced, lost their homes. The plan to retrain the insurrectionists was shelved the same week. The department didn't dare return this group to precincts. Instead the rehired were placed in something called the Neighborhood Stabilization Unit. The unit, which was used to flood bad neighborhoods with cops, was really just a holding pen for department incorrigibles. Guys would stay there until they screwed up, and then they would get bounced out of the department. The dutiful and proud wanted to be cops so badly that they ignored the insult of the gloried ticket-writing assignment completely.

One of those places the NSU squad covered was Crown Heights, Brooklyn. Trimboli hated the NSU duty, but he actually liked Crown Heights and the 71st precinct. The cops in the 71st thought Joe was nuts. In NSU, you had weekends off and never actually had to arrest anyone. Joe Trimboli wanted out of a good summons detail to work in a jungle? The guy must be batty. On the day Joe switched into the precinct the inspector called him into his office. "Let me get this straight," said the commander. "You requested to come here. Do you know where you are?"

"Yes," Joe answered.

"Let me tell you something," the boss said. "If you came here to drink or gamble, I'm going to fuck you. This command is nothing but a bucket of blood, and if you don't watch what the fuck you're doing you'll get hurt. I don't know why you came here, but if you came here to be a cop, you'll find plenty of action.''

The precinct was a bucket of blood, but Joe was surrounded by cops and bosses who gave a damn about the NYPD. Cops had to fight their way home every night. On the first night, Joe knew he was in a different place, almost a domestic Vietnam. No one even went to roll call. The cops, who were all warriors, ignored sergeants!

Later he actually saw a cop burn the roll call sheet — just put a match to it. Cops ran the precinct; sergeants and lieutenants were petrified of lowly patrolmen. The rank-and-file cops would destroy your car if you got bossy with them. Still, they were making some tremendous, death-defying arrests. There were no louts in the place and absolutely no corruption. The guys just had an aversion to orders and bosses. Joe Trimboli couldn't have been happier.

The precinct was so violent that only two guys walked foot post; it was that dangerous out there. Joe Trimboli had one of the posts. He knew every shop owner on Nostrand Avenue between Empire and Eastern Parkway. Nostrand Avenue was one of the toughest commercial blocks in Brooklyn — the first one to burn in a riot.

Everyone in the neighborhood knew that the cops liked to sit and have lunch in a certain place, a pork store. One day an out-of-town robber drifted in and robbed the Chinese restaurant next door. The cook came running into the pork store and announced, ''I'm being held up.'' A couple of engorged cops stumbled out the door, looked, and found this fellow standing in the middle of the restaurant with a pistol in his hand. Joe turned to the guy who had the post and said, ''Shoot him.'' The cop said, ''No. No.'' So six other cops leaned into the doorway and started yelling, ''Drop the gun. Drop the gun.'' The stupid bandit wouldn't drop the gun. He was shot, many, many times. The only guy to get a medal in the attempted robbery was the guy who refused to shoot the robber.

The goal for all cops was to get into plainclothes. The only thing better than being a city cop was being a city detective: NYPD blue is nice but NYPD gold was better. Joe Trimboli wanted a detective's gold shield more than he wanted to breathe. He was transferred into the precinct's anticrime unit, which was a hybrid unit for would-be detectives—guys who were still on patrol but wore civilian clothes. Joe then hooked up with his first real, and credible, partner, a slightly older fellow named Ronnie Donahue. The first time they pulled out of the precinct together, they spent two wordless hours. Finally Ronnie said, "I don't know if I want to work with you."

"Really," Joe answered. "Well, then let's go back to the precinct, now. And fuck you too."

"I don't know if I can take the time to train you," Donahue said. He then explained that he had just gotten rid of a partner who was silent and stupid until it came time to take credit for an arrest. Then the self-promoting dullard found his voice, lied about what happened, and got them both in trouble. Donahue was honest. When the DA asked him if that was the way it happened, Donahue answered no. The bout of honesty would haunt Donahue for another ten years and cause him and his partner to part badly.

"You got some pair of balls," Trimboli told Donahue the first day. "You're gonna train me? You don't gotta train me. I'm no potato farmer from Suffolk County. I'm from Brooklyn, pal, and I know the street."

But Joe Trimboli was wrong—he did need to be trained. Luckily Joe's new partner was extremely giving. Not only was Donahue physically courageous, he was also constantly putting himself in harm's way. Donahue was a special cop because he was intelligent enough to listen. He had a way of reading people on the street and seeing into their souls. The other cops used to joke that Donahue had X-ray vision. Trimboli and Donahue once were looking for a four-man robbery team. The team had been sticking up stores all day. No one could find them.

Ronnie passed a car and announced, "That's them."
And it was. But when the cops ran up to the car, one of
the robbers pulled a gun, staring at Donahue. Another
began to yell, "Shoot him. Shoot him." Joe, standing to
the right, was also ready to let one go. Technically, it
was time for somebody to die. In that instant, another
police car pulled up, and the robber dropped his gun.
Donahue and Trimboli saved the perp's life by not killing
him. There was a big difference between what these cops
did and didn't do. It was the difference between a tolera-
ble and a superb cop.

"This must be your lucky day," Donahue dead-
panned. "You should be going to the morgue and instead
you are going to jail."

That year the team got fifty medals—setting a police
department record that still stands today. They were both
lucky and good. One afternoon they were simply walking
down the street together when Donahue looked at a guy
and said, "He doesn't smell right." The guy stopped,
stared at the cops, reached into his jacket, and came out
with a loaded gun. Trimboli thought he would go into
full cardiac arrest. Donahue had the presence of mind to
say, "Thanks, sir, we'll take that." The bad guy threw
his gun into the street and ran.

The duo was promoted to the precinct's RIP unit—a
robbery detail that was handling about forty-four cases a
week that year. The whole thrust of a cop's career path
was to make arrests and get the gold shield. Trimboli was
making about three gun arrests a week that year. He lived
with Donahue in the grand jury room; they became collar
junkies—they needed their daily arrest fix. Their reputations became legendary. And if a day passed when they
didn't arrest someone or get involved in a chase, they
actually felt bad. They went through a type of detoxifi-
cation on those days. These cops were antiunion because
they never believed a cop was off duty. The job was all
day every day—you were either in court or on the job.
There wasn't time for any kind of life away from the

department. Once Trimboli even drove to a perp's house in the projects on his day off. He called the guy on the phone and actually promised to come up and kick the guy's butt if he didn't surrender immediately. The guy came downstairs and got into Joe's personal car and drove with him to the precinct in cuffs. The other cops were amazed. One of them called Trimboli aside and said, "Joe, the other guys think you are a fucking psycho. You just can't do this. Someone is going to report you to the union."

But Joe and Ronnie had some incredible experiences and exploits. The prosecuting attorneys would just look at them and say, "You've got to be shitting me." One night a guy had walked out of an apartment building, spotted them, dropped a paper bag, and run away. Trimboli wasn't going to chase the guy—he didn't do anything wrong. So Ronnie walked over to the bag, picked it up, and showed Trimboli. Cash. Lots of it. By the time they looked up the guy was gone.

"Hey, mister," Donahue said in a very low voice. "You forgot your bag." And then almost to himself, "Oh, damn. I guess he's gone."

The cops got back in the car and drove directly to the precinct. Donahue turned in the money, fifteen grand in small bills, every penny of it. Donahue had a signed voucher to prove it. Trimboli loved that. But he couldn't help poking fun. He found a couple of guys, winked at them, and waited for Donahue to come into the squad room. Then he said, "Yeah. That stupid fucking Donahue. He actually turned in found money. What a fucking asshole. Could have paid the mortgage."

Donahue didn't see the humor in the joke because even then cops were stealing. Though none of them worked with Donahue and Trimboli directly, good cops already knew the bullshit excuses for stealing. Drug money was big-time in Crown Heights in the early 1980s. And cops who tried to explain away stealing by saying they were frustrated do-gooders were just criminals explaining away their criminal behavior.

Trimboli might have worried that they had done the wrong thing by turning in the money. If so, he soon realized how right their decision was. One afternoon a young cop from his precinct started chasing a drug dealer on foot. The kid outran his backup and wound up face-to-face with the dealer. The cop was shot seven times at point-blank range. Joe Trimboli was driving into work when he heard the news. He then drove directly to the hospital and wound up standing in the emergency room. As saviors go, the surgeons were composed and deliberate. Trimboli was in the room listening as the doctors tediously removed one slug after another from the cop. The reclaimed bullets were dropped into an aluminum pan on the floor next to the bed. You never forget that sound. Officer Joseph Trimboli never did. That is what drug war sounds like, he realized: bullet fragments wet with a cop's blood hitting an aluminum pan with a tinny ping.

The young cop lived but was forced to retire on three-quarters pension. Trimboli saw him years later at an Honor Legion dinner. The kid looked genuinely happy to be alive, and Trimboli was delighted to see him. He realized as he looked at him that the whole thing was about choices. Joe Trimboli could have stolen the money—the paper bag was right in his partner's hands—but they didn't take the money. That was the kind of cop Joe chose to become, and looking at the kid who was shot by a drug dealer made Joe proud of his choice.

Joe Trimboli had taken the sergeant's test shortly after returning to the job. He missed making the grade by a point and then got busy chasing criminals with Ronnie Donahue. Indeed by the time Trimboli teamed up with Donahue, he no longer cared about making the grade of sergeant, he wanted the gold badge. Making detective was the only target that mattered anymore. The cops who graduated from anticrime and RIP units together were finally transferred into the precinct Detective Squad. Still, they were so-called white badges doing gold badge

work. Again their names went on the list. Donahue got
the first call. Trimboli was about to follow him into the
police department's elite circle when the department no-
tified him that he was being made a sergeant. Trimboli
was crestfallen—not only was he not going into the squad
as a sergeant, but now he was going back to patrol. Trimboli was really hurt when he saw his assignment. He was
going to the 77th precinct, the police department's unof-
ficial dumping ground. Trimboli knew the neighborhood—the heart of black Brooklyn. He had been poach-
ing arrests there for years.

He got there in September 1983 and it was—even
then—a wild place. On Trimboli's first tour, he watched
a beer truck pull into the enclosed precinct parking lot.
And in through the back door came a workman pushing
two beer kegs on a hand truck.

"Sarge," the guy asked Trimboli, "where do you
want this?" A daytime beer delivery to a New York City
police precinct? Trimboli feared for his job; he began
to shake.

"Sarge," said the desk officer. "I'll take care of
this."

And he did. The beer was for a private club located in
the precinct basement. By then corrupt cops in the city's
most notorious police precinct were already conducting
nightly raids of their own on neighborhood drug dealers.
Not to arrest them, mind you—but rather just to tax
them. Cops in the 77th precinct would see a drug spot,
run to the phone, and call in shots fired at the location.
Then the precinct's rogue cops—from the midnight
tour—the so-called Buddy Boys, would rush in to rob
the dealers. On occasion the cops even took a tour behind
crack barricades to sell tins of coke. Sometimes they
would borrow equipment from a fire station in the precinct and rush off to bang through crack house doors with
sledgehammers. Other times the cops borrowed ladders.
Thirteen cops were arrested in a sting at the precinct. It
was the biggest corruption investigation since Knapp and

Serpico. One cop killed himself. Everyone wanted to kill the two cops—Henry Winter and Tony Magno—who turned on the others after being caught.

Trimboli knew all the cops who were arrested. For a brief time, they were his guys. Hell, Magno and Winter even drove Trimboli home to South Brooklyn in their squad car one day. The cops parked their patrol car, came into the house for a whiskey shot, and then drove back to the precinct. Drinking on duty was illegal as hell, but it was the smallest transgression in the city's most infamous station house. Hell, precinct cops were riding shotgun for drug dealers the same week.

The precinct commander, Inspector Donald Bishop, would never hurt a cop, and that was his problem. His cops were stealing everything in the precinct that wasn't bolted down. Bishop was demoted and transferred, finally retiring. The 77th precinct was a very strange place to work unless you were a detective. It turned out that the best detectives in the city worked in the same building with the most corrupt cops in the city.

"I could solve a lot of crimes here," said the precinct's detective squad boss, George Duke, "if they'd let me go downstairs and round up suspects at our roll call." Most of the detectives, who were among the finest in the city, went on to huge jobs in the police department; Duke became head of the department's Major Case Squad. But a lot of people around him were wearing wires. Once he was asked about the secret to his success. "I never talk to a cop in this precinct," he said in reference to the abundance of tape recorders, "unless he has one foot in a bucket of water."

Shortly after Trimboli got to the precinct in September 1983, Inspector Bishop called him in for a chat. There was an old police building on Washington Avenue, Bishop explained, the former 80th precinct. The department was going to open the decrepit place and call it the 77th precinct annex, and Bishop wanted Trimboli to work there. On the first hour of his first tour, Trimboli wound up in the old captain's office drinking coffee. He walked to the window and looked out to see a guy rolling up the steel gates in front of his store to begin the day's business. The guy waved and smiled. Joe then looked into the store behind the proprietor and quickly spit out his coffee on the window. The guy was opening a numbers parlor for business in broad daylight, directly across the street from a police station. Joe was going to bust the guy's operation that morning. He called the main office for permission, where a lieutenant said, "Not so fast, Sarge. Aren't you new here?" The diligent lieutenant promised to call somebody in public morals to handle the raid, but they never came. There was no such thing as morals, either public or private, in that corruption-ridden precinct. When Trimboli transferred out of the precinct in February 1984 the guy with the numbers joint was still standing there every morning, smiling and waving at the sergeant. The situation was very demeaning, but Joe never wanted to rob the guy. Hell, all he ever wanted to do was blow the creep's store to smithereens.

Trimboli was transferred again, this time to Fort Greene. The precinct was starting an RIP unit, and Trimboli was the perfect guy to whip the unit into shape. He spent two years there, and the cops were more than a little crazy to make the project work. Trimboli once learned that three armed robbers were in a project apartment. He drove there, borrowed some uniforms from the maintenance workers, and asked the real custodians to shut off the building's electrical power. The juice was cut to a twenty-story project. Joe walked into the apartment with a pair of wires. He tested all the outlets and announced, "Yeah, you have no power." He saw all three of the robbers sleeping in the apartment. The cop with Trimboli began to sweat. The make-believe custodians pardoned themselves and left. "What if they recognized you," the guy with Trimboli said. "We would have had a shoot-out in the apartment."

Another cop said, "What if someone in the building

is on a dialysis machine? If you cut off power, Boss, you definitely killed them.''

Trimboli was a little nervous about his stunt. He felt a whole lot better when all three guys came outside and the police moved in to arrest them. On another occasion the cops were after a stickup man nicknamed Big Lips. The guy was sticking up everyone in the project he saw: old ladies, very old men, even young kids walking home from school. They were all targets, only the cops couldn't get close to him. The guy lived in the middle of the project and could see the cops coming, no matter what kind of car they were driving. So Trimboli had this idea: He would deputize a city ambulance. The ambulance crew drove into the project, lights and siren flashing. They backed up right to the guy's building. There was Big Lips, sitting on his stoop expecting someone to be rescued, but when the door to the ambulance burst open, Trimboli and two cops reached for their bad guy. Big Lips was delivered by ambulance to the precinct.

It was a good detail, but it wasn't a detective unit. The guys were cracking robberies, not homicides. Murder is not only the ultimate crime but also the ultimate case. Joseph Trimboli wanted to be the best; he wanted to solve murders. The progression seemed natural. The first crime he had ever solved—all those years ago—was the case of a stolen car. Trimboli's many medals proved that he was a good investigator, but there seemed to be a roadblock in the middle of his career path. How does a cop with a sergeant's rank get into the Detective Bureau? No one was going to make the bureau out of an RIP unit. Still, there had to be a way, and one day, two guys came to see Trimboli and offered a different kind of career path: the Field Internal Affairs Unit. The two guys who came to see him, Tony Vecchi and Jimmy Weppler, were both good cops. One was a sergeant in FIAU, the other was on his way to lieutenant. The fastest way into the bureau for a sergeant, they told Trimboli, was through FIAU. The job didn't have to be forever; do two years

with us in Internal Affairs and then get yourself transferred up and out.

Joe Trimboli wasn't buying it; he knew the truth. Joe
Trimboli hated FIAU. He felt the same about FIAU as
any other cop: It was bad news. Cops who worked in that
unit were bad guys. Still, the RIP sergeants would all be
transferred back to patrol. So these two guys came into
Trimboli's office—guys he knew and trusted from the
old days—and said, "Joe, you could come with us."
When Trimboli wanted to know specifically what the two
supervisors did for the Field Internal Affairs Unit, their
answer was what Joe wanted to hear. "We don't do any
heavy shit," one guy said. "All we do is petty bullshit.
We don't do heavy cases. Internal Affairs does the big
anticop stuff. We just keep the fellahs in line. We give
people complaints for wearing their hats wrong, for
working jobs without permission. Stuff like that. Nothing
permanent." Trimboli was almost relieved. He didn't
want a job locking up cops. The idea for him anyway was
to use this job to make the Detective Bureau. Trimboli
liked cops and wanted to work with them again. Cops
who lock up cops can never safely work with cops again.

But the stigma of being assigned to the FIAU unit reporting to IAD was huge. Trimboli couldn't deny how
he felt about cops who worked there. You were taught
that Internal Affairs was the enemy. Real cops hated
them. Cops all felt that the people who worked in Internal Affairs were losers. They were turnarounds, people
who would sell out their mothers to get ahead. They
weren't real cops. They didn't have the guts to come out
on the street and work with real police officers. They just
wanted to hide there and get a soft job where they
wouldn't be threatened by the criminal element. IAD
people were to be avoided at all costs, even socially, especially socially.

So Joe Trimboli knew that if he walked into a precinct
as a member of FIAU, he would be a pariah. Everybody
would step away. Being stared at silently by cops had to

be a lousy feeling. He remembered looking at members of FIAU when he was working in a precinct they visited and thinking these cops were three-headed fucking monsters. So when Joe, a real cop with a tough streetwise reputation, mentioned that he might go into the FIAU, even the guys in his own RIP unit were pretty ruthless in their damnation.

"Joe," one of the sergeant's own subordinates said quite loudly, "how the fuck could you do this shit? How can you work with those rat bastards?"

The question was good, possibly even fair. Trimboli was tormenting himself with similar questions. Why would a street cop—a real street cop with laurels up the kisser—choose to work for those bookworms and pretenders? And the truth for Joe Trimboli was pretty simple. He wanted desperately to serve as a Detective Squad boss. He could do FIAU for a year, or so he believed.

The interview process did not go very well. The panel of three inquisitors loved Trimboli, but he didn't think very much of them or their questions. They had soft hands, he noted, and smelled of cute cologne. They asked him the usual integrity questions. "Okay, Sergeant, you are on patrol and you find somebody is taking money. What would you do? Do you confront him? Will you warn him? Will you come to us? Would you put a wire on if necessary to trap a cop who you knew was dirty, and we told you was dirty?"

The questions were kind of jolting. Answering them in the positive violated Trimboli's being and fiber. But again, Trimboli knew why he was there and why he was going through twenty questions. The only way left for him to travel into the Detective Bureau was to go through these stumblebums. There were guys in FIAU, Trimboli knew even by then, who were quite horrible, the department's most worthless investigators. They were in the division to avoid detection. IAD was the worst dumping ground in the department. How could the IAD cops even find out what was going on in a place like the 77th precinct? Hell, these guys in IAD were thieves, he realized; they did no work and drew a check on the city's coffers. That made them as bad as cops "taxing" drug dealers. The guys who Trimboli actually met in FIAU were piss-poor detectives who could not go out in the street and actually catch a cop doing bad because these cops had never been in the street before. Even the good guys in the Internal Affairs Unit were disinterested in their work, and part of Trimboli was glad for that. Ultimately Joe began to look at time spent in the FIAU as a prison sentence. The sergeant was going to do one year hard in FIAU, he decided, on his way to the Detective Squad. He was a real cop with real medals on his chest and a reputation for stepping into tough situations, no questions asked. Most veteran Brooklyn cops knew that Trimboli was squared away, and those who didn't know could find out. If before promoting him to the Detective Bureau the department needed Joe Trimboli to inspect that fellow cops had their hats on straight, so be it. Joe had already made the vow not to hurt another cop, and if Internal Affairs never arrested another patrolman, that would be fine with Sergeant Joseph Trimboli. Although Joe had never been a duty shirker, he figured he could dog it for a year if he had to.

From the beginning, investigators were struck by the sergeant's procop attitude. Most of the cops who came into FIAU got a fair shake from Trimboli. He usually cleared guys of allegations, and the word went out fairly quickly. Cops started lining up to have their cases investigated by Trimboli. Joe started to develop a reputation. In precinct houses throughout Brooklyn North they were saying, He's not just your run-of-the-mill Internal Affairs scumbag, this guy actually likes cops. What the hell could he be doing in FIAU? The other sergeants started to resent him. They felt Trimboli should be a hard-nosed ballbreaker like them. What was the sense of being in FIAU, his bosses asked, if you weren't going to break cops' chops?

Most of the guys in the unit were married and lived on Long Island. Some of them worked in FIAU for the simplest of reasons—they liked the hours. Imagine being a cop and being able to set your work schedule and have weekends off.

The first case Joe got was the so-called Big Poop Caper. Some cop got drunk at home and took a shit in his girlfriend's drop ceiling. The defecation fell on the floor and ruined a rug. After he'd spent ten years wrestling with bad guys in the street over loaded guns, this is the job they gave Sergeant Trimboli to investigate. He went out to the apartment and saw the rug and the stain. He asked the woman, "Did you see him do it?" No, she said. Then he called the cop in, read him his rights, and turned the tape recorder on.

"Officer," Sergeant Trimboli wanted to know, "did you take a shit in that woman's ceiling?" The cop started to laugh, and so did Joe, realizing the absurdity of his new job. Joe knew the cop was guilty. The cop knew he was guilty. But the cop realized that Joe wasn't going to solve the caper by taking a freaking stool sample. Joe marked the allegation "unsubstantiated" and thought, Gee, they really do get shit cases here. The cop walked out of Joe's office laughing.

Joe was going to try and not lock up any cops; that would be a terrible thing. He would have to give cops a command discipline or two—maybe even dock them a few days of vacation. The cases, he believed, were all going to be administrative bullshit.

And then one night during the summer of 1986, Joe began to feel differently. He walked into the squad room one day when the officers were listening to an Internal Affairs radio. They were doing an integrity test in Joe's old precinct, the 77th. A drug dealer named Benny Burwell was being paid by the department to wear a wire and offer two cops, Henry Winter and Tony Magno, money. The cops in FIAU were listening to a watcher giving a play-by-play description of the setup and cheering on the bad cops.

"Take the money," one FIAU cop yelled.

"Get some," said a second cop.

And then everyone in the room.

"Take it. Take it."

Finally Winter and Magno went for the bribe money. They fell, and a whole precinct toppled with them. The cops in the room with Trimboli started to cheer. But Joe Trimboli knew the cops who took the payoff, and he was disgusted by them. Once they had even worked for him, and he had considered them the toughest guys in his squad. He rode them firmly and watched them constantly. Supervision was the key. If you let these guys go, they would wander. As a patrol supervisor, Trimboli never gave Winter and Magno space to screw up.

Now, Joe felt as though his stomach would empty. He felt equally upset to be working with cops who loudly celebrated police corruption and misdeeds. Joe felt that cops who cheered obscene cops were equally rotten. So he wanted to get out of the room and away from the FIAU officers. But when the end came and the precinct fell, Trimboli had to go and take guns away from some of the thirteen cops who were being arrested.

The bosses thought one of the cops, a black woman named Crystal Spivey, might kill herself. He drove out to her home and suspended the cop. She was definitely dirty. Internal Affairs cops had videotaped her riding shotgun for a drug dealer as he drove a cocaine shipment across Brooklyn. Still it was an intense assignment— arresting a fellow cop. At one point Spivey became scared. She had been hoping to turn informant herself.

The special prosecutor had tried to convince her to make this an interracial issue. Corruption was split along racial lines—white cops didn't trust black cops to steal, and vice versa. But everyone trusted Officer Spivey. The prosecutor had only the corrupt white cops; now he needed corrupt black cops. Spivey was his only black cop, but a lot of dirty black cops were in the precinct who wouldn't allow Winter and Magno, two white cops, near them. Investigators still believed that one black cop in the precinct killed two drug dealers sitting in a car. Two black cops played on a drug dealer's baseball team nicknamed the Wild Bunch. The second baseman, nicknamed Nuke, was convicted of half a dozen murders by the time he reached twenty-one. The case could have been substantial. But someone leaked word of the secret corruption case back to the precinct. Spivey never got the chance to wear her own tape recorder on dirty cops, so she ran inside and put it on when she saw Trimboli, wanting him to think she was working for the prosecutor. Joe realized what was going on immediately.

"Let's go, Crystal," Sergeant Trimboli said. "Give me your gun and badge. And shut off that tape recorder in your pocket. The case is over for you."

The job and Trimboli's assignments were changing with the advent of crack. The rock was everywhere, and corruption was suddenly everywhere too. Trimboli wasn't being asked to look into allegations about cops' bathroom habits anymore. Six months after he was assigned to FIAU the allegations suddenly started getting serious. A lot of cops were being accused of either stealing cocaine or using it. IAD didn't really want a part of these cases. The guys in IAD were spit-and-polish bosses mostly. They didn't deign to go out in the street looking for trouble. After the 77th's case broke, the department was in no hurry for another police scandal. The police commissioner, Benjamin Ward, refused to investigate other problem precincts. He told Special Prosecutor Charles J. Hynes, "There is no other corruption. Leave my department alone." One of the prosecutor's people went to a computer and studied brutality complaints against cops throughout the city. Brutality was the first form of police corruption, and silence was the building block. If cops saw other cops smack suspects and said nothing, it was only a matter of time before cops looked the other way on outright thievery. So Hynes had a printout that seemed to show there were half a dozen precincts

where cops had too many outstanding brutality complaints and corruption allegations. The two precincts
mentioned at this meeting were the 75th precinct and
Brownsville's 73rd precinct.

"If you say the word, we can clean up the whole department," Hynes said.

"Forget it," Commissioner Ward was heard to say.
"My department is clean. I don't want to hear about any
more corruption."

The commissioner's order went down the ladder: The
PC doesn't want to hear about corruption cases. So IAD
just quit them. In particular, IAD quit drug cases. They
got out of the drug business, history shows, just as crack
hit the city. The drug and the chance for corruption were
now on every corner, but the PC didn't want to know.
No one had to tell IAD, the most political arm in the
police department, twice. The old head of IAD, a scary
unmovable investigator named William Guido, retired as
the 77th precinct toppled. No police commissioner had
ever dared to tell Guido how to investigate police corruption. He would have cursed out the boss and ordered him
handcuffed. At the end of 1986, the new IAD chief, Daniel Sullivan, effectively quit looking for bad cops in the
drug business. IAD—the parent company, if you will, of
FIAU—simply stopped working on allegations of drug
activity. Union officials at PBA, incidentally, couldn't
have been happier. They were terribly embarrassed when
thirteen police officers were arrested in the 77th precinct.
One committed suicide after admitting his guilt to a
newspaper reporter. The union could now say all drug
allegations were a scheme against cops by smart drug
dealers. The public liked that fiction, but not as much as
the next round of corrupt cops, who were suddenly free
to become the bad guys.

"When I came to the commissioner with corruption
cases, I felt like he wanted to shoot me," Sullivan later
admitted. So Sullivan saved himself and shot them down
first. IAD still had cases but quickly farmed out the work

to field offices like Trimboli's squad in Brooklyn North. FIAU cops became the overworked grunts of internal police investigations, and the officers in the Brooklyn North FIAU were swiftly overwhelmed.

The cops Trimboli was looking at weren't just wearing their hats wrong, these cops were wrongheaded, period. Some of these cops seemed to have become cops just to get high. The Watcher was confused. The folders said these guys were cops, but his street instincts said he was going up against real bad guys. To make matters worse, he had little or no help. And what, really, was Joseph Trimboli's role in all this? He was a cop, and a hardworking one. But go after cops? Especially when the top brass didn't seem to care? He wasn't sure anymore. Amazingly, he still had this drive.

"They gave me an investigation to do," he would explain years later. "It just wasn't part of my nature to look the other way. People who know me when I was a cop working in the RIP unit and when I was a detective knew that if you gave me an investigation, I was the last one you wanted to be looking. Because I wasn't going to stop. I was going to just keep on coming until I proved or disproved what happened, and that was my mind-set in every investigation. You told me to do something, I'm not going to let politics come into play here, especially not with something as serious as drugs and cops. They just don't go together. It was totally contrary to what I felt morally obligated to do. To look the other way and let a corrupt cop exist on the streets, I couldn't do that. I took an oath. I couldn't look away."

One day Joe Trimboli got a phone tip about a cop in East New York's 75th precinct. An anonymous tipster called IAD to say the officer was a cokehead. IAD quickly lateraled the case to Sergeant Trimboli. The FIAU cop wanted to be careful—anyone could pick up a phone and say anything about any cop. In fact a lot of drug dealers were calling the cops then and making bogus claims against cops who had or were about to arrest them. There was even a piece of paper out being circulated by drug dealers that instructed criminals in the proper way to make an allegation against a cop. The police union couldn't tell you enough about that scam. It was proof, they said, that every allegation ever brought against a cop was phony.

So Trimboli started to take a look at the cop, who was coming in late for work every night. He was in a downward physical spiral, deteriorating by the second. He was obviously a coke fiend, but it wasn't Trimboli's job to arrest the cop. That was IAD's job. He phoned them after four days of watching him and said, "This guy's going down tonight. He's losing it. The guy is never going to survive another tour." IAD did nothing.

By chance, Trimboli did his own observation of the guy that night. Old habits were hard to break. It was tough to quit the surveillance when you actually began focusing on a bad cop. The cop reported to his post and started snorting coke, in uniform, right in front of Trimboli. He spotted the cops in the unmarked Plymouth Fury watching him and ran into a Chinese restaurant. He stayed there all night. When the place closed, the workers carried him out and propped him up against a telephone pole. Trimboli walked up to the stupefied cop and removed the cop's gun from his holster. He never even flinched. It was dangerous and scary. The sergeant went to a pay phone and called the cop's boss. Finally, they sent a car for the stupefied officer and carried him back to the precinct. The officer refused a drug test the same night. Finally the cop came face-to-face with Joseph Trimboli.

"You're dogging me," he said. "But you're not chasing the other cops in the Seven Five getting high." Trimboli pressed him to say more, but the cop passed out first. He was suspended, and ultimately resigned with permission, and never said another word to IAD about his precinct. Trimboli retired for the night, angry with IAD for leaving the job of busting a cop to him but wondering what it was that the officer meant by other guys in the Seven Five. There were no repercussions because IAD answered to no one.

———

THE VOICE OF THE WATCHER

The first time I saw Michael Dowd I knew he was dirty, but the first time I really followed him was when he was a twenty-five-year-old punk doing a summer detail at Coney Island. DuBois had already left the force. He resigned in the midst of allegations that they were stealing from drug dealers and off dead bodies, so DuBois up and joined the Suffolk County Police Department. Right in the middle of the investigation the guy quits. And the department lets him go, no questions asked. The original allegation is in the spring, and it's the fall of 1986 before Dowd gets back to the precinct. He spent the whole summer getting drunk on the Coney Island summer detail. So I go out to East New York to check him out. Dowd is working a four-to-twelve tour at Martin Luther King Park, about half a mile away from the precinct. So I drove out there and waited. Michael shows up and he's with a guy in an adjoining foot post, Walter Yurkiw. Walter is a clean-cut 75th cop, or so I think. He's six foot three with red hair and looks like Frankenstein walking around with Dowd. So I pull up about a block away, then I see a car pull up—the sergeant's car. They both walk over to the car and pass their memo books through the window for the boss to scratch. They watch the boss go and then hightail it to Dowd's own car, which is parked on the same block. They both climb in and take off, abandoning their post. I never knew where they went. An hour later they returned with some food—so who knows?—maybe they just went to lunch. They stayed in their car the whole night. They never even bothered to go to their post. At 11 P.M. they drove back to the precinct, and Dowd drove like a madman. It would be very hard, I guessed, to tail him. It was no big deal. So the guy left his post and had lunch. It was a variation of having your hat on backward.

We spent a lot of time talking to former prisoners. No one would say Dowd ripped them off, and we didn't have the manpower to arrest every guy who Dowd ever arrested. He hasn't collared that many, but the department just doesn't seem to care if the allegations are true or untrue. But during these observations I hadn't seen Dowd with any known drug dealers, and the dead don't complain, so there was no way we could confirm the allegation that Dowd was stealing from dead bodies. So the FIAU bosses (and this was their first mistake with Dowd) said, "Close out the case, unsubstantiated." The boss said to bring him in and you can write him up for violations of the patrol guide. But don't ask him or tell him about the drug allegations.

It was bullshit. We didn't work the case, really. What we found was minor. The interesting thing is that, normally, if you have a drug allegation against a cop, and you don't find anything, you just close the case. You never tip the cop. Calling Dowd in was a mistake. We let him know right from the start that we were watching him.

So I brought them both in and sat them down at the table. Dowd first. There was a tape recorder on the table between us. The guy came in holding his hat and laid it on the table with his memo book. I was sitting down. You don't stand up and shake hands; your positions are clearly defined. By definition and seat assignment Dowd is the Dirtbag Cop and I'm the Watcher. I introduced myself by name. Dowd comes in with a union lawyer and sits down. Dowd is very nervous, he keeps looking around, wild-eyed. He seems to be thinking this should be more of an interrogation, and he's right. I read him his rights from the patrol guide and advised him to answer the questions. The bosses want to close the case with misconduct noted. The lieutenant, who is sitting next to me, never says a word. The silent treatment is his act.

So Michael Dowd is sitting in a small room with no windows staring at me. I give the date and ask his name and shield number. He says, "My name is Michael Dowd . . ." and so on. I tell him you can refer to your memo book at any time if necessary. I ask where he was that day and where he was working. He admits to everything, which is really nothing. A lot of cops are nervous in this situation. But getting to know Michael Dowd over the course of years, this was the only time I ever saw him exhibit fear; he was always cocky. The thing I realized that day is that Michael Dowd will be cocky as long as he's not cornered. Once he's cornered, the curtain comes down, the act ends, and the true Michael Dowd is revealed, and the cop turns out to be a pussycat. His being scared shitless at this hearing sent bad signals to me because all we're talking about here is a patrol violation. I mean you can't even take time from the guy. His demeanor was inappropriate for the crime that he committed, so to speak. We have nothing about the other stuff, really, but even then, I don't believe the allegations to be false. It hasn't been borne out by the investigation, but there is something wrong with Michael Dowd. It hasn't been proven here, but the guy is full of shit. And he's too nervous for this kind of silliness.

So Dowd takes off and he's so agitated that he leaves his department radio on the table behind him. I motion to the lieutenant and say, "Give it back?" And the boss says, "No, write this up, for failing to properly secure department property." Which was total bullshit. Here is this guy robbing drug dealers and stealing money from dead bodies and you go after him for misplacing a radio. This is the kind of slipshod investigation they were doing in Internal Affairs.

Dowd leaves and in comes Walter Yurkiw, who is the consummate bullshit artist. This guy is a born actor; he should have been given a SAG card. He comes dancing into the room, I mean literally hyped up, ranting and raving and cursing. Dowd comes in meek, mild-mannered, and scared. Here comes Yurkiw screaming. He fucking was screaming and trying to divert us from what's going on. And Walter screams, "That motherfucker." Meaning Dowd. "That scumbag. If I had known that he was being looked at, I never would have taken a post with him. I would never have gotten in a car going with him anywhere. And now I'm in trouble because that scumbag was doing some bullshit and I didn't know about it. I would never work with him. Sarge, I ain't never been in trouble before, I don't do this shit. I don't do that shit. I don't get caught up in the crap. I'm just a model cop. This is what happens when you work with scumbags like Michael Dowd." And that was the end of it.

Dowd was definitely the leader. He always walked a step ahead of Walter. Yurkiw was the cowboy; in fact that's what they called him at the precinct. We took five days from them, and that's the only time Michael Dowd was disciplined by anyone within the New York City Police Department. The lieutenant with me hated Dowd, and he doesn't believe any of this crap. This isn't shit in a ceiling. This is a drug allegation, and these guys are laughing at us. The next time I see Walter Yurkiw he'll be snorting heroin and robbing stores at gunpoint while on duty. But now, they're mocking us. We're cops and we can't touch them. The lieutenant looks at Dowd's radio and says, "Joe, this is the perfect way for you to close out your case. Bang him." We took him for eight days' pay. I hated them both, really. The cop who is a drug dealer and the cop who doesn't want to catch a drug dealer. They're both equally pitiful because each one is feeding off the other. So getting Michael Dowd like this isn't enough; it will never be enough. I promised myself that day: This guy is shit and someday I'm gonna get him.

The question people always ask is, Why did you even bother with Michael Dowd? Why did I alone want to chase Michael Dowd until the end. Why did I fight so hard. *Why did I lose my family over him, why did I fight the police department so hard and lose my good standing in the police. Why did I ultimately have to quit and move on. I've thought about this a lot. Part of the answer is the corruption; it was this kind of corruption that drove me crazy. It wasn't just the idea of a cop stealing—they've been stealing for as long as they have been wearing badges. If detectives' shields were really made out of gold, cops would steal them too. It was the drugs that bothered me. Knowing there was a cop out there wearing the same badge as me and playing a part in the killing game, and no one in the department seemed to care. It made me twisted. It was the injustice of the thing. I am not some high-minded moralist, but I had seen the destruction, I had seen the death, and you never actually recover from it. I'm not talking only about cops killed by drug dealers. That is too simplistic. I am talking about the everyday killing that only a cop sees. Only a cop knows the perversity of drugs. He sees the death. He smells it. He wears it home on his clothes. It's there when he hugs his kids. And a cop joins in this business? That bothered me; that will always bother me.*

Every cop can tell you about his first encounter with drugs and death. You never forget it. Once when I was working in the 71st precinct out in Crown Heights, Brooklyn, I was called to a location where a door was ajar. I walked in the house and started down the stairs. As I got to the bottom of the staircase I saw a pair of legs. There was a guy hog-tied on the floor. His feet and his hands were tied together, and then the feet were tied to the hands. He was shot once in the back of the head while he was tied. He was lying on the floor, and the moment he was killed he defecated, so there was shit all over him. And across from him, maybe ten feet away, was this beautiful, young, nude black girl. Evidently she had been in the shower when whoever came into the apartment surprised her. They cut off her arm at the shoulder with a steak knife. They cut off the arm right at the shoulder. Just dropped the arm and the knife right there. The arm was lying on the floor next to her like a piece of meat. Her eyes were just staring up at the ceiling. They were bulging. And I could not conceive of the pain those eyes experienced. On the table in between these two was all this drug paraphernalia. He knew his murderers, they came to rip him off and wound up killing them both. They were probably tortured. Maybe she died first, and he watched them cut off her arm. Maybe she saw the arm lying on the floor next to her before she died. The terror was unthinkable. But the possibilities are endlessly terrifying. It is just another story of a drug deal gone bad. But there was another person in the apartment.

When I turned and looked toward the bedroom, there was a two-year-old girl standing there, crying. She had apparently witnessed the butchering of her mother and father. I ran in and grabbed the child. I hugged her and shielded her eyes with my hand, which looked huge on her. The child was shaking. I was frozen, I couldn't say anything. We were both whimpering. The other cops came in and took the child. She was taken out and comforted. I remember the apartment flooding with police officers, and as I stepped out I confronted a frantic family. They were screaming, trying to gain entry, and I just looked at them. As I walked out I heard the cop behind me say, "You really don't want to go in there. They're dead and you really don't want to see them this way." That was my first encounter with that kind of drug violence. It is a vivid memory.

Over the years I would see all kinds of wanton violence and carnage. Crack has totally destroyed our society. Anything powerful enough to destroy maternal instinct and make a mother sell her ten-year-old daughter for a hit has got to be something from the devil. The amount of heartache and grief that is brought upon the users and their victims is something I think we have to pay for every single day. So no, I wasn't a one-man crusade to stomp out drugs. That would be a crazy, overwhelming ambition. But when the time came and I knew a guy like Michael Dowd existed, and he was supposed to be one of us, who was supposed to protect your daughter and mine, and when I came to realize he wasn't protecting but was causing all of this death so he could make a few illegal bucks, I wanted him. I wanted him so bad, I could taste it. He had to be brought down. And whenever I forgot that, whenever things looked impossible, I heard the little girl whimpering in the apartment.

5

THE DOMINICAN

He had come to America from a wooden hovel at the dead end of a squalid alley in the Dominican Republic. He discovered gold on a cement street corner in New York. No, trees do not grow in Brooklyn anymore, but cocoa grows in every park. Gold bubbles up white and dusty out of the ground. The corner is recognized as "turf" throughout Brooklyn and coveted throughout the nebulous drug world as "a spot." Oh to be young, armed, and dangerous in Brooklyn with a spot. The world—especially East New York—was yours for the taking.

City sidewalks had cracks, sure. Everyone knew that. But now, at least in Brooklyn, they also had José Montalvo—the one they called Chelo. The Dominican was filling every prized East New York intersection with uppercase crack. Though young Chelo had once surrounded himself with a pack of braying, sickly mongrels in a San Francisco de Macorís alley, the drug dealer now seemed to move in a mink cloud—all of his subordinates dressed in furs. Chelo's henchmen seemed to share the personality and disposition of his old dogs, but at least the companions now licking at his heels were wearing finer fleeces.

Chelo was just another unemployed illegal alien

among the 350,000 Dominicans living in New York City, but he quickly learned that Americans were crazy for cocaine and that Colombians were scared to sell it to them directly. Cartel bosses from Cali needed street-corner salesmen in Brooklyn. They needed Chelo or someone like him to make door-to-door deliveries of coke. Chelo had no problem taking chances and he had no problem pulling the occasional trigger. Half of every dollar he made went back into the organization. He was a RICO case waiting to happen.

Within a few years, Chelo was even being listed by narcotics investigators assigned to the New York City Police Department as a "reputed drug kingpin." On the streets, people didn't need the cops to tell them Chelo was as big as the drug world got. By then, Chelo was a walking deity. He was the perfect character for New York gangster lore: the big bad guy with a heart of gold. Chelo was revered by young Hispanics in the same way that young Italian wanna-be gangsters worshiped John Gotti, who made his bones as a kid in this same Brooklyn neighborhood of Brownsville. Where once there had been Lucky Luciano and Murder Inc., there was now Chelo and a new company of homicide. They called themselves La Compania—the Company.

So much of the life Chelo dreamed about was a tired gangster cliché. So what if Chelo traveled through the ghetto like an incarnation of the stereotypical Superfly—only badder and richer? Chelo didn't invent the ghetto or the persona. As a kid he saw the gaudy pimp on a movie screen and worshiped him. Superfly was one of the only movies about America Chelo could remember seeing while growing up in his one-movie-projector town. Superfly was this Dominican kid's role model, his Mickey Mantle. Chelo was living the "gangsta life" years before the invention of rap music and the "living large" ghetto mentality. By 1987 Chelo was traveling through the New York ghetto with everything but his own theme music. Chelo never saw that movie *Scarface* until he came to Brooklyn, his theater in San Francisco de Macorís was behind the urban gangster myths. Still, from Capone to Superfly, to Montana and Chelo, it was all the same gangster tale, just different scripts.

Chelo was the biggest cocaine dealer in the worst part of New York. He covered himself with leggy blonde models, colorful leather pants, and enough dead animal skins to fill a medium-size zoo, and wore the skins from endangered reptiles on his feet. When Chelo moved, gold glistened and metal clinked. He was a walking show window, a gaudy mannequin come to life. He traveled by white limousine to his home in the Bronx. He cut his coke deals in Washington Heights and dealt crack cocaine on two major markets in East New York. And as the traditional urban gangster, Chelo was as charming and ruthless as the old-time hood he replaced.

One afternoon Chelo was hugging kids in the street, and the next day he had the kids' mother shot for stealing from him. La Compania dominated street-level distribution of cocaine in principally two spots. The gang was making $200,000 a week at two corners: Norwood and Fulton, and Pitkin and Pine. The cocaine was generally packaged in quantities known as "twenties," which contained approximately one-half to one gram of coke and sold for twenty dollars apiece.

La Compania's enforcers were regarded as lethal and prolific. They intimidated people, beating customers as well as workers. When they suspected a worker of stealing, they simply kidnapped his wife. If the suspicions were strong enough, they raped his wife and killed his kids. Hell, if Chelo could have made boots out of your skin, he would have done that too.

Members of La Compania were the ultimate capitalists. They simply eliminated competition with an Uzi burst to the head. All disputes were settled by the gun. They were extremely well organized. La Compania would and did assign its members different roles, including sellers, runners, lookouts, deliverers, packers, money carriers, drivers, managers, bosses, and enforcers or hitmen. Members and associates of La Compania operated various packing offices throughout the city where cocaine was processed and packaged. The bags were further assembled into "bundles" consisting of ten twenty-dollar bags. These bundles were then transported by members of La Compania to "stashes" and distribution locations, then sent out to "spots," or retail outlets. These spots were manned seven days a week and twenty-four hours a day. There were three shifts in a La Compania workday—designed to coil_ide with the three changes in shifts at the nearby 75th precinct.

The enterprise worked, in part, because most of Chelo's gang members were first-generation American gangster. With every new American immigrant group—Irish, Italian, and German, Jew and Gentile alike—the gangster comes over first. The cops and lawyers, maybe even a mayor or two, come later. There is nothing more American than the outlaw. Chelo saw it in the movies, so it must be true. The Old West existed then, even in the 1980s, for Citizen Chelo.

The only way Chelo was going back home from America was either as an icon or as a corpse. There was no middle ground back home, just burying ground. A high stone wall surrounded the ancient cemetery in the middle of town. No one was actually buried underground in the place because you only rented eternal space in the poor man's cemetery. Still, the good and bad were housed in adjoining crypts if a dead man's survivors could pay the rent. If you went afoul of the landlord, the village gravedigger moved you out and burned your bones.

Chelo had learned an important lesson in his hometown: Drugs can save you. His hometown—which is located about one hundred kilometers southeast of Santo Domingo—had been seeing its sons returned home from New York. There had been two hundred murders of residents in the town of 250,000 between 1985 and 1993.

All of San Francisco de Macorís's dead kids were casualties of a war they happily enlisted to fight in, and most returned home to be buried. The poverty of the dead kids only seemed to add to the fundamental sadness of their stories.

There was nothing noble about poverty, the people of San Francisco de Macorís said. But greatness was relative, and a kid could only make it off the island in one of two ways—as either a major-league baseball player or a big-league drug dealer. Take your pick, middle infielder or middle man. But decide fast, said the elders, there is no shame in riches.

The economy of San Francisco de Macorís was controlled, for the most part, by people who made their fortune trafficking cocaine in New York. There was even a section of town filled with gigantic, ice cream–colored pastel houses and swimming pools where rich Dominican-Yorks came home to retire. They drove many cars, covered themselves with golden trinkets, and pointed satellite dishes toward the sky. Suddenly there were all-night, open-air discos at the edge of town as well as a Mercedes-Benz dealership to go with the one car wash and no traffic lights in the world's first cocaine boomtown. The once-proud farming town was quickly transformed from poor and ramshackle to gaudy and wildly futuristic. Narco Village, as they called the community, looked as if it had been modeled by a set designer from the movie *Scarface*. The architecture was Early Miami Vice. One section of the village was a hodgepodge of turrets, domes, skylights, castle walls, and flying saucers.

The neighborhood looked exactly like what had actually happened. Uneducated people had been given thousands of dollars. The lucky came home alive— sometimes with slugs in them, sure, but rich and alive. The smarter ones didn't go back, instead they taught teenaged urban commandos at a boot camp for drug dealers in a former rice paddy now nicknamed Camp Cocaine. The money had changed the smiling, sleepy disposition of the town into something crazed and nocturnal. Everyone who was school-age dreamed of going to New York, making money, buying the Don Johnson clothes, and returning home a rich champion.

So Chelo dreamed of the trafficker's life. It was a wanton, bloody reality, punctuated by gunfire. But it was the only gospel Chelo believed in, the only teaching he followed. He had pistols and raging aspirations to go with his mink-skinned Dominican-born minions. Now the gangster needed one more thing: He needed a cop.

The immigrant gangster needed Michael Dowd. But not, as it turned out, as much as Michael Dowd, young New York conqueror, needed a vacant-eyed drug dealer from some Dominican back alley.

Joe Adonis was a drone, as were all of Chelo's workers. Actually Adonis was a wanna-be drone because Chelo wouldn't let him sell drugs full-time. Adonis's father owned Joe's Grocery, a bodega in the middle of the 75th precinct. The place sold all the standard provisions of the age and place: soda pop, doughnuts, beer, cigarettes, and the occasional twenty-dollar tin of coke. The old man would have sold more coke if he could, but La Compania was putting a lot of would-be drug-dealing rival bodega owners out of business. They accomplished this with bullets. Who needed the headache, frankly, identified with a gunshot wound to the head? The old man liked cops, but not because the police uniform stood for anything anymore in the 75th precinct. The old man preferred people standing in his store—even cops. Even the worst customers, he discovered, didn't like to rob his bodega in front of witnesses.

In post–Italian-dominated gangsterism in Brownsville and East New York, the bodega had replaced the barbershop as the neighborhood hangout. You could go there and measure out your life over a cup of coffee. Indeed in the neighborhood, people started talking about something nicknamed "coffeepot racketeers." The uniformed cops from the 75th precinct were good soda and cigarette customers. One of the cops who came into the place regularly was a cop with short brown hair and a mustache. The silver nameplate above his uniform pocket said DOWD. The old man knew him as Mike the Cop. That's how everyone in the neighborhood knew Officer Dowd. He was simply Mike the Cop. In fact, it didn't take much to notice Mike; all the old man had to do was look up. Mike the Cop was in the place every day, at all hours. He didn't walk his beat but the bodega aisles at all hours. He was the cop who came in the store and loudly demanded free cigarettes and soda. Even then DOWD was a four-letter word.

Michael Dowd's new partner was Kenny Eurell. The other cops called him Scummer. It was the perfect nickname. The blond-haired foul-mouthed confederate was also from Suffolk County. Eurell had worked most of his police career as an inside man. Scummer hated police work because he was afraid of getting hurt in the street. Ironically, Eurell harbored plans to hurt himself on the job. He was going to fake an injury and retire early with a tax-free pension. That was his big dream—to steal a pension from the city.

As it was, Eurell was a plague hoping to happen. He was listed as a "chronic" abuser of sick time, calling in sick a total of twenty-four times even before he hooked up with Michael Dowd as a partner. All that Scummer knew about police work was that citizens paid taxes and that cops stole pensions. Eurell was constantly complaining about Long Island taxes; letters that he wrote complaining about assessments were published in his local weekly paper. He typed up a letter about the waste of taxpayers' money and then jumped in his car, driving sixty miles to fall asleep—at taxpayer expense—in his squad car. Like Dowd, Eurell believed the police pension was just one more thing to steal from the city. Other cops dreamed of making big busts; Eurell fantasized about busting a big bone. A case of whiplash—even fake whip-lash—would be a dream come true. Every time Officer Scummer drove through an intersection in his patrol car, he pressed his index finger against the windshield and prayed for an accident. So even before Eurell became Michael Dowd's partner, he had decided to become a professional thief. It was a perfect partnership.

Kenneth J. Eurell grew up in Rosedale, Queens. He was an athletic kid with all the ambition of a bowling team captain. This is not to say Eurell was ill suited for work patrolling the country's most furious and dangerous landscape, but he was a bit of a country bumpkin. The only weakness he thought to mention on his application was, ahem, hay fever.

"I can't breathe when I drive through large fields," cautioned the would-be urban centurion. They are still laughing at the police academy over that admission from the recruit.

The son of a carpenter, Kenny Eurell never created anything with his own hands more permanent than fists. He was a mean-spirited child who neighbors say liked to torture pets. Upon his graduation from Catholic high school in Rockville Centre, Long Island, the electronics instructors at a local BOCES training program told him he should think about a career in custodial work. Instead, in January 1981, Eurell joined the police department.

In a section of his application marked Conclusion and Recommendation, Police Officer John McKeen wrote, "Candidate is single, resides with his parents, and has no debts. He was prompt for his personal interview, neat in his appearance, and was candid and cooperative throughout this investigation. He has never been the subject of any negative police action and nothing of a derogatory nature was uncovered during school, employment, and residence checks. Based on an evaluation of the candidate, and his past history, recommend APPROVAL."

Kenny Eurell never wanted to be a cop in the big, bad city. He was a bigot, and the thought of rushing into black and Hispanic neighborhoods was unsettling. However, there was a waiting list for the Suffolk County Police Department, so Eurell turned his attention to New York, and the city, unfortunately, settled for second best. As a New York City cop, Kenny Eurell was headed for the broom detail when he met Michael Dowd. Instead of sweeping the station house, Eurell figured he could clean house in the neighborhood. Why just steal a pension when you could steal bundles of cash outright? He wound up in the 75th precinct his first year after getting out of the academy. The department loved him. The silent cop couldn't be accused of being a ranting lunatic. Kenny Eurell wanted to stay hidden for twenty years.

"This officer is a credit to this command," wrote his sergeant, George Carruthers, after Eurell had worked in the 75th precinct for six months. "His common-sense method of handling the many types of jobs that arise in this command is an inspiration to the many new members of this department that have been recently assigned here."

Kenny Eurell was the perfect cop: dumb but invisible.

"This officer shows a willingness to work if given the proper opportunity. This officer has good career potential and will be an asset to the department."

"I concur with this evaluation," wrote the boss, Lieutenant John J. Maloney.

By this time Eurell noticed the opening that Michael Dowd offered to a thief of his own limited competence.

Joe Adonis was a leech and a cokehead. He wouldn't work a legitimate job, and he believed everyone was trying to beat him out of a dollar. He hated the neighborhood he lived in and despised everybody who had the audacity to work for a living. Adonis believed in nothing, he carried on about nothing. He even occasionally planned to rob his own father's grocery store. So it figured that Adonis gravitated toward Police Officer Michael Dowd, the insufferable deviate.

"Joe, you are a total loser," Dowd told Adonis shortly after meeting him. "In fact, you should have been a cop."

"I know," Adonis sighed. Both men laughed.

The cop and the drug dealer began to hang out together. Dowd would come into the old man's store, particularly on Friday nights, and invite Adonis to join him for cocktails at Bailey's Bar. The first time he stopped by the place Adonis was surprised at the number of off-duty cops in the place. He counted a dozen, but he probably missed the female cops.

"Do you see that guy?" a drunken Police Officer Robert Dowd once said to Adonis, pointing to his brother Michael as he stood in the middle of Bailey's Bar. "I love that guy. He is my hero."

And that is how choir practice went. Occasionally the guys would drive out to a reflecting pool near Kennedy Airport and shoot off their guns, but the cops only did that sort of drunken carousing while they were on duty. Adonis only saw the crew when they were off duty. New York City cops and East New York drug dealers drank together in Bailey's Bar until the dawn came or they passed out, whichever came first.

A bond began to grow between them. Adonis was clearly a street bum, but who would disapprove of dirtbags in a social circle filled with drunks, cokeheads, and deviates? By now Michael Dowd had reduced his own desires to two simple objectives: getting high and getting laid. That was the depth of his ambition. So Joe Adonis was perfect company because his own aspirations didn't run much deeper. They began hanging out at another bar called the Normandy and a couple of by-the-hour hotels bordering Kennedy Airport.

Then one night, there was a social breakthrough of sorts. Michael Dowd pulled out a tin of cocaine in front of Adonis, and soon the Crew was snorting together every night. Sometimes Adonis brought the cocaine, on other occasions one of the Dowd boys had the coke. The cop never wanted to buy coke from Adonis. At first, the dealer was puzzled. Then he realized the cop was stealing product on the street.

Dowd's Crew was well established by now. You had Walter Yurkiw, who was absolutely wild, downright scary, Adonis believed. The cop wasn't just loud, he was practically a crackhead. But Yurkiw wasn't the only coke-crazed cop in the Crew. The cops were a better, even more closely knit gang, Adonis had to admit, than the guys in La Compania. Within a few months after they started hanging out in Bailey's, Dowd started to bring stashes of coke into the place and laying it out on the pool table for Adonis to admire and taste.

"We stole this today," Officer Dowd bragged to Adonis. "We're really very good at stealing."

The cops had coke on them all the time. Adonis was hearing on the street about their nightly raids. The drug dealers—including Chelo—weren't sure what to do with them. One dealer who was doing coke business out of Joe's father's store decided to stay in business by paying off the cops. The dealer, who was named Adam Diaz and working out of a bodega on New Lots Avenue, was doing a huge business and building an organization to rival La Compania. Adonis watched Adam give weekly payoffs to Dowd and Eurell. Then one night Dowd showed up at Bailey's driving a brand-new red Corvette.

"How much did that cost?" the jealous drug dealer wondered.

"Thirty-five thousand," replied the cop.

Yurkiw was upset with Dowd and the Crew for making peace with the Diaz organization. He saw them all as foreigners and easy marks. Yurkiw liked knocking down doors and stealing drugs. He was still a cop, dammit. Why did Officer Yurkiw have to agree to be bought off when he could just steal the coke and sell it himself?

Dowd had a new scam going. He was selling coke along with his partner, Kenny Eurell, out on Long Island. The cops could steal from losers in New York City by night and sell the same cocaine to Suffolk County losers by day. The cops began addressing each other as "Officer Loser" and left Bailey's Bar each morning joking that the gathering of the Loser's Club had gone exceedingly well.

Adonis wanted to smack one of the cops once, when the cop insulted him professionally. He walked into Bailey's Bar one evening still fairly sober himself after the cops had been there for a while. Michael and Robert Dowd were as high as Adonis had ever seen them. Yurkiw's eyes lit up as he spotted Adonis. He rushed over and handed the dealer a folded package of stolen cocaine.

"Yo, that product will cost you twenty dollars, man," New York City Police Officer Walter Yurkiw said.

"Fuck off, cop," said the drug dealer. "What kind of loser do you think I am anyway, Walter, that I need to buy your stolen coke? You guys are cops, remember? I am a real drug dealer."

The police department's Internal Affairs action desk received a phone tip on November 17, 1987. It became the first entry in FIAU 87-424.

"I don't want to give my name," the caller said.

"You don't have to," the Internal Affairs cop said. Someone in another room had already hit the Record button. It was against department policy then for police officers to turn in other cops anonymously. This was the least of the department's indiscretions.

"There is a cop who is telling the owner of a bodega on New Lots Avenue about drug raids," the caller continued. "Two cops, actually. They are getting eight thousand dollars a week to protect the operation. These cops are also shaking down local drug dealers. They steal the dealer's drugs and then give them to a friend to sell. This friend of the cops owns a radio and car alarm store on Atlantic Avenue."

"What else?" the cop asked. He spoke in a bored

voice that said he had heard hundreds of similar complaints.

"I am associated with the bingo hall next door to the
radio place," the caller said.

The cop needed a little more information. He didn't
actually want it, but the police bible demanded it.

"Do you know any of the cops' names?" the cop
asked, his disinterest already showing.

"Yeah, I think I know both of their names," he said.
"They are both white guys. One is named Michael
Doug—yeah, that's it. Michael Doug. The other guy is
named Ken Eurell. They both work here in the Seventy-
fifth precinct, I think they're partners or something."

"Thank you, sir," said the cop. He didn't mean that
actually. But all police work was form.

"Anything else?"

"No, but I may call back," the caller said. And then,
click, he was gone. The cop moved to the personal records. He looked down a roster of 75th precinct cops and
spotted the names pretty quickly. Not Mike Doug, but
Police Officer Michael Dowd, badge number 22310.
There, too, was Police Officer Kenneth Eurell, badge
number 10482.

The IAD cop picked up the phone, and somewhere a
case file was opened. All of the information ever needed
to take Michael Dowd down had just been offered in a
three-minute telephone call. It would take six years and
a cataclysmic shock to the police department to prove the
caller right. But it was all there, on the first page. All of
the information was correct. And all of it was about to
be ignored.

The case was given to a young inexperienced cop from
the FIAU office named Skye Williams. One of the first
things Officer Williams did was drive out to the bingo
hall and start asking specific public questions about cops
taking payoffs. She did find Auto Sound City—the place
where they dealt with car radios and coke—because another allegation had been phoned into IAD the month

before. An anonymous male complained uniformed cops were drinking beer in the place and openly smoking pot. The caller, obviously a local businessman, had called the precinct to complain about double-parked cars outside Auto Sound City. The caller said he also saw the dealers beating a man with a baseball bat.

"**M**ove them yourself, shithead," said the cop who took the original unrecorded phone complaint in the 75th precinct. "Do you want one of us to come up there and get hit with a bat?"

The new year opened with a fresh set of phone calls and allegations against Michael Dowd. An anonymous male called the Crimestopper Hotline on January 14, 1988, and said, quite plainly, "Officer Michael Dowd is selling drugs. He has purchased two homes on Long Island with the money and another house in Virginia. He also bought a red Corvette. The cop is a male white about twenty-five to twenty-six years old. Five foot ten and a hundred thirty-five pounds. His license plate number is VBL380."

Even at this early point, the investigators appeared lost. But Michael Dowd sounded like the real deal. In a crack piece of investigative work, Officer Williams drove to suspected addresses looking for cops in broad daylight, during work hours. Surprise—she never saw any cops. Officer Williams filled out work sheets but never actually observed Police Officer Michael Dowd doing anything wrong during his work hours.

Apparently soon after this, someone within Internal Affairs suggested the bright idea that they split up Officers Dowd and Eurell as partners. This would have broken the golden rule of police investigations: Never let them know they are being watched. Word leaked back to Dowd and Eurell that FIAU is looking at you.

———————

In 1987, I'm doing my own work on some other cops, in Brooklyn North precincts. These guys aren't robbing anybody themselves just yet, but they are both severe cokeheads. Granville Davis is the sergeant handling the new allegation against Michael Dowd. I have other work, of course, but Michael Dowd is my hobby. I keep myself available to get this guy. Everybody knows that I'm interested in Dowd after my experience catching him off duty with Yurkiw. Dowd was sent to Coney Island after I grabbed eight days' vacation from him. He was drunk all summer on foot post. I went to see him a couple of times, and by chance he looked alive and alert. I never lost sight of him or interest.

Granville Davis was a good, conscientious guy. He was a dedicated individual, but he was a slow, methodical worker. I don't mean that in a derogatory fashion. That was just Granville's personality. It would drive you crazy; you wanted to push him sometimes. He'd do things one step at a time. I believed they should free us all up to go after this guy. We should drop everything and put people on Dowd twenty-four hours a day, seven days a week. After all, this was new for us. We'd rarely get a specific allegation against a named cop, and now we were getting two and three allegations against Michael Dowd. Always drugs. Amazingly all of the cases on Dowd were passed to the field office from Internal Affairs. I always thought that was crazy. If IAD wasn't looking at guys stealing money from dead bodies and taking $8,000-a-week bribes from drug dealers, what were they so busy looking at? Was some New York City cop a serial killer? Was their work so big or important that Internal Affairs had to farm out Michael Dowd to the second team?

My memory of Granville Davis was one of total frustration. He said to me, "You know, I tried to follow that creep Michael Dowd today, and guess what he did?" And then Davis told me something that took me right back to the night I tried to follow Dowd leaving Martin Luther King Park on his illegal lunch. So I said, "Granville, what happened?" He says, "Well, you know, I started following the fuck—Dowd drives so goddamn fast, you can't believe what he pulled on me. I'm following him on the highway. He jumped the center divider and went against traffic in the opposite direction to get away from me." Granville was extremely upset. I sat him down and said, "Granville, you got burned." And he looked at me and he got a little upset when I said that but it was just the two of us talking. I said, "He did it because he picked you out. You got burned. Don't feel bad. We all get burned. If anybody thinks they don't, they're full of crap. But you got burned big-time. And you better be careful of him because if he's jumping dividers and going against oncoming traffic to get away from you, then the guy is very screwed up." So, all we know at this stage is that Michael Dowd is totally fucked up. We've got allegations and cases against him. But there is a total lack of sense in the office, even then, that we've got to do anything about this guy. There is no commitment. All of these cases have come in on the same guy, and nobody is lifting a finger to do something, to actually coordinate a campaign to get him.

It's funny, but I felt that some of the anonymous tips against Dowd were coming from other cops. The jargon used to describe him was police talk, the terminology belonged to cops. So that just cemented a feeling I had always had about Dowd. The guy is so wild that even the cops he works with are dropping dimes on him. He is that outrageous. Even cops in the city's most rough-and-tumble precinct—the 75th—think Michael Dowd is too slimy to be a cop.

But I also had my sources. Every cop has to have his sources, even among drug dealers. You have to cultivate guys you can go to in the pinch on both sides of the badge. So I had a friend who worked in the 75th precinct. He was the guy I went to originally and said, "What do you think of Michael Dowd?" and he said, "He's a piece of shit. Why?" In November of 1987, I run into my friend outside the 75th precinct and he looks at me. And *the look says, I gotta talk to you. But he ain't going to talk to me in front of his precinct. He is a cop. And I am Internal Affairs. I know the score. Policy is policy.*

So I walked away and he called me up at work and said, "I want to talk to you." We met and took a walk in the street near my home, and my friend says, "You remember the guy you asked me about?" I said, "Yeah." He says, "You are on the money." I said, "What are you talking about?" "He's dirty." "What are you talking about? Give me more." "Joe, I can't give you a whole lot more. I don't want to get involved in this shit. I got family." And the whole bullshit. I promised him, "Look, I'm never going to put on paper what you tell me. But give me something so I know where I am going. You tell me I am right, tell me why I am right, and I will never let this thing go. I'll stay with this guy until he dies."

Then he told me, "You know his sister-in-law gets her hair done at my wife's beauty parlor. And she always talks about him. She says her brother-in-law is dealing drugs and that the cops never catch him. She says the guy is living high off the hog and acting like a big shot. And her husband—Michael Dowd's brother Edward— has got nothing. He's a struggling fireman and stuff like that." So now I'm thinking, I wonder if Michael Dowd's own sister-in-law is dropping hints to us and ratting him out. It was possible. And it is still possible. A few of the anonymous callers were female. So now I have a direct link into Michael Dowd's family, and they are telling me he is a dirty rotten motherfucker.

I reported straight to the beauty parlor, looking for work as a janitor. It was the easiest tail I ever did. Surveillance by appointment only. The sister-in-law had to make an appointment. And I was there for the next scheduled rendezvous, just listening in. Actually, I went there for a beard trim. She was carrying on in the seat right next to me. I saw her and she saw me. She wouldn't talk about Dowd with me sitting there. But I went back to the office and looked her up. Sure enough. She was Michael Dowd's sister-in-law. They lived right in the neighborhood. My friend was very concerned and scared. He told me the next day, "Joe, we don't do beards. I would prefer you don't come back here." And I understood. The sister-in-law could always ask questions herself. The beauty parlor was owned by the wife of a cop who worked in Michael Dowd's own precinct. You don't have to be too smart to figure out that you may be creating a problem for your brother-in-law here.

I never went back. I didn't need to. My friend the cop had given me something nobody else could ever give me. He let me know that someone inside the family was complaining about her brother-in-law the drug dealer. I did feel a little guilty about this kind of access. It was a little like sitting next to the priest in the confessional and listening. I knew I couldn't pass this information along to the New York City Police Department because the bosses would trample on my friend's career. I made the guy a promise. I knew from that point on that I would never again treat Michael Dowd as a "possible" suspect. I knew for sure that was bullshit. I couldn't articulate it to my bosses, but I just kept telling them, "I know the truth about the guy." You know, it's funny now but I've never told anyone that story before. Not the cops. Not the Mollen Commission. After all these years no one knew the truth behind my Michael Dowd secret until now.

THE INFORMANTS

The cop was named Rivers. No one remembers, anymore, what happened to him. They say he quietly
moved on from the 75th precinct to other police business.
Officer Rivers worked in the Narcotics Division and was
assigned to something called the Tactical Narcotics
Team. If all of this had worked out correctly, Rivers
could have been a huge name. He would have been the
hero on the front page of the newspaper. Officer Rivers
should have been a starting point, but now the name is
just a word on a sheet of paper in the back of a four-
hundred-page IAD file marked MICHAEL DOWD. All that
followed over the next seven years—from all of the corruption allegations to the arrests and committee hearings
and back to the arrests again—indeed all of the resulting
police scandal that is the Michael Dowd case can now be
traced back to a simple arrest made by someone named
Rivers. He arrested a drug dealer who was paying cops
not to get arrested. No one on either side knew that at the
time. But imagine the drug dealer's surprise when he saw
Officer Rivers. And imagine too Officer Rivers's as-
tonishment, years later, when he heard about Michael
Dowd.

The buy-and-bust operation that ensnared Adam Diaz
was typical. The TNT unit sent an undercover into 439

New Lots Avenue to buy cocaine. The building was dangerous because it was run by the legendary drug dealer named Chelo. The drug buy was made in the bodega, called the El Dorado Supermarket, on January 8, 1987. Diaz, caught behind the counter, was named in summons 1501 and charged with selling cocaine. A year later, the arrest was quietly voided.

Adam Diaz was the linchpin in this whole operation. He was the one person who knew Chelo and Michael Dowd equally well. Diaz worked for Chelo, and Dowd worked for Diaz. It was a tidy, profitable relationship. If someone had tried to turn Diaz into an informant, after his arrest by Rivers, this whole matter would have ended. Diaz was the one man who could give investigators a drug kingpin and a gang of corrupt cops. But no one bothered to talk to him or even bothered to try and find him after he made bail. By then Adam Diaz was starting to work with another dealer named Baron who owned a car stereo shop where they filled cars with cocaine and guns. The place, Auto Sound City, was located in the heart of East New York on Atlantic Avenue. The place was moving carloads of coke all around the city, no questions asked.

The name Adam Diaz was right there in the police file. Skye Williams, the first investigator working on Michael Dowd full-time, got a list naming dealers in that building who could have been paying off Michael Dowd. There were ten names that year. Adam Diaz was one of them. Williams never found Diaz or the others. They turned out to be just names on a page in her file.

All of what followed was avoidable. By early 1987, Michael Dowd and Kenny Eurell had been working on the dealer's payroll for over a year. Adam Diaz used to say "hello" to the cops on the street while cops were getting shot by drug dealers all over New York. But Dowd and Eurell couldn't have been nicer to the drug dealer, and Diaz was their secret provider. By then both cops had wives, children, and mortgages. To everyone in their neighborhoods, Dowd and Eurell were admired young fathers. They were, as neighbors bragged, "on the job." Dowd was the darling of the local volunteer fire department. Eurell was talking about coaching a Little League baseball team. His wife, Dottie, was Miss Personality of her West Islip neighborhood. At work, both cops were just as nice to a guy everybody in the neighborhood recognized as a notorious, gun-toting drug dealer.

By then Chelo was in control of the whole neighborhood, and Adam Diaz was his principal lieutenant. Chelo had taken control from a rival gang by killing them all. Diaz and a dealer named Paulino operated a stash house for Chelo. They were working their way up the ladder, buying cops along the way. Adam had said nothing to the cop upon his first arrest in January. He said nothing to them. The cops hit the stash house a second time on November 12, 1987. The drug dealers were kind of chagrined. Why was Chelo paying cops from the 75th precinct to protect them when the *policia* were still showing up to bust his people? This time the narcotics unit arrested six people. The narcotics unit was now hurting Chelo directly. They were interfering with La Compania's balance sheet.

Five days after the arrests at 439 New Lots, one of the dealers apparently got mad enough to call the police and complain. The anonymous caller dropped a dime on the corrupt cops. It was the infamous Michael Doug call.

"Michael Doug and Kenny Eurell are being paid off by drug dealers," the caller said. He also claimed that they shook down drug dealers.

Somewhere in the NYPD, someone in the great blue bureaucracy started to type out a police form. One official report, called a Communication Referral, was sent to Chief Sullivan's office. The case was filed IAD case number 87-2712. It was stamped and received by Frank C. Corcillo, the assistant chief and commanding officer. It was referred to the Patrol Borough in Brooklyn North on November 20 by the chief of the police department, Robert J. Johnson, Jr. From the start, at least on paper anyway, senior officials knew about the allegation against Michael Dowd and his partner. Years later Johnson would retire with a full pension, after he went partially deaf at a Rolling Stones concert in Shea Stadium. He was never asked to explain his apparent blindness in the Michael Dowd affair.

Oddly, the original intelligence on Michael Dowd was extremely precise. According to IAD, the case was received on November 17, 1987.

"A call to the IAD action desk from an anonymous male who refused to identify himself. The subjects inform the owners of a grocery store on New Lots Avenue and Vermont Street of impending drug raids at the premises. In addition, these subjects visit the grocery store and collect $8,000 a week. Also, the subjects shake down local drug dealers, confiscate their drugs, and give them to a friend to sell. This friend also has a radio and alarm store located at Atlantic Avenue and Crescent Street. Complainant refused to identify himself but indicated that he would call back with additional information."

That night the department sent someone out to inspect both locations. Detectives easily discovered 439 New Lots Avenue. It was a notorious grocery called the El Dorado Supermarket. The bodega, a well-known drug spot, was run by Adam Diaz. Police determined that the Atlantic Avenue location was Auto Sound City. If someone did even the most cursory investigation, they could find the arrest report for 439 New Lots Avenue. No one knew the name "Adam Diaz," yet there were only a half dozen names to know. They could have checked on Diaz with Officer Rivers. The auto store was run by Baron Perez. That was the first time they heard his name. Diaz and Perez are the beginning and the end of the Michael Dowd case. An investigation that might have been solved in the first month was allowed to fester for the rest of the decade and poison the entire body of the New York City Police Department. What should have been known in five minutes took the police department more than five years to learn.

Joseph Trimboli was not surprised to be back on the Michael Dowd case. Once you start to believe that a cop is capable of stealing money from a dead body you know he might do anything.

Trimboli began his busywork then. He staked out the locations on those days Eurell and Dowd were supposed to be working. He figured out that Auto Sound City was the same place Skye Williams had been looking for cops smoking pot. That allegation had been received a month before the payoff tip. The first thing he had to admit, as a police supervisor, was that if his investigations of Dowd had been fully staffed and coordinated, Dowd would have been caught long ago. But, IAD wasn't interested in catching Michael Dowd, who now had no reason to fear FIAU cops.

The shooflies, as internal investigators were nicknamed by rank-and-file patrolmen, were easily spotted by Dowd and Eurell. Still, the rogue officers were wary. The special prosecutor tore down the 77th precinct, and those cops were amateur thieves. Now everyone in the know was saying that the East New York precinct would fall next. Did the department know about Dowd and Eurell too? The word was that the cops were in trouble, and there are few secrets in a precinct locker room. Everybody was hearing that Dowd was going to be arrested. The 75th precinct, it was rumored, was about to go up in smoke. Certain PBA delegates in Brooklyn seemed to know about the Dowd corruption allegations, and they apparently discreetly shared the information.

The next file in the case referred to a complaint received in early 1988. Again the complaint was anonymous. A man called the Crimestopper Hotline and alleged that Dowd was selling drugs and buying property on Long Island. This caller also claimed that Dowd owned property in Virginia. The caller seemed to know Dowd or his family. He gave the cops a physical description of the cop and a plate number for his car. This complainant claimed that Dowd had faked a line-of-duty injury when he was stabbed by a disgruntled drug dealer.

Dowd had begun to drink incredibly heavily, and he was high for most of the new year. He was acting crazy around the Sutter Avenue station house. A lot of cops were astonished that Dowd hadn't been arrested yet—they thought his drug addiction and thievery were obvious. Some, wary of the 77th precinct scandals, accused Michael Dowd of being a rat.

On one of these occasions the precinct was on an outing to Atlantic City. The bus was full of cops. The rumors about Dowd spread quickly.

"Dowd is a rat," cops whispered. "He is wearing a wire."

Michael Dowd also heard this rumor, and he couldn't have been happier at the opportunity to prove it false. He stripped down to his underwear and paraded down the aisle, making it obvious that although he was probably crazy, the cop was not a rat. The cops stuffed bills in his underwear and laughed. It was hard for the cops not to like Dowd; he was irreverent and funny. But he was also obviously high, a crazy drug user. That made some of the cops even more scared. This cop is on the loose and on the level? Now that was terrible, they agreed. What if they ever needed Police Officer Michael Dowd as a backup?

It would have been easy then to take the case away from Trimboli and put a team of IAD cops on Michael Dowd. This investigation needed a big-time commitment from the department. Amazingly, nothing was forthcoming. You had a series of serious allegations about one cop. And Michael Dowd wasn't even arresting anyone, so he couldn't possibly argue that drug dealers were trying to get back at him.

Michael Dowd was a loser, everyone agreed. He had no shame or grace. He drove a $35,000 Corvette to work and sped off to one of four homes on Long Island. He was paying another $15,000 in property taxes alone. Still, no one bothered to notice. It would have been simple to listen in on his phone conversations, but the order was never given. For some reason, cops did not want to get up on other cops' home phones. It was an unwritten rule that you did not monitor their conversations. Michael Dowd talked about drugs a lot on the phone, and that was how he would finally be caught in May 1992 by Suffolk County narcotics investigators.

The cop was daring the department to catch him either doing cocaine or stealing money and drugs. It was too soon after the disgrace of the 77th precinct scandal, so the department just turned their collective backs on his misdeeds. No one wanted to know or even hear bad things about another corrupt cop. Like most criminals, he flourished in a dark vacuum.

Michael Dowd had no home life anymore. Separated, he had fallen for Kimberly Welles, a bleach-blonde cop from the precinct who was the mother of a young child and liked to say she was between husbands. Officer Welles appeared every bit as reckless as Officer Dowd. She spent many nights with him at Bailey's. They were an accident waiting to happen. The integrity control officer at the precinct, Armstrong, now began to fear for his own job and career. He was about to split up Eurell and Dowd—and spread the cancer—when Trimboli stepped in and told him to leave the suspected cokeheads together as partners.

Michael Dowd got, even by his standards, extremely drunk and high on Saint Patrick's Day, 1988. He came to work glassy-eyed and disheveled-looking and threatened to beat up a sergeant who suggested he go home sick. It was obvious he had been smoking crack. Finally Dowd pulled a gun on the sergeant. The cops in the 75th precinct, even the bad ones, had seen enough of Michael

Dowd. Now the crackhead cop was threatening to shoot them. Kenny Eurell had been forewarned about Dowd's condition and quickly took a sick day.

The bosses had seen plenty of Dowd. He kept a bottle of vinegar in his locker, believing the old wives' tale that vinegar covered coke in a urine test. The new commander of the precinct, Deputy Inspector John Harkens, wasn't going to put up with Dowd and his Crew. He was going to run them out of the place. He was a no-nonsense boss who hoped to see Dowd, specifically, thrown off the police force. He wanted to order the cop to take a urine test, correctly assuming that Dowd would flunk it. But the PBA delegate saved Dowd at the last second. He said the bosses didn't have "probable cause" to suspect Dowd of smoking crack. Before Dowd could be ordered to give a urine sample, they rushed him into an alcohol treatment program. The Farm can be a second chance for cops who drink too much to reclaim their lives. It is a fireable offense for a cop to use illegal drugs in the NYPD. Admit drug abuse and you lose your job. End of story. So a lot of cops now blame their coke problem on booze, which is an allowable abuse. Once a cop gets in the Farm, he is golden. No one asks him for a urine sample. So once again the union stepped in to save Police Officer Michael Dowd.

Dowd did thirty days in the drunk tank. He never stopped drinking or doing drugs, mind you, but he kept well hidden for the month. Eurell was taken out of the Fifth Squad and put on precinct foot patrol. He was still raising hell by night out in Suffolk County, but his case wasn't a priority yet. No one cared about a cop sitting up on the Farm; he wasn't their problem now. In April, Michael Dowd went to see the department psychiatrist for counseling. He wasn't even a danger to himself, the doctors said.

The state special prosecutor for corruption, Charles J. Hynes, lost his appetite for catching dirty cops around this time. And that was a shame. The creation of the

Special Prosecutor was part of police corruption folklore, yet it was another smoke screen.

In 1972, the Office of the Deputy Attorney General for the investigation of the New York City judicial system had been established by Nelson Rockefeller. There were ten executive orders issued by the governor under section 63(2) of the executive law and the judiciary law. The first five orders under the executive law superseded the five New York City elected district attorneys with respect to cases arising out of, or related to, the New York City criminal justice system. The latter five were under the judiciary law. They established an extraordinary term of the Supreme Court to sit, as needed, in all five counties of the city.

This Special Prosecutor's office was the governor's response to the Knapp Commission and gave them ultimate power over all New York City corruption cases. That commission's written report began with the sentence: "We found corruption to be widespread." The Commission insisted that District Attorneys' offices cannot effectively deal with police corruption. Essentially, it stated that district attorneys must rely on the very department that they want to investigate. Police thyself was the edict. At its best, it is an arrangement that invites the derailment of serious police corruption probes before they get too high and too wide. District Attorneys, even good ones, cannot be expected to combat police corruption. Those offices are swamped with street crime and staffed by overworked prosecutors who do not have the time or the expertise to handle police corruption cases effectively.

In 1950, twenty years before Knapp, a gambler named Harry Gross created a huge scandal. He made massive and regular payoffs to protect his operation to about one hundred officers who ranged from the rank of patrolman to full inspector.

"Twenty years from now, there will be another police scandal," predicted Justice Burton Roberts, who was

Bronx DA at the time of Knapp. "I cannot tell you why. I cannot tell you why Halley's Comet comes over the skies every few years, but it does. Corruption will be back, too."

Police corruption in New York was on a twenty-year cycle. Frank Serpico was replaced by Joe Trimboli. The Knapp Commission was ultimately replaced by the Mollen Commission. An Internal Affairs investigator, now a well-known IAD captain, even told Burton Roberts how police corruption would be different in the future. This time, he predicted, the corruption would be drugs and brutality.

Why? The organized pad of the Knapp era was too organized. Too many people knew you were involved. Any of the people who knew what was going on could rat you out. But when drugs arrived on every corner in New York, there was suddenly a new temptation. Cops could get in and out of the corruption business silently and quickly. The individual "score" was much more lucrative, and there was little incentive for a replay. Cops would be stupid to deal with the same pusher. The cops had a saying about this: Don't take checks and don't go back. And that is what you see with modern police corruption—pockets of one to five officers with drugs.

The brutality is part of this.

By 1987, Hynes appeared to be a watchdog in name only. He had lawyers working in his office who were losing many of the 77th precinct corruption cases. The losses were fairly remarkable as the prosecutor had tape recordings in all of those cases. He also had the rogue cop Henry Winter sitting in the witness chair, but juries hated Winter. They didn't believe his testimony or trust his tapes. Half of the arrested cops walked. One named Frank Lauria, Jr., was made the PBA poster boy that year. He was supposed to be an innocent man who was persecuted by a reckless, cop-hating prosecutor. Frank Lauria must have known he wasn't going to fool a Brooklyn jury and the police department, so he resigned quietly. A year later, Lauria was hired as a detective by the Mount Vernon Police Department. A proper background check with NYPD was never done. Then, in 1994, the FBI heard about these corrupt cops in Mount Vernon. They sent in a fictitious drug dealer, and Frank Lauria, Jr., robbed him. This time he was on videotape. The PBA said nothing.

After the 77th precinct scandal, Joe Hynes had his conversation with Police Commissioner Ben Ward. The PC wasn't going to help him put more cops in jail. So, claiming the police failed to bring him solid allegations, Hynes effectively quit the corruption business. He had moved on to other things and became a savior to the city on race issues.

The governor appointed Hynes to investigate a racial attack at Howard Beach. Hynes did very well in that case, trying the matter himself. The city needed him to win the case and convict a group of white teenaged racists who chased a black kid to his death on a highway. Hynes won convictions against most of the major players, but at a price. All of his assistants were busy with the Howard Beach matter; they had no time to investigate matters of police corruption. No cop in the city realized it at the time, but the special prosecutor for corruption was out of the police-watching business by the summer of 1988. Unless a uniformed cop marched into a bodega, gun drawn, and robbed the place, he was not going to get arrested by the special prosecutor.

No one was admitting this sleight of hand. Hynes, a decent man, wanted to run for district attorney in Brooklyn and couldn't afford to be accused of abdicating his job. So the cops investigating the Dowd matter were invited to the special prosecutor's office on April 14, 1988.

It should have been a major meeting. It should have been the starting point for an enormous internal inquiry. It wasn't. And today, everyone who was at that meeting wants to forget the gathering ever happened. It is embarrassing for public officials to admit now that they screwed up big-time. The meeting was never mentioned publicly at the Mollen Commission hearings, but some of the first cops to fail miserably at catching Dowd were assembled at Rector Street that morning. Granville Davis was the investigating officer. Skye Williams was there; so was the commander of Brooklyn North FIAU, Captain Stephen Friedland. They met with Dennis Hawkins, the special assistant to Special State Prosecutor Charles J. Hynes. They were there to discuss Michael Dowd.

If the cop had gotten their full attention then, Michael Dowd would have been a career case for Hynes. It would have been as big as Howard Beach. But Hawkins didn't have the bodies to go get Dowd, and incredibly enough, he wanted no part of Dowd. He was meeting with the press every day back then to tell them how wonderful a job his boss was doing in the Howard Beach trial. In effect, Hawkins jerked off the cops, telling them to get more information themselves. He suggested that the cops look at Dowd's 1040 to see if the cop was reporting his income to the IRS properly. He said there was not enough information on Dowd to justify a subpoena of Dowd's financial records.

Six days later Dowd was released from the Farm. He went to a bar and celebrated. The cop was back in business, only unarmed. The department was afraid of him and suggested he get psychological help. They assigned him to the motor transport division, stationed at the Whitestone Pound. The cop now was guarding towed cars. How much trouble could he get into?

Hawkins kept the FIAU investigators thinking he was interested in helping them. The police department still had no idea how much Dowd paid for his property. No credit information could be released without a court order. Hawkins kept promising, but said he could not issue the order without more information. Eventually he just stopped taking their calls altogether. The prosecutor became known as NA Hawkins, as in Not Available

Hawkins. Repeated calls in May and June of 1988 went unanswered. And once the special prosecutor's disinterest became evident in the 75th precinct, the rogue cops went absolutely crazy.

———————

So now they figure they have a free ride. There is no stopping these cops. In 1988, the cases continue to come in on Michael Dowd but it's a bad joke. You can't go into the office and meet an investigator who isn't working on a Michael Dowd case. And they're not even working together on them. Then in July 1988 Walter Yurkiw gets locked up for a stickup at 923 Livonia Avenue. He robbed a store on his way to work. It was incredible. But that is how crazy the thing was getting. He was with a couple of other guys from the precinct, Chickie Guerva and Jeffrey Guzzo. Chickie is a former cop from the 75th now working at Bailey's as the bartender. Guzzo just got suspended from the 75th after he did a faceload of coke in front of another corrupt cop. The second cop turned Guzzo in to get IAD off his own back. They are all wonderful, stand-up guys.

It is July 2, 1988. They go into a location called R & T Grocery at 923 Livonia Avenue, and they stick up the place. They kidnap the owner of the place and take him out in their car. The owner is later interviewed by my people. And the story this guy told, it sent a chill up your spine. When they took him, they put him in the back of Yurkiw's car. On the floor in the backseat. They were going to teach him a lesson, scare him. As it turns out, they did the stickup at the behest of a drug dealer. It was all tied to La Compania. The owner was named Lugo. Two years later Chelo killed everyone he could find named Lugo.

As they were leaving the scene, they see a police car, a blue and white, from their own command. There are two rookies in the car, and they drop in behind Yurkiw.

But don't forget, Yurkiw is whacked out at this point in life. He is doing coke on the front seat while he is driving. He is doing Eight Balls, parachutes, cocaine, and heroin. He's got Chickie in the front seat with him. He's got Jeffrey Guzzo in the backseat with an illegal 9 millimeter. He was allowed to quit the force that year after failing a drug test. He drank so much vinegar that he pissed blood. They call it retiring with permission. So, back in the car, they've got this guy on the fucking floor. And all over the car are drugs, scales, crack pipes, and cash. So the last thing these "cops" can allow is a routine stop by other cops. They ain't getting stopped. Yurkiw's comment on this state of affairs was, "If they pull us over, kill them." A report of "shots fired" at another location came over the air, and the uniformed rookie cops broke off their tail to respond. They would never know how lucky they had been.

When I was told this the next day, I didn't need to hear another word about Walter Yurkiw ever again. I would follow him to the ends of the earth. He was going to kill a cop from his own command? I wanted him. I wanted Yurkiw and I wanted Dowd. To make this even more offensive was the fact that Yurkiw's brother Paul had just gotten the shit shot out of him. He was a cop with emergency services, and he was set up by a drug dealer when he went to help a broken-down car on the side of the road. Your brother is a hero cop who was shot and you don't think twice about taking down one of your own? Amazing.

The store owner, Lugo, eventually went to the cops and spotted Yurkiw's car in the lot. Yurkiw had robbed the bodega and then gone to work. He hid out in the precinct and parked his car in the lot. The arresting officers went crazy. Yurkiw was upstairs getting dressed. He was as high as a kite. Yeah, he went to work and left the shit on the backseat of his car in the parking lot. Yurkiw went to work and the guys from my office went to the precinct to investigate the case. Yurkiw was wearing an

NYPD baseball cap. We just thought the cap was part of a disguise. Who would think a real cop robbed a place and took a hostage while wearing a department cap. You can't make up this kind of stuff.

When my guys came back from the precinct with their tale, all sorts of sirens went off in my head. This was the guy I knew from Michael Dowd. We had all these investigations on Dowd. All of these drug allegations. We knew about Bailey's by then. We sat on the bar while they looked for Guzzo and Chickie. No one was supposed to know about the place. Dowd was still going there. So was his brother Robert and Kimberly Welles. The guys investigating Chelo were also watching the place. And still the cops came. One day while we were sitting there, watching, these dopes from IAD burned the place. The IAD cops were looking to arrest Chickie, the bartender. If they were smart, IAD would have arrested Chickie at home, but they rushed in and arrested him in front of the whole place. They ran him out of there in handcuffs. The location was burned. For obvious corruption, this was last call. Bailey's was ruined as a place for dirty cops and watchers. No cop ever came back. Just like that, IAD blew up the biggest watering hole in the city for corrupt cops. Their decision to arrest Chickie Guerva in Bailey's was not only lazy, it was also mindless and self-defeating. Why burn Bailey's Bar like that? This was their clubhouse, their after-hours hangout. Bailey's Bar was to the corrupt cops what the Ravenite Social Club was to John Gotti. We should have slipped in, like the FBI did with the Ravenite, and wired the place for sight and sound. We would have had all these corrupt cops on tape. Instead, we watched IAD tear the whole thing down in front of our eyes.

Only Yurkiw was still carrying the badge, but I still looked at all three of these guys as cops. I went back to the office and pulled the bible. The bible was the logbook, with a listing of all the cases that came into our office and how they had been closed. It included cases going back three years, and all of the anonymous complaints. "Unidentified male white, plainclothes, unmarked car picking up drug dealers at the conduit." "Unidentified male whites doing stickups." "Criminal impersonation of police officers." All the stuff where nobody had ever been identified. And here they were. Oh Jesus, fifty or sixty complaints. Just pertaining to this MO. Never mind the rest of the corruption in the 75th precinct. The 75th precinct was far outdistancing everyone. So I saw that and I saw these three cops. I went to my captain and said, "Captain, that's them." He looked at me and said, "What are you talking about?" And I told him. "All of this shit for all of these years, that's them. That's why we have never been able to get them. They are doing stickups in their own command, out of uniform, with their own cars. So every time we'd go to look for them, to see who was working in plainclothes that night, we would miss them. It wasn't an anticrime detail. Cops in the 75th precinct had already been rocked by that scandal. These crooks were uniformed cops working their own plainclothes detail." He looked at me and said, "This is one isolated incident." And I said, "I don't think so, Captain. I don't think it is isolated at all. I think these are the guys."

He didn't agree with me, but he admitted we might have a more serious problem. It only takes about nine days after the stickup for the captain to become convinced we needed to do a whole lot more. He came to me and said, "Joe, I think what you have got to do is head a self-generated team." I was going to create a proactive case. He said, "Set one up in the 75th precinct, but be careful. I don't want it to appear we are homing in on a specific group of people or persons. Just do it. Our relationship with IAD has been very poor. So make it general. And another thing—all of the corruption cases involving Dowd and all of those other people now belong to you. You're getting all of them."

I felt good because Michael Dowd was always my pet

project. Now he is my job, period. Granville Davis and Skye Williams were both done with the investigation. I had been working on the guy off and on for two years. And I wanted this investigation. The word I was getting back at the precinct was that Dowd was supposed to be there for the stickup. Everybody believed that Dowd was part of the group that was doing stickups. So when they didn't see him get arrested, they were sure he was a rat.

But we learned the only reason Dowd wasn't there that night was because he got scared. Yurkiw was too fucked up even for Michael Dowd. The special prosecutor should have been embarrassed. They knew about Dowd. They knew about Yurkiw. And nothing happened. They wanted to tell us about a potential tax problem. It was bullshit. Dowd should have been locked up. We should have had a team investigating him. Now I had the case. And I was determined to see it through. I had a clear mission. Now I needed help. I needed informants.

It was the collar to end all collars. Again, it should have ended Michael Dowd. Two cops from the 75th precinct were sitting in their marked blue and white car. Police Officer Robert Harvey was assigned to drive his sergeant, Anthony Caldarola, around. That night, September 11, 1988, Sergeant Caldarola was on loan to the 75th precinct from the 77th precinct. As the patrol supervisor, his job was to drive through the precinct and check up on the cops. He would sign their books once he had finished checking in on them. Beat cops call this getting a scratch.

At about 10:30 P.M., while the cops were parked at the intersection of Warwick and Belmont avenues, they almost suffered the big scratch. Another car came flying through the intersection and nearly smashed into their parked patrol car. A black and white 1981 Oldsmobile ignored the stop sign, barely missed them, and screeched off. The cops gave chase, hitting their lights and siren. It was not their job to arrest anybody tonight. But this was a tough one to ignore.

The cops saw the driver toss a paper bag onto the rear seat. Sergeant Caldarola retrieved the bag and opened it. Inside were four small bottles containing what looked to be cocaine.

"Where is your license?" Sergeant Caldarola asked.

"It's under the visor," he said. "You can keep it."

The sergeant flipped the visor, and another paper containing several clumps of white powder fell on the driver's seat. There was also four hundred dollars tucked in the visor.

"Let's make a deal," said the driver. "It's yours."

The driver was placed under arrest and driven back to the 75th precinct. His name was Joe Adonis.

They did a little more investigating at the scene and discovered that the car ignition switch had been removed. The cops believed this was a very hot car. Harvey searched the glove compartment and found a pair of imported handcuffs and keys. There was also a rotating red dome light. Apparently this guy Adonis liked to play cop.

There were three photographs on the front seat. In one photo, the subject was holding an Uzi machine gun. The poses seemed to suggest that Adonis was a serious fellow. Harvey did a quick search under the seat then and found near the electric seat track another plastic Baggie with a pound of cocaine inside. Adonis had $787 in cash on him.

"Keep it," Adonis said repeatedly. He never knew cops to be shy before.

Adonis said he just got the car back. It had been stolen from him the week before. He admitted the cocaine was his. He also told investigators he had tried to bribe the cops.

"The offer still stands," Adonis said.

The car was then taken back to the 75th precinct park-

ing lot and parked in a slot not far from where Walter
Yurkiw's car had once been discovered. By coincidence,
Adonis and Yurkiw used to park their cars next to each
other in the lot outside Bailey's Bar.

The paperwork started again. The bribery arrest became IAD log number 88-934. The nervous Patrol Borough Brooklyn North duty captain wrote out a report in
his own hand on four pages of white legal paper. It was
addressed to the chief of the department. By noon the
biggest of bosses in the NYPD knew about Joe Adonis
and the cops in Bailey's Bar. The distribution list for the
report was equally impressive. It went to Pamela Hayes
at the special prosecutor's office. It landed on the desk
of Inspector Petrunti at IAD. It went to Operations. It
also went to the 75th precinct. Everyone knew about the
arrest. But only a few people knew the whole story.

They called out the big boys at 3 A.M. No one bothered
to call Joe Trimboli. Lieutenant Tony Vecchi was driven
to the 75th precinct by the investigating officer, Sergeant
Kenneth Carlson. The cops could barely believe what
they heard. It was so fantastic, actually, that Carlson believed Adonis was lying. But it was all true.

Joe Adonis said his father owned a bodega at 924
Blake Avenue called Mr. Joe's Grocery. Joe said he
works in the store with his old man and knows most of
the cops from the 75th precinct from their trips to the
store for beer and soda. On occasion, he said, the cops
even pay for what they take. Michael Dowd never paid.
He was very clear about that from the start.

"He is like us," Adonis said.

Adonis began to know Michael Dowd, ahem, socially.
"Adonis mentioned the following specific locations,"
Carlson later wrote.

Bailey's Bar, Brooklyn; Normandy Bar, Cypress
Avenue and Cooper Avenue; the Hilton Hotel and
the Holiday Inn, both at Kennedy Airport. He said
there were other bars they went to together but he

can't remember specific locations. They would go for drinks and to pick up women and sometimes they would snort cocaine together. This would take place in bar bathrooms or in hotel rooms after they picked up women in the hotel bar. Sometimes Adonis would supply the cocaine and they would share it with Dowd. Adonis never saw Dowd purchase cocaine, but the police officer never asked Adonis to purchase cocaine for him. Adonis states there frequently were other people with them including Dowd's brother, a police officer. He sometimes went with them and that he saw this individual snort cocaine on occasion. He does not know the brother's name but was introduced to him by Michael Dowd as his brother and believes him to be a police officer because he has seen his gun and shield. Based on descriptions, the other people who would occasionally go with them are believed to be Yurkiw and Guzzo and Guerva. Adonis states that he is unable to provide any single date or time when this activity occurred. He knows that Dowd drove a red Corvette and had been in treatment for drinking. He last saw Dowd about two weeks ago, day and time unknown, when Dowd came into the grocery store. They did not go out and there was no narcotics use that day. Adonis knows that federal authorities recently raided a grocery store at Atlantic and Van Siclen. He claims not to know any people involved but knows that they had the drug operation at New Lots and Vermont prior to moving to Atlantic. He states that the operation has since been moved to an auto repair shop at Atlantic Avenue and Crescent Street.

Joe Adonis was everything the internal investigators could have ever hoped for. Obviously the dirty cops trusted him. He knew about Dowd. He knew Walter Yurkiw and his Crew. He knew about Bailey's. He knew about New Lots Avenue and the dealer named Adam. He knew a federal case had happened in there somewhere. He even knew about Auto Sound City. IAD should have rushed in right then and wired Joe Adonis for sight and sound. The experts tell you this is how you build a case. Use Adonis to get Dowd. Use Dowd to topple a half dozen corrupt precincts. Ultimately this is a version of what happened. But first everyone who came in contact with Joe Adonis had to screw up. Given the history, it came as no surprise.

The mistakes began with Sergeant Kenneth Carlson. The first cop to meet Joe Adonis didn't believe him. This mistake in judgment allowed Michael Dowd to roam free for another four years. At every point, Carlson's original mistake was expanded and multiplied. Everyone in the business of overseeing the police—IAD, the DA, and the special prosecutor for corruption—missed the boat with Joe Adonis. Only one man believed from the start that Adonis was the link needed to bring Michael Dowd to justice. His name was Joe Trimboli.

But even before Joe got involved with the would-be informant, the battle lines were being drawn. Sergeant Carlson called the special prosecutor and actually managed to get NA Hawkins on the telephone. Carlson informed Hawkins of the result of his interview with "defendant" Joe Adonis. Hawkins promised to follow up this investigation. Then Hawkins hung up the phone, sighed, and disappeared for another three months.

———

When Adonis got locked up in the 75th precinct, this is where Kenny Carlson and I started to part company. Instead of being friendly, we became barely civil. Adonis got locked up and, continuing his pattern, tried to bribe a couple of officers. They sent two lieutenants over with Sergeant Carlson and a tape recorder. No one ever called me. So they went over and came back with this tape and work sheet. The guy says he knows Dowd. He knows a lot of people. He is the Rosetta Stone to police corruption out there. They lock him up with a kilo of powder that turns out to be cocaine. Don't forget that point.

When they come back to the precinct, the captain shows me their work sheet. I have this case now. I have all of the Dowd cases. And no one called me. I'm livid. One of the lieutenants is my friend Tony Vecchi, the guy who talked me into coming into FIAU. These guys are professional watchers, they are supposed to know better than this. The next day, when they bring the case to me, they really downplay the value of Adonis. I looked at them and said, "You have got to be kidding me. Why wouldn't you at least let me know about this?" And their attitude was, "Did you see Adonis?" And I said, "Of course not." "Well, he's a piece of shit. He's a dirtbag and don't believe anything he says. He couldn't possibly associate with cops. The shit in the back of his car isn't the real deal, it's baby powder."

I distinctly remember that. Of course the stuff was coke. Adonis was the real deal. We had some very heated words. When I asked him later why he didn't let me know about this, he said, "Because first of all the shit in his car isn't real. Adonis is too small-time. He's a dirty scuzzy guy, and cops would never trust him the way he's saying they would. I just feel he's throwing names around. He's bogus." I left the room. At this point I felt their hearts weren't into the investigation. They were just going through the fucking motions. There was a little jealousy and animosity in the office then. I had just been singled out and given that investigation. They had been overlooked. So now they overlooked Adonis.

I asked for permission to go see Adonis in the Brooklyn House of Detention. Everybody knows him as Joe Adonis, but his real name was José Arroyo. I went in the next day with another sergeant from the office named Gus Mulrain. You're let in a big steel gate at the front of Atlantic Avenue, and you show your ID to correction

guards. They guide you over to a spot where you take
your gun out, aim it at a sand bar, and remove the bullets. You hand the bullets and the gun to a guy on the
other side of the partition. They lead you through another
steel door and put you in chairs inside a little glass cubi-
cle. And you sit there and wait.

   I will always remember the first time I saw Joe Adonis.
They took his cuffs off and let him walk in, wearing an
orange prison uniform. He is scared shitless. He comes
over and extends his hand to me, and I shake it. He sat
down opposite me and took a look at my partner. I said,
"It's okay." He stared at me and said, "You know, man,
I want to talk to you, because nobody ever shook my
fucking hand before. They treat me like fucking dirt."
"Let's get down to business," I said. "What is going on
here?" So he started to tell me the whole story. He said,
"My name is Joe Adonis. I know a lot about cops receiving payoffs and doing drugs in the 75th precinct. I know
Michael Dowd, Kenny Eurell, Walter Yurkiw, Jeffrey
Guzzo, and Chickie Guerva." "Do you know anything
about stickups, Joe?" "I not only know about the
Stickup, I know about other stickups." "How do you
know about them?" "I set 'em up, man." "You set up
the stickups?" "Yeah." Adonis says he set the thing up
with Michael Dowd because the guy named Lugo was a
rival drug dealer and Adonis wanted to hurt him. "Was
Michael Dowd involved in this?" He said, "Yes, Michael planned it. Yurkiw and Guzzo were his boys."
Then he explains, "Michael don't take part in the stickups themselves. He isn't a strong arm." He used the plu-
ral form of the word—stickups. "There has only been
one stickup," I say. "No, man, there's been lots of
stickups. I know because I have been involved in them.
It isn't always the same guys. I plan the hit. Michael gets
his boys and they go do their job. Then we meet again at
Bailey's with Chickie at the bar. The back room has a
pool table, and it opens into a blind alley, so it's pretty
safe. And when they come back from a stickup, Yurkiw

will be carrying the bag over his shoulder like a big shot. He'll carry the shit in through the back door. And there will always be ten or twelve cops waiting in the room because they know Yurkiw went to do a stickup and they're waiting for drugs. Walter will open the bag and throw it on the pool table. Everybody gets a chance to take some of the stuff, and what's left over Yurkiw takes and sells. In fact one time Guzzo was pissed off because he wanted an extra ounce and Walter made him pay for it with his piece of the take. Guzzo was really pissed off because he felt Walter should have given it to him for free."

Adonis talked about going with the cops to hotel bars and picking up women. Some of the women in the Crew, Adonis said, were cops. The cops trusted Adonis to hold their guns. Sometimes, he said, they had orgies together. The cops treated Adonis well, they liked him. They gave him the cuffs and the rotating police light. Dowd was playacting cop. Why couldn't Adonis?

Finally the prisoner turns to me and says, "Trimboli, I can't do time. I'm twenty-three years old. I can't do twenty years. In fact I don't want to do no jail time at all." I told him, "If I go to somebody for help, are you willing to talk to them?" He said, "Absolutely." So he got up and I specifically got up and looked him right in the eye. Then I shook his hand. He looked at me and stuck his hands through the partition so they could cuff him again. He looked at me and nodded.

Me and Gus walked out of the building. And when we got outside, Gus turned to face me. He was shaking. He said, "Joey, do me a favor. Don't ever fucking bring me with you on something like this again. I don't want to hear it." Gus did a lot of investigations the same as I did. We felt completely different than my old friend Vecchi and Kenny Carlson. My gut reaction was this guy is holding back some, because he still wants to make a deal. But he knows about Auto Sound City and New Lots Ave too. He mentions a guy named Adam who used to *work for his dad. The kid doesn't want to rat out his father. That makes sense. He also doesn't say anything about Eurell using drugs.*

Anyway, I positively don't buy what the other three investigators have told me about Joe Adonis. You have to put this in perspective. With hindsight, we know that every single thing Adonis told us was true. But it was all new then. And the cops did not want to hear it or even believe it. They had the whole thing handed to them by a street dealer facing no real time, and no one wanted to know the truth or even take a chance on his being right. So the agreement is made that I am going to see the special prosecutor with this. Charles Hynes is too busy with Howard Beach. The guy IAD wants me to see in the SPO's office is named Dan Landes. He is in a Queens courtroom every day helping Hynes try the murder case. Still, a bribery case falls under the jurisdiction of the special prosecutor for corruption. The SPO doesn't have to ask anyone for permission if he wants to make a deal.

Later, they told me, "I can cut this deal myself." But no one wanted this case. IAD had already told me, "You are on your own with this. We can't give you any manpower or money." Then at the last minute, when they heard I was going in to see Adonis, IAD got nervous. They wanted to send a lieutenant with me. I went in without him. I needed help, not a baby-sitter. The IAD guy went in alone after me. He heard all the same stuff. Only he ignored it and called me cursing for seeing Adonis without him.

I was beginning to feel like a schmuck, which is how they wanted me to feel. I was not going to just quit, and I was not going to move on. I was going to get Michael Dowd. By then, that was my function in life. To the observers, I looked peculiar. But that is what the department wanted people to see—an insane chaser. I was playing the traditional role of department zealot. If enough people decide you are crazy in this department, it frees them to walk away. No one has to listen to a fanatic.

They can freeze him out. They can't silence you, but if no one is listening to what you are saying, what good is a voice? This is the way the NYPD handled Frank Serpico too. They made him seem like an unreasonable man. When bosses got tired of hearing Serpico, they quietly hinted the cop was probably nuts anyway. And the "nut job" label dragged Serpico down. It made him disappear. I was determined not to surrender.

Sure, Joe Adonis was a dirtbag. He was a scumbag, too, but he knew what the fuck he was talking about. I was very happy that day. I believed in my heart that Michael Dowd was finally going to jail.

7

THE CHASE

The tug-of-war between good cop and bad cop was really just beginning. The police department was about to abandon Joe Trimboli. He was one man alone. Michael Dowd was getting all the benefits afforded a police department employee. He was anonymous and insulated. The union was there to protect him. The city did not want to know about him. The special prosecutor had given up on finding him or even cops like him. The drug dealers couldn't have been happier. Michael Dowd wasn't working for the city anymore. He was working for Adam Diaz. And Michael Dowd delivered in the crunch.

The dealers told Mike the Cop that they needed to know when the narcotics cops were coming. Adam Diaz was still smarting about his arrest a year earlier. The case had been dropped, but it could have been worse. Diaz could have been stuck in jail for a long time. The only reason the cops had even been able to get close to him, Diaz argued, was because Michael Dowd let down his guard. Dowd called in sick and Diaz spent the day under arrest. Talk about payback. So Diaz wanted to have ears. He needed a police radio. He needed to hear the cops talking their way into his nest next time.

"A radio is not a problem," Dowd told Diaz before he went off to the Farm. "If you want a radio I will get you a radio."

That night Dowd stole a handheld radio from the detective squad room. He handed it to Diaz and even told him how to use it. The dealer gave him a pistol as a gift. Now Diaz and La Compania could hear the cops coming. It was blasphemy of the worst kind.

Once Dowd got away with stealing a department radio and giving it to Diaz, the rogue cop got braver. He began to warn the drug gang when federal agents were in the area. Dowd would call a beeper number and alert Diaz to raids. The warning was pretty simple to read: 911. Dowd was a valuable watchdog. Occasionally when one of the NYPD's Tactical Narcotics Teams hit the area, they would assemble at the 75th precinct. Dowd would watch their roll call and put the numbers 911 into the beeper. The drug dealers would rush to shut down their operations. Officer Dowd, the protector in the blue uniform, was protecting the drug dealers.

The cop was being paid well—about $4,000 a week in the beginning to outfit the gang with badges and guns. Most of the money could be picked up in an envelope left for Eurell at Auto Sound City on Atlantic Avenue. Dowd wasn't a coward when it came time to get paid. He would go to the place himself, in uniform no less, and pick up the envelope from Baron Perez. Auto Sound City was the perfect place to drop drugs. On occasion Dowd would drive his own red Corvette right into the garage. Baron Perez also drove a red Corvette. The mixup was part of the corrupt police officer's cover. Dowd used to keep stolen drugs and guns right in his trunk. Baron Perez would remove the illegal contraband from the trunk and replace it with cash. Sometimes, especially in the beginning when no one was looking at them, Dowd and Eurell would drive their patrol car into the garage. They drove out of Auto Sound City extremely happy customers.

The ten cops in Dowd's Crew were ambitious thieves. A few grew downright frothy when Dowd talked about stealing. They set goals for how much money they would steal in a day. On normal summer tours, they would steal $200 a day. They got more greedy, however, around the holidays. They tried to steal $500 a day around Christmas.

By the start of 1987, even before the cops from the 77th precinct scandal were on trial, Dowd was feeling brave again. He was making $8,000 a week from a drug dealer who wanted tips and the right to brag to his friends that he had a New York City cop on his payroll. Dowd split his time between Bailey's and an isolated Jamaica Bay inlet nicknamed "the Pool." They drank at the Pool, did coke, and fired their weapons into the air. They also plotted drug raids there.

"The Pool was a good place to hide," Dowd used to brag to his crooked compatriots, "from the police." In the 75th precinct there was a new rallying cry.

"Meeting at the Pool tonight," Dowd would yell. And there would be half a dozen cops there for choir practice.

After a while, Dowd wasn't even sure who he could trust to steal anymore. Once, called to a shooting crime scene on Sutter Avenue, Michael Dowd grabbed a stack of $100 bills. He thrust as many as he could into his front pants pocket. At the last second, Dowd looked up and saw a sergeant staring at him.

"Has that been properly vouchered?" the sergeant asked. Dowd panicked. He turned everything in. Later he saw the sergeant. "You had the money in your damn pocket," the sergeant said. "You should have kept it."

The cop had no pride. No amount of money, he felt, was too small to steal. Sure, he would steal from the occasional dead body. But he wouldn't stop just there either. Once Officer Dowd happened upon the scene of a burglary. There was a complainant in the house when Dowd got there, but the complainant was just a kid.

"Where is your mother?" Officer Dowd wanted to know.

"At work," the cop was told.

Suddenly, Michael Dowd saw opportunity. The kid

didn't know where his mother kept her valuables. So Dowd suggested that the kid call his mother and ask where she kept the stash. The kid called and Dowd listened in. By the time the kid hung up the phone, Michael Dowd had emptied the secret drawer of $600. He was very proud of himself too. The money meant nothing to him, but it was a fortune in the ghetto. Dowd asked the kid to hand him the phone.

"Yeah," Police Officer Michael Dowd announced. "They got everything."

The mother cried on the phone for a very long time. The dirty cop wasn't even embarrassed. He went to Bailey's that night and bought drinks for everybody.

"We are just making money off the job," Dowd explained. Good cops, he explained, were cops who wouldn't turn in bad ones. Dowd rolled drunks, sniffed lines of coke off his patrol car dashboard, and generally stole so much money while working as a New York City police officer that, on occasion, Michael Dowd even forgot to pick up his own paycheck. It was nice work if you could get it. By this time, the IAD bosses had heard a lot of rumors about Michael Dowd. But no one believed what they heard. The Internal Affairs cops, showing little imagination, questioned what two patrol cops could contribute to drug dealers to earn that much in bribes.

"What do two guys in a radio car know about narcotics raids?" quipped a smirking Robert Beatty, the IAD honcho, years later. And the answer was, Not very much, but more than the drug dealers.

Still, La Compania needed more from Dowd. They had all the guns, radios, and badges. It was nice to be warned occasionally of an impending drug raid. But it didn't seem to either Chelo or Adam Diaz that Mike the Cop was doing enough to earn his money. So Chelo came up with a mission for him—a road show actually. It happened just before Michael Dowd got scared of losing his job and his chance to steal. There was a guy in the Bronx named Juan who Chelo wanted dead. He had given Chelo a lot of trouble. He had shot up a couple of his places, he had stolen money from him, and he had smacked around a couple of his women. Then the rival dealer quit Brooklyn to hide in the Bronx. He lived in the middle of a nice block and wouldn't come out of the house. Juan would not come to Chelo, and Chelo would not chance going to Juan. So one of the guys went to Michael Dowd and Kenny Eurell with a suggestion.

"You guys are cops," the dealer said. "Go into Juan's house and 'arrest' him."

It was a wonderfully dangerous caper. Dowd liked the idea. Eurell was nervous. No one knows to this day whether Eurell was in on the move or if Dowd dressed someone up to look like Eurell. Dowd was definitely there. And so, unfortunately, was Juan. The cops drove up to the house in the middle of the day in the summer of 1988. They were supposed to go to the Spofford Juvenile Home to drop off a kid. They did that and swung down a ramp off the highway to visit Juan. It was a wonderful cover. If anyone ever saw the cop car in the neighborhood, Dowd had a great answer. "Oh, we drove a kid up to Spofford and got lost." But no one noticed the patrol car. Dowd knocked on the door and went in. Juan was carried out in handcuffs. Juan was not, incidentally, surprised to see cops from the 75th precinct. He had done a lot of things wrong in the neighborhood, and it was normal for the cops to send a car for him. Dowd drove Juan straight back to the corner of Norwood and Fulton. It was darker now.

"Get out," Dowd said.

"Here?" Juan said. "But this isn't the precinct."

"Get out," Dowd said, again.

The prisoner was still in handcuffs. Chelo and his boys were standing right there in the shadows. They stepped forward as Juan climbed out of the backseat. Juan bucked when he saw them and realized his predicament, but it was too late. Juan went quietly and was never seen again.

Michael Dowd and Kenny Eurell split $10,000 in the ultimate police scam. If anyone in IAD was interested—and they weren't—this was how two cops in a patrol car could help a narcotics gang.

The story didn't end there either. The doomed man was executed, investigators were later told, and dumped in the Hudson River. His body was never found. He is still carried on a missing persons report. This information was turned over to IAD in 1991. That should have been the start of an all-hands-on-deck search for witnesses. By then, one federal informant was telling investigators all he knew about the case. What should have become yet another starting point in the Michael Dowd case became another dead end. The case died in a file cabinet at Internal Affairs. A witness identified Dowd from a photo spread. "That is Mike the Cop," the federal witness said in 1991. "He did the kidnapping." Amazingly the witness was never reinterviewed. No one ever even told Joe Trimboli about this case or identification.

Chelo, the informant told federal agents, was paying Michael Dowd as much as $8,000 a week in 1991. But the drug dealer was impatient with Dowd and Eurell's work. He threatened to kill the cop for being too greedy. Dowd warned Chelo of impending drug raids and homicide investigations, the federal informant said. He also advised them to do most of their drug dealing during shift changes in the 75th precinct. Police presence in the area then, Dowd said, would be minimal. So Chelo's people would drive to the corner of Norwood and Fulton or Pine and Pitkin to do their deals at 4 P.M. and midnight. The cops were off the streets then. When they returned, Chelo would close down. Customers knew all about the shift changes. As tired cops returned their patrol cars to the precinct, and fresh cops lined up for roll call, coke-heads in East New York lined up twenty deep to buy tins of what they all called the Shit.

My marriage fell apart. I was never home. I was consumed by this case, and probably a little wacky. By now, Dowd was separated from his wife too. But he split because he's high all the time and can't keep his dick in his pants. I was just consumed with this case. I abandoned my wife emotionally. I was a terrible husband. I couldn't concentrate on my own life anymore. Life was just something that happened between those hours when you worked. Once I went with my wife's cousin, who drove a Corvette, to Michael Dowd's house to do surveillance. He never knew it, but he was doing surveillance. I know it was way out of line, but that is how consumed with this case I became. I was doing stakeouts with people who came over to barbecue steaks.

By this time, I learned Michael Dowd was with Kimberly Welles all the time. He was staying with her and was with her at Christmas that year. I am sitting on all of their houses, all of the time, watching. I don't have time to be a husband. I am failing my own little daughter. I am the only person on this case, and I am working on my days off. I am watching these guys get drunk and I am watching them with their families. I see Kenny Eurell water his lawn and playing with his kid. I am watching this while eating my own Sunday dinner in the car. Imagine a good Italian eating baked ziti in a parked car outside of a corrupt cop's house on a Sunday afternoon. My mother called to say she was ashamed of me.

I would be watching these guys and cursing them out. You only need to get lucky once on surveillance. And I was putting myself in a position to get lucky. I would get out of the car and get close to them. I followed Dowd into a 7-Eleven once. This was in Brentwood. I was standing at the front counter buying cigarettes. Dowd bought beer. "Excuse me," he said. I stepped back to make room for him. I could smell his aftershave. It was Brut. I wanted to look him in the eye. I did, but he didn't

*even remember me, he was probably too fucked up.
Sometimes I sat next to them in restaurants. I liked being
invisible. I liked being the Watcher.*

*I lived in Seaford, which is about thirty miles from
Michael Dowd's house in Brentwood. I would come
home from work, stop in Seaford, and then go to work
on Michael Dowd's house. Sometimes I would sit there
all night, watching. I left my family alone. That's a
shame. I can never reclaim that time. I was unkempt then
with a really long ponytail. I had a full, scraggly beard.
Did they ever make me? They probably did. Was I taking
chances? Yeah. But I didn't know any other way to do it.*

*In the beginning, they let me do weekend observa-
tions. I was watching Dowd's house with Kenny Carlson.
Kenny had a pickup truck; he's like a fucking farmer this
guy. We had gone to a doughnut place and we both had
coffee sitting on the dashboard of the car, and I just took
a bite of a fucking doughnut. And who comes out of
Michael Dowd's house but the king of the castle followed by this big tall redheaded guy. They're both getting into the red Corvette. And Kenny says, "Who the
fuck is that?" I said, "Take a good look, Kenny. That is
Walter Yurkiw." He says, "Get the fuck out of here. Are
you kidding me?" This is maybe two weeks after the
stickup. I says, "No, that's him" and Kenny is yelling,
"Holy shit. We got him." It was a great find. We had
them together right after Yurkiw made bail in the stickup.
We both thought it was fantastic. I couldn't wait to get
back to work and give them this one.*

*And the reaction was much different from what we
expected. They shut us down—no more weekend observations. The captain called us in and told us he couldn't
give us any more weekends because the chief couldn't
spend overtime on this investigation. IAD called me and
actually said, "We don't think this is so bad because he's
not a convicted felon yet." WHAT? Yurkiw only does
stickups, carries cocaine around, and kidnaps people. It
ain't bad enough? At that point I am not telling them*

Dowd is hanging out with Yurkiw, I am telling them Yur-
kiw is living in Michael Dowd's own house. The guy
from IAD called, and I will never forget his words:
"After all, they are friends, there is nothing wrong with
that." Even Kenny thought that was significant. Michael
Dowd was living with a coke-snorting armed robber.
This wasn't an allegation. We saw this with our own
eyes.

Finally I told the captain, "Hey, wait a minute, boss.
This is a significant thing here. We've linked Michael
Dowd with the stickup crew." But they shut us down
anyway. The chief, Thomas Gallagher, said no more
weekend work. He was frightened for his own career.
He once called allegations of police corruption "career
threatening." You couldn't move up the fast track in One
Police Plaza with a scandal around your neck.

I was watching Yurkiw a lot. You couldn't help it. You
would drive to Michael Dowd's house and there he would
be. He also lived with Michael's brother Robert Dowd
for a while. I would go to his home and sit a block away.
You had to be careful out in Suffolk County because you
can't just sit. People see you sitting there, they come out
of their house, they call the police, there's all kinds of
nonsense. This gets more attention from the police than
our surveillance. At one point I had a very near confron-
tation with Walter Yurkiw. I came down Apple Street in
Brentwood, right off the main drag. I always used to
come in through the back roads from Mike's house. I
could use the back streets from Robert's house and
to come up on his brother's house and not be seen. And
I could always see who was behind me. And this time I
made a mistake, I got careless. I came right off the main
road and made a left on Apple. I go past the house, turn
around, and who is coming down the street right at me?
Walter Yurkiw. It's dark out, so at first I think I am okay.
But Walter picked me up immediately. I could see his
fucking eyes. He zeroed in on me. I started down the
street because I didn't want to panic, but I gave it more

gas. I looked in the rearview mirror, and there is fucking Walter, throwing a wild-ass U-turn. I said, "Fuck, this is bad." Because I know that I am going to get into a huge confrontation. Walter couldn't have been in a good mood; he had been arrested again for beating up his girl-friend and threatened a witness in his case. Not the best time for a confrontation. I hit the main corner and hung a right to head back to the highway. And here comes Walter whipping down the street trying to get in behind me. And that's when I hit the gas and jumped onto the parkway. Walter missed the ramp. That was the closest any of them ever came to getting me. Even coked out and everything, Walter Yurkiw made me going by him in the dark. He would have made a good watcher, I guess. That was the scary part.

THE SCHEME

No one wanted to make use of Joe Adonis. Joe Trimboli could not believe he had been abandoned with the self-generated case and a willing informant. But no one he talked to in either the police department or the special prosecutor's office seemed to care about catching Michael Dowd and his corrupt band of crooks. The SPO had Walter Yurkiw in the bodega robbery.

Reporters knew more than the police department wanted to know. Two industrious police reporters from the *New York Post* went out to find Yurkiw in Brooklyn. They found him too—stoned and stumbling around his block. Yurkiw began talking about a corrupt band of cops from the 75th precinct. He had a lot of terrible things to say about Michael Dowd. He also mentioned a cop named Mackey. Yurkiw claimed that the cops were holding up drug dealers and stealing money. In the still-foaming wake of the 77th precinct scandal, the charges seemed wild and even obscene. But then they always do. The police department was counting on doubters.

Yurkiw also talked about some murders. He said the cops he worked with were killers. The reporters later remembered that he was pretty high at the time. He was afraid of going to jail. He did not, however, talk about specifics. If someone came around to listen to him, Yur-

Police Officer Joe Trimboli in 1983, receiving his promotion and sergeant's badge from then Police Commissioner McGuire.

Charles Hynes, the former state special prosecutor for corruption and Brooklyn D.A. at the time of the hearings.

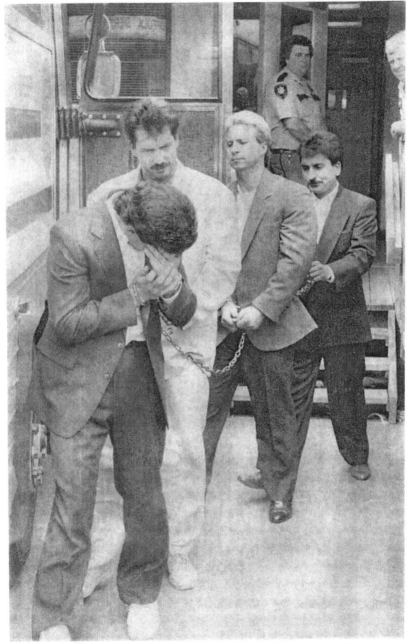

Thomas Mascia, Michael Dowd, Kenneth Eurell, and Daniel Eurell (front to rear) after their arraignment on drug-dealing charges.

Suffolk County D.A. James Catterson, with his dog, Hammer. Catterson was responsible for bringing Dowd to justice for his drug dealing on Long Island.

Former police commissioner with former state appeals court judge Milt Mollen when he announced that Mollen had been selected by Mayor Dinkins to monitor an independent commission investigating allegations of police corruption.

Michael Dowd testifying at the Mollen Commission hearings about his criminal activity and abuse of his position.

Joe Trimboli felt very mixed emotions over the commission. He had hoped this would expose both the police corruption as well as the system that allowed it to flourish.

Twenty years after the Knapp Commission spotlighted police corruption through Frank Serpico's efforts, the scene is revisited by the Mollen Commission as a result of Trimboli's five-year investigation.

Michael Dowd being sworn in prior to testifying before the Mollen Commission, the creation of which was sparked by his arrest.

Joe Trimboli finding the Mollen Commission to be a frustrating experience, and not an opportunity to truly speak out about police corruption and cover-ups.

10

11

Daniel Sullivan gestures as he testifies before the Mollen Commission. Sullivan led the Internal Affairs Bureau throughout the 1990s, but claimed that he knew little or nothing about his division's investigation of Michael Dowd.

Police Commissioner Raymond Kelly testifies before the Commission. "They tried to paint themselves as typical police officers gone astray; the truth is something else," he stated.

Joe Armao (right), head of the Mollen Commission investigation team, conferring with his boss, Milt Mollen, during the hearings.

Michael Dowd's wife,
Bonnie, wipes tears as
she is escorted away
after Dowd's initial guilty
plea in Federal Court.

Judge Kimba Wood
wasn't swayed by the
Mollen Commission
and handed down a
stern sentence on
Michael Dowd.

kiw hinted that he would talk. The reporters, both alert, experienced people, couldn't write an unsubstantiated story. But they could do something. Ultimately, their information was discussed with Internal Affairs. The reporters told the chief, Daniel Sullivan, what they knew. The chief assured them he was looking into the matter. He promised to keep them posted. Once again, nothing ever came of it.

No one ever told Trimboli about Walter Yurkiw's meeting with the reporters. His cops-as-stickup-men theory about the 75th precinct could have been confirmed by Yurkiw in 1989. It was not Yurkiw's last offer to cooperate with investigators. Yurkiw was a rat in waiting. But even without Yurkiw's confession Trimboli realized there was a whole lot more happening in the 75th precinct, and no one wanted to know about it. He called the SPO office daily in November of 1988 trying to set up a meeting with Dan Landes. The prosecutor was presently on trial in Queens, his secretary said. She took his message and then took it time and time again. Trimboli then went around Landes and began to call the attorney for Joe Adonis directly. Landes had set up a meeting with Adonis and his lawyer but never showed. The attorney, Dellicari, seemed interested in talking.

Finally, on December 2, 1988, six weeks later, Captain Friedland, Lieutenant Tony Vecchi, Sergeant Kenny Carlson, and Joe Trimboli met at the SPO's office with Dennis Hawkins and Dan Landes. According to the work sheet Trimboli prepared, they discussed "possible avenues of investigation and new modes of approach." Whatever that meant. Mr. Landes stated, according to the work sheet, that he had nothing new to add to the matter of the 75th precinct investigation. He promised, however, to get a photo album of cops in the precinct and show it around. That would help with surveillance, Landes insisted. He also said he would not entertain a visit from Adonis. Trimboli was ready to explode. He persisted, however, and set up a meeting for December 13, 1988.

Trimboli filed the following report about a three-hour meeting in the special prosecutor's office.

The undersigned was present at the offices of the special prosecutor. The purpose of this visit was to conduct an interview of Mr. José Adonis in the presence of both Mr. Landes and Betty Barros, special prosecutor's office. At the onset of the interview (held in the conference room) Mr. Adonis was apprised of his legal standing relative to information disclosed by Mr. Adonis during the course of the interview. Present at this time was a Mr. Anthony Dellicari, attorney for Mr. Adonis. Shortly before the actual interview, Mr. Dellicari excused himself on the premise that some of the information disclosed might come into conflict with clients he may have or may not have at the present time.

Mr. Adonis restated statements previously made relative to his friendship with P.O. Michael Dowd. He restated that he had socialized with Dowd and his brother, a cop from Queens, along with P.O. Yurkiw, P.O. Guzzo, and P.O. Guerva. Mr. Adonis indicated that he had set up the first of several stickups at 923 Livonia by passing the information on to Yurkiw and company on the premises. Mr. Adonis stated that he stood across the street and watched Yurkiw, Guzzo, and a third Unidentified Male do the first stickup. The unidentified male is listed as M/W 6'0" 200 pounds with a beard. (Named Spenser?) Continuing, Mr. Adonis said he set up this location because he had an argument with the owner of the location. Mr. Adonis indicated that Yurkiw, Guzzo, and Guerva hit the place on a regular basis, culminating in their July arrest. Mr. Adonis stated that while he was not present for additional robberies he was present at Bailey's Bar several times when Yurkiw, Guzzo, and Guerva came in with the proceeds of their robberies consisting of from one-half to a pound of coke. At least eight to ten officers were at Bailey's when some of this contraband was passed around. Later it was removed to an unknown location. Present at these times were P.O. Michael Dowd, P.O. Robert Dowd, P.O. Yurkiw, P.O. Guzzo, P.O. Guerva, P.O. Eurell, and a number of others not known to him by name. At one point Mr. Adonis expressed surprise that Mr. Guzzo had charged him for some coke they had taken during a robbery. Investigating officer asked Mr. Adonis about P.O. Eurell, and he stated that while Eurell had been present when the narcotics were taken into the bar and was present when the other officers were using it, he had never taken any of the drugs himself. Mr. Adonis stated that at one point in time his father had rented out his store to a dealer named Adam. This location is 934 Blake Avenue, Brooklyn. Mr. Adonis stated that P.O. Eurell and P.O. Dowd came into that location on a regular basis and did take payoffs from Mr. Adam to protect his drug operation.

Continuing, Mr. Adonis indicated that when his father found out that Adam was selling drugs at the location he forced him to move out. Adam then moved his operation to a building around the corner from Auto Sound City on Atlantic and Crescent. IO reminded Mr. Adonis that he previously told IO that drugs were being placed inside the autos at Auto Sound City and he said we misunderstood him. The dealers would park their cars at Sound City and walk around the corner to pick up drugs and/or guns at the other building. They would then leave the location on foot with the drugs and/or guns that they had just picked up. IO asked him about the cars they had parked at Sound City, and he stated they would leave them there for weeks or months to have stereo

systems installed. He told the IO, "You know, drug
dealers do have more than one car." I asked Mr.
Adonis about Baron (manager of Sound City) and
his involvement in the drug operation, and he indicated that he did not know if he had any involvement. Baron probably knew what was going on but
he had no direct involvement. He was a middle man.
Mr. Adonis restated P.O. Dowd did deliver drugs
for Adam but now indicated he did not know if he
has continued to do so since he went to the Farm.
He stated that he would be willing to view photos of
the 75th precinct cops in an effort to determine the
identities of the other officers at Bailey's during
drug distribution and use. In addition, Mr. Adonis
indicated that when he and the 75th cops socialized
they would usually get rooms at one of the airport
hotels. It was not their practice to stay at the bar
because they would usually bring women to the
hotel with them. Mr. Adonis indicated he did not
know whether or not any of the women were female officers.

Later Adonis was handed a phone. He knew the number of Auto Sound City by heart. He dialed the number
and asked to speak to Baron Perez. The dealer got on and
talked nicely to Adonis.

Trimboli secretly recorded this meeting to protect himself. He turned the tape over to a captain, who gave it to
a lieutenant. The bosses wanted to enhance the sound.
One week passed and then two. Still, no tape. Finally
the lieutenant said the tape was ruined. It was as if the
conversation never happened. In early 1989, however,
Trimboli learned the tape had been turned over to IAD.
They were secretly monitoring his investigation of the
75th precinct and Michael Dowd. All the information
quietly disappeared into a "tickler" file.

One day Kenny Carlson walked into the FIAU office
smiling. His relationship with Trimboli was getting a lit-

tle bit better, but it was not as good as it had been before IAD tried to hide Joe Adonis's existence from Trimboli. But now Carlson was holding a piece of paper and smiling.

"I hate to do this to you, Joe," Carlson said.

"What?" Joe asked. Carlson handed him the piece of paper. It was a work sheet of an interview with a burglary suspect named Ralph Pittman. He had just been debriefed by a member of the Staten Island District Attorney squad.

"He says he has information on the 75th precinct," Carlson said.

"Oh fuck," Trimboli said.

Carlson pointed to a name on the bottom of the work sheet, Michael Dowd. Ralph Pittman hadn't mentioned the cop by name, but he did say the cop drives a red Corvette and is on the payroll of the Dominican drug dealers. Trimboli was still trying to talk Landes into using Adonis. And it was not going particularly well. The Howard Beach trials were over, but Joe Hynes was getting ready to run for Brooklyn district attorney. The special prosecutor, everyone sensed, was about to become extinct.

"This is fucking great," Trimboli muttered. He had another witness tying Dowd to dealers. IAD was gone, taking the prosecutors with them. And the guys Trimboli worked with were laughingly heaping more cases on him. He was still one cop alone, but even the Watcher was starting to see double.

The first crime Michael Dowd ever permitted was the sin of hubris. The cop believed that he somehow mattered. More important, he believed that in the end his ego would save him. He couldn't be caught stealing because he was Michael Dowd. He was too smart for the chasers and the watchers. Oddly enough one of the first defenses offered by a criminal is intelligence. "Would I be stupid enough to do that?" And the cops think, Yeah, that would be stupid to rob the place you hang out in every day at gunpoint. Once in Queens this guy named Barry Coker walked into his neighborhood bar behind a metal walker. This was his disguise. Barry pulled a pistol and robbed the place. Later the bartender told police all she knew. "Barry Coker strolled in here with a metal walker and robbed the place." People do not commit crimes because they are smart. People do dumb things because they are, well, dumb. So when a killer says to a good detective, "Would I be stupid enough to do that?" a good detective will say, "Yeah, you are that stupid. You didn't kill your mother because you were smart." But for some reason, people always expect criminals to be smarter than they are.

Michael Dowd was stupid because he believed he was an original—a prototype if you will. Occasionally, even with cops, that happens. You come across a dumb one who doesn't know his history. Each generation of thieves perceives itself as the first. They think that just because the guys in the 77th precinct got caught, that doesn't mean they will catch me. I'm too smart to get caught. In truth, Michael Dowd was a fairly slick criminal. His ability to recognize a tail and ditch it frustrated investigators. Ultimately, he only got caught because he got unlucky. But Dowd made a lot of stupid mistakes before then. It was only luck and the stupidity of the IAD that kept him in uniform all those years. At any point investigators could have put a tap on his phone and caught him.

Since July of 1988, the Central Robbery Division in Queens had identified a pattern of commercial robberies in which two "perpetrators" had been identified. They were identified as Michael Walsh, thirty-five, of Elmhurst and Joe Guglielmo of Ozone Park. They did fifteen robberies, the majority of which involved Radio Shack stores. They would walk into a place, ask to see police scanner equipment, and tell the clerk they were police officers. When the stuff was on the counter the police impersonators would pull their guns and commit the robbery. They would steal cash and the scanners. That made them robbers and the supreme police buffs. They also robbed a Pioneer supermarket in Ozone Park in July. The two guys walked into the store and held it up. A third guy drove the getaway car. No one could identify the getaway car driver. They also robbed a bakery and a couple of Knapp Shoe stores.

The robbery investigators said, "Some cop buff is robbing scanners and police footwear." Noting the name of the shoe store (Knapp Shoes as in Knapp Commission), they joked, "It must be Revenge of the Knapp Commission nerds."

On December 8, 1988, a stolen rental car was recovered in the Bronx by the 41st precinct. The cops, all geniuses, never opened the trunk. The car was returned to the Avis yard in Queens. Later that day, a man later identified as Michael Walsh approached an Avis security guard and identified himself as Sergeant Donahue from the 5th precinct. He told the guard he had to inspect the car that was recovered by the 41st precinct. When the guard told him he would have to verify his identification, Walsh left in a brown Oldsmobile along with a white guy who had a mustache. The guard called the precinct and learned there was no such person as Sergeant Donahue.

"If this guy comes back, dial 911," the cop said.

The following day Walsh came back and saw another guard. When the man who identified himself as "Sergeant Donahue" turned the corner and got into the fenced-in area, the guard dialed 911. Walsh was arrested. The trunk was full of goodies, including three stolen scanners and a bogus sergeant's shield, a correction guard's shield, a bogus transit police shield, an FBI light, handcuffs, a room key to the JFK Holiday Inn, and a loaded .38 caliber Colt revolver. The gun had been stolen from a cop in the 32nd precinct in 1982.

After being arrested Walsh made admissions about the robberies but wouldn't talk about anyone else involved. He also admitted stealing a limo with a cellular phone in it. His partner, Guglielmo, still had the limo. A review of phone records showed that calls were made to the 75th precinct. In September, a Queens cop had stopped Walsh's partner, Joe Guglielmo. He was suspected of stealing something from a car. During the process of identifying himself to the cop, Guglielmo exposed a current New York City PBA card that had a shield number on it. He said his father was a cop. The cop let him go but remembered. The cop informed IAD of the incident. A subsequent investigation revealed that Guglielmo was wanted for car theft. They were professional police impersonators. The PBA card belonged to Michael Dowd. He had only one and had never reported it stolen.

No one called Trimboli. Carlson was sent to find out what he could about Michael Dowd, even though he had zero interest in him by then. He didn't find much. Amazingly, a sergeant for Queens FIAU had even called Michael Dowd to come in for an official interview, called a GO 15. Cops must answer questions in exchange for limited immunity. The sergeant never called Brooklyn FIAU to see what they knew about Dowd. The Queens sergeant chose to believe that someone had stolen the police union card from Dowd. After all, the impersonators had a lot of other stolen goods. In a vacuum, Police Officer Michael Dowd's answer—"I lost the card six months ago"— seemed logical. The cop was given a slide. "He couldn't have been stupid enough to give his PBA union card to a gang of police impersonators," the sergeant said. But he was wrong. Years later investigators learned Dowd sold the card. He also drove the getaway car. If Michael Dowd could sell his NYPD badge, why not a union card?

By now IAD was telling everyone connected with the Dowd case to disappear. They even put the orders in writing. Captain Friedland placed a call to Internal Affairs on November 22, 1988, and spoke to another captain. Friedland wanted bodies. IAD told him they would not offer any assistance in this case. They had no cars and equipment to spare. Another captain from IAD called Friedland back shortly.

"We can't help you," said a captain named Nacokivz. "But keep us abreast of what you learn." The captain also told Friedland that Trimboli's investigation would not come into conflict with any existing IAD investigation.

"We have nothing going on in the 75th precinct," Nacokivz said.

Trimboli's captain called Thomas Gallagher, the chief of Patrol in Brooklyn North. The chief shrugged his shoulders. Trimboli filed an innocuous report. The bosses all signed it. The summary was the only work done on Michael Dowd that week.

That same month an IAD cop stumbled upon some information. A reliable informant used in a case on Staten Island had mentioned cops in the 75th precinct. He had helped the FBI in the past in a case against corrupt correction guards. Clearly the guy had a track record. Ken Carlson went to see the guy, Ralph Pittman, in the Brooklyn House of Detention on November 18. The informant said the FBI had sent him to nose around the 75th precinct. In August 1988 he spent nine full days in the precinct. Whenever anybody asked what he was doing there, Pittman said trying to avoid being killed. He said he saw cops in the precinct dealing coke. He identified a photo of an officer who he said was the main supplier and picked out two other officers as dealers. He also stated that a male white officer in the precinct was a runner for the Colombians. Pittman said the guy in the Corvette picks up large amounts of cocaine from their distribution spot—Auto Sound City at Atlantic and Crescent. This officer also set up spots that were robbed by the officers arrested in July. He identified other cops and a female who hung out with the cop in the red Corvette.

This was all interesting to Trimboli. Pittman had Dowd and the Corvette right. He had Auto Sound City right. But he also had a whole different group of corrupt cops working as drug dealers in the 75th precinct. He had the names of four cops who were dealing coke out of the

75th precinct. They all worked in plainclothes. He knew Dowd and he knew the four cops.

Trimboli thought this tale was incredible. But it got even worse. Pittman said he had a girlfriend in the precinct, a civilian who was a coke fiend. She bought drugs from these four cops. He has a name for this woman. Trimboli passed this information along to Landes. If the prosecutor believed the informants he had two major headaches in the 75th precinct. Landes didn't seem interested. He didn't want to make a deal with Adonis because he was an A1 felon. A bad deal with Adonis against a Brooklyn cop could hurt Hynes in the election. Pittman seemed crazy. He had been stabbed in prison. But he was only a two-bit burglar. The woman he mentioned in the precinct did exist, and she was Pittman's girlfriend. But incredibly Landes could not find the woman. The Staten Island DA, Landes insisted, wanted to put the two-bit burglar away as a predicate felon. Landes balked at using either informant to make a case against a New York City police officer. While Pittman was in prison, he had been stabbed for apparently ratting out some correction guards. They wouldn't protect him against the other inmates. He called Trimboli from the infirmary.

"Hey, I told you what was happening," Pittman said. "But fuck a deal. I just need to go upstate to prison. Get me the fuck out of here."

"I will," Trimboli said. "But you have to be straight with me."

"All right," Pittman said. "I've been holding back on you because the girl in the precinct is my girlfriend. And what happened was she got a bad coke habit. She couldn't pay for the coke no more. So the cops what they do is make her give them blow jobs for coke. And I don't want that because she is my lady."

"So what did you do about it?" Trimboli asked. "Did you confront the cops?"

"Nah, man," Pittman said. "I went down there and started selling drugs for them."

Trimboli could not believe this story. But once again he told Landes this latest installment. The prosecutor hated Pittman. He didn't want to use him. No matter how hard Trimboli tried to get Landes to use his influence, he could not get the Staten Island DA to drop his burglary case. Besides, Landes insisted, we can't find this woman. So he let Pittman drift away. Which was too bad, really. Two years later, when an embarrassed police commissioner ordered investigators to find out what went wrong with the Dowd case, they found the woman in twenty-four hours. Trimboli was never allowed even to look for her, but five years later, she had the same memory of her days in the 75th precinct as Ralph Pittman. By then, it was too late to do anything about Michael Dowd or the cops he left behind in the 75th precinct.

The next month, Trimboli got a call from another inmate, named Dennis Washington. This informant didn't and couldn't say he was friends with the cops, but he did have good information. Washington knew the location 924 Blake Avenue. It was the bodega run by Joe Adonis and his father. Washington said the father was in on the drug dealing with the guy named Adam. Washington said cops were pulling up in front of the place in expensive autos. He said Adam paid off the cops. Some of the cops were dealing drugs. Washington wasn't looking for a deal. He just wanted to share information.

Back to Michael Dowd, working in the Whitestone Pound guarding cars that had been ticketed and towed. He couldn't be much help to anyone. Unless you were a drug dealer. The Dominicans were quite clever. They built secret compartments into their cars that would open by hydraulics. You touch a button on the steering wheel and you had a great place to store drugs. Couriers were moving product from Washington Heights into Brooklyn and the Bronx using these compartments. Cops couldn't find the hiding places, so no dealer had to worry about being stopped by lawmen while moving cocaine, guns,

or cash. On occasion those cars would be towed. A
dealer would rush outside to find his car and his stash
gone, and that's where Dowd helped out. So the corrupt
cop was still on the payroll and working.

Joe Trimboli used to go to the pound and study Dowd
through a pair of binoculars. He regularly watched him
from the roof of a building across from the Whitestone
Expressway. On the first day Joe climbed onto the roof,
he met another cop on a stakeout. This cop was older and
assigned to watch the miscreants on modified assignment
in the pound. He worked for FIAU, but no one knew
about him. Trimboli had never met him before. The
owner of the building was mad at the old-time detective
for going home with a set of his keys. Trimboli inter-
vened, called the other detective at home, and made a
quick peace between the forgetful detective and the angry
landlord. The old guy figured he owed Trimboli a favor.

"Listen," the grateful detective said, "I know who
Michael Dowd is and I don't want to know what you are
doing. But IAD sent me the work sheet on his case. It's
about something that happened at the pound. I shouldn't
know about it, but you should."

IAD was icing Trimboli by now. They had a precinct
with twenty-five to thirty dirty cops. No one wanted to
face the problem. They didn't want Trimboli uncovering
the problem and embarrassing the department. Now the
old man had been told something by IAD.

The Feds apparently were doing an investigation at
Auto Sound City. No one had admitted the operation yet,
but it wasn't a secret. Hell, Adonis knew about it. So
through his own informants, Joe knew the dealer named
Adam was involved. But no one in the special prosecutor's office could find out where Adam was. Dan Landes
told Joe the Feds told him that Adam was in the Dominican Republic. When Trimboli asked Landes what
Adam's last name was, the prosecutor replied, "You
know, I forgot to ask them." So Adam was working for
the government. So maybe here was the phantom parallel

investigation again. Someone, somewhere, was going to get Michael Dowd.

But Trimboli could never get good, specific information on Adam or the federal case. If IAD knew, they weren't sharing. Landes did know, and he wasn't saying. The Feds sent two informants into Auto Sound City. They were there to make a buy. Baron Perez ran the play, Michael Dowd was in plainclothes. He carried a gun, shotgunning the marriage between dealers and buyers. The buyers saw him standing against the wall snorting cocaine during the transaction. While the buy was being made, an edgy Dowd walks over to Baron. The manager opens a door and hands Dowd a packet. The buyers had no idea who Dowd is.

About a month after the guys made their deal with Baron they got their car towed. They went to the U.S. attorney and got him to sign a letter. Then they went to the pound. Lo and behold, who do the informants see? Michael Dowd. They look at him and realize he's the guy who shotgunned their transaction. And he's wearing a police shirt and dungarees. Holy shit, they both thought, this guy is a cop. Amazingly, Dowd didn't recognize these two guys as federal operatives. That would have been some scene: shoot-out at the Whitestone pound. They went back to the U.S. attorney's office and spoke to an investigator, who filled out a work sheet. The work sheet was passed from the Feds to IAD. Yet again, no one told Trimboli. They refused to give him the information.

Joe quietly called the U.S. attorney to find out more. Actually, they knew a lot more. The Feds had a major dealer who used to pay off Dowd. Sergeant Trimboli realized then that if the Feds had wanted to arrest Michael Dowd, they had enough by 1988 to get him. But the Feds were working the whole deal. Chelo and dirty cops. The case involved about twenty homicides. It would take two years to close the circle. But at least Trimboli knew that someone was doing the right thing. He figured that even if he stayed shut down by IAD someone would catch Dowd. Someone out there, Trimboli believed, was running a parallel investigation.

Charles Rose, the Chief of the Narcotics Unit in the Eastern District, knew an awful lot about Michael Dowd. He filed a report that landed quietly in the lap of IAD. Rose made arrangements to have both would-be informants interviewed. The witness was named Elvis Quezada. He was a major partner in the operation near Auto Sound City. He was asked if he was paying protection money to any cops from the 75th precinct. He said yes, he was paying money to two cops, Chickie and Mike, through an acquaintance named José Caseras. Adam Diaz along with Caseras owned the El Dorado bodega at the intersection of New Lots and Vermont avenues. He was paying Mike about $4,000 a week for protection. Quezada said that the Caseras operation was hit by the Feds and Mike tried to tip the dealers off but they misunderstood the warning. Caseras then disappeared for about six months, and when he came back he set up shop with Quezada on Atlantic Avenue. He hired Mike, who brought in Chickie. They would watch the outside of the place and call in warnings on their beepers. The secret code was twenty-four. That meant the Feds were coming and they should shut down for twenty-four hours. The dealers paid the cops $3,000 a week. Quezada was shown a photo array of Dowd and ex–Police Officer Guerva. He identified them both.

———

Quezada and Caseras were busted by the Feds. They were big players in Chelo's crew—La Compania. And at one point Carlson came in with a work sheet from Charles Rose. He dropped it on my desk. He was getting out of FIAU. He was going to work with detectives. He didn't want any part of this Internal Affairs stuff anymore. He was going back to work with the regular guys.

He just wanted to get out of that office in one piece. So, I could see the Feds had more. They were very helpful. They gave IAD everything they asked for. They even let a sergeant named Buckley interview Quezada. They would not let us meet the informants who saw Dowd in the pound though. The only rule was that the Feds didn't want us to use these guys on the witness stand. We couldn't blow their Dominican investigation. And that made sense. The Feds caught these guys. The Feds owned them.

So nobody in Internal Affairs wanted to know much about the Dominican drug dealers. Carlson was a good cop, but he was taking the party line: "Trimboli is crazy with the Dowd stuff." It gave him someplace to fall. Carlson wanted to bury the case. God forbid it was real. I wasn't mad, I was furious. IAD never told me about federal informants. But I found out about them and chased them down on my own time. I called Charles Rose. It bothered him terribly that there were cops out there in Brooklyn working with drug dealers who assassinated cops. I asked Rose permission to debrief his informant. By then, Rose admitted the Feds were pretty much done with them. One of them was even out on bail.

I called Caseras at home. He was in Manhattan, and he said he was ready to do time. I asked him if he wanted to make a deal, and he replied, "If you are asking me if I was present when my boss paid off the cops, yeah I was there and I know all about the payoff." I told him, "Listen, you don't want me stumbling around in your Manhattan neighborhood. Why don't you come to Brooklyn and we'll sit down." He said, "Fine, I'll come to Brooklyn." But he never came. I never heard from him again. I was never able to get in touch with him again. I don't know to this day what happened to him.

The amazing thing is that Landes knew about these two guys all the time. He had seen the reports about their conversation. He was privy to information on Dowd and the payoffs. He was privy to what was going on between the 75th precinct and the U.S. attorney's office. Landes never told me when I spoke to him about Adonis and Dowd that he already knew there were two guys saying the same thing. But he knew it was right there in black and white on a work sheet, in his file.

Maybe he didn't want me to know about the federal investigation. Maybe he didn't want to expose himself and Hynes to this kind of attention. How could Hynes, in good conscience, give up his job as special prosecutor and allow the state to shut down that office in this scandal? Hynes wasn't corrupt either. He was just ambitious. So maybe he never knew. Maybe Landes was smart enough never to tell Hynes what was happening.

People stopped going with me to see Landes and Hawkins. They abandoned me and sent me to all of the meetings alone. No one ever went with me to see a prosecutor again. In the end—when this whole thing blew up—it would be my word against theirs. "We didn't simply quit the case," Hynes could argue. "Trimboli didn't bring us good stuff. It's his fault." Clearly, I was being set up for the big fall by the police department and the special prosecutor. They had their bad cop. His name was Trimboli. The only winner in this was the genuinely bad cop, Police Officer Michael Dowd. He was still carrying a badge.

———

The New Year broke in 1989 with what should have been an incredibly huge break in the Dowd case. Joe learned from one of his sources that Dowd was planning a vacation and was supposed to leave the next day. So the Watcher drove out to the Whitestone Pound to meet the police lieutenant running the compound. The most conspicuous criminal in the police department couldn't help bragging to the other cops. He told everyone he was going on vacation to South America with his new blonde girlfriend. In fact it was Dowd's anniversary, January 26—on that same day in 1982 Michael Dowd became a cop.

"Did Officer Dowd happen to mention where he was vacationing?" Trimboli asked. Surveillance of a whole hemisphere could be tough.

"Yes, he did actually," the lieutenant said. "He said he was going to see new friends in the Dominican Republic."

Joe Trimboli couldn't have invented this scenario. Obviously, Michael Dowd felt safe again. He was still being paid by Dominican drug dealers, including Adam Diaz. There was no question about that anymore. In Joe's case folder he had work sheets based on conversations with half a dozen informants. He had operatives telling him that Dowd was making as much as $8,000 a week in payoffs. And now Dowd told his friends that he was going to the Dominican Republic to see his drug-dealing pals. Sergeant Trimboli drove straight to Kennedy Airport from the Whitestone Pound. How delicious, he thought. The investigator was going to follow Michael Dowd into a foreign country. The possibilities for corruption, the Watcher believed, were endless.

He visited each airline that had a flight scheduled for Santo Domingo that day, January 26. Trimboli didn't catch Dowd boarding any of the flights. Joe spoke to the head of the Port Authority Internal Affairs police, who advised him he did not find the name Dowd on any passenger lists for that day. Those IAD cops weren't much more help than his own.

Still, Trimboli believed that Dowd was stupid enough to leave the country and go visit drug dealers in the Dominican Republic. He did some soft talking to a Pan Am flight attendant and got a passenger list for the week's flights. There were only two listed passengers. There it was: "M Dowd." The cop had a reservation for January 30, 1989. He was flying Pan Am flight 2223 at 11:45 P.M. But the flight manifest held another surprise: "Ms. K. Welles." If Joe was right, Officer Dowd would be traveling to the Dominican Republic with Police Officer Kimberly Welles of the 75th precinct. Trimboli was

ecstatic. Dowd had been driving Kimberly's car to and
from work for a week. Joe checked the precinct roster
and she was right there, just like Joe remembered her.
The pieces were finally falling into place.

Enter IAD.

———

*So as soon as I found out who she was and where she
was going, I went to my boss. I told him what was going
on, and he immediately called Internal Affairs. And I
told my boss I wanted to be on a plane to the Dominican
Republic. I wanted to follow them down. And he objected. And IAD vehemently objected. And then a
strange thing happened. I got a phone call back from
Internal Affairs giving me permission to go to the Dominican Republic. Captain Friedland called me into his
office then. "Well," he said, "you know you got permission to go. But I just want to tell you one thing. I'm
not going to object to your going, but I am going to deny
you the right to go." I was stunned. I asked him, why?
"I just want you to understand something. The police in
the Dominican Republic are not the police. They're
thieves. They are all on the payroll of drug dealers. It is
not like you can go down there and confide in anybody.
And it's not like you even know your way around down
there." What he said made a lot of sense. Maybe I
shouldn't have gone. But IAD should have sent a team
of people; why am I one man alone? Where is the DEA?
This is Drug Dealing 101 for them. This is not a case for
Joe Trimboli anymore. Michael Dowd just upped the
ante.*

*Nobody knows this, but I made secret provisions to go
myself. I had people in the Dominican Republic who
were going to bring me into the country as a relative.
They were going to keep me in their house near Santo
Domingo. These were people I knew from Long Island
who came from the Dominican Republic. Like most*

Dominicans, they were good, hard-working people. They were going to bring me into the country as a cousin and secrete me in their house. We made the arrangements. But we decided against it at the last minute. My captain ordered me not to go, and I wondered what would have happened to me if the department found out I went down there.

Over the next five days I was on the phone trying to reach an American Embassy and the DEA. Once again, nobody is helping me. No bosses, no IAD, no direction, no help. I am on the phone in my office in Brooklyn trying to set up a stakeout in Santo Domingo. Even the guys I was talking to had to be thinking: If this is big, why doesn't this guy's boss call us? I speak some Spanish. That helps a little. But we have thousands of Spanish-speaking investigators. Where were they?

I finally got through to the chief counsel, who put me in touch with the DEA. They had to be thinking, Don't the DEA and NYPD have a joint task force in New York City? Why doesn't this dopey sergeant call them? I had, and they hung up on me. I believe Dowd is going down there for a drug meet. That is my information, and I explain it to them. I have two cops coming down there, one male, one female, here are their descriptions. I ask, "Could you tell me where they go and who they see?" All I am asking for is a soft tail. That was the simplest request I could make. IAD could have had the army follow him. The following day Dowd left New York with Officer Welles. The cops were holding hands. But there was another surprise. Walter Yurkiw trailed behind through the lounge, dragging their luggage. And, so, they went to the Dominican Republic. My people saw them get off the plane on the other end, and they followed Dowd and Welles to some place called Casa Campo, a $500-a-night hotel. I didn't know it at the time, but Adam Diaz was there waiting for them. Some people said Adam owned a piece of the hotel. It was no coincidence. So I called the DEA from New York again

and say to them, "What I need to know is for you to let
me know who they meet while they are down there."
And that's when he told me, "Well listen, you gotta understand, we have other priorities down here. We might
be able to get to this, but it is not a priority. We will try
and help you." Later, the DEA told me Dowd and
Welles were on a "flying holiday," whatever that means.
They promised to obtain the phone records from the hotel
but never did that either. It was amazing to me. I was
sitting in Brooklyn trying to organize a tail in the freaking Dominican Republic. IAD could have done this in a
second. They knew about Dowd. They knew about my
case and they knew about the federal case. Did they think
Michael Dowd was innocent, wrongly accused? They
didn't do anything because they didn't want it done. It
would have been embarrassing. It might have blown up
in Brooklyn. Big bosses' careers may have suffered. You
can't trust police to police the police. They get hung up
on too many competing agendas.

I was furious with Dowd and seething at IAD. I
reached out to a guy I know with the Port Authority police. And I told him, "Long shot, but let's search these
two idiots on their way back into the country at Kennedy.
Anyone stupid enough to go down there may be asinine
enough to bring coke back." So I spoke to somebody at
the airport. He said, "Okay, we can randomly pull up to
ten people off a flight and just check them." When they
came out of the area they were searched. Actually their
bags were searched. I wanted them searched bodily, but
no one did that. Walter Yurkiw was there, watching.
Dowd was cursing and pissed off. He pulled his badge
and NYPD identification. He could not believe that he, a
badge-carrying New York City police officer, was being
searched by what he called rent-a-cops. And Dowd was
objecting very loudly to Yurkiw, of all people. "I can't
believe this shit. Do you see how they are treating a guy
on the job?" Actually, Yurkiw got mad too. He
screamed, "Now you know how I feel. When they ar-

rested me, they tossed me too." They found nothing in
the luggage. Five years later Dowd would say to the Mollen Commission investigators, "That was Trimboli trying to get me at Kennedy when I came back from the
Dominican Republic, wasn't it? Well, it almost worked.
If they had searched us, they would have found the
coke."

———————

Kimberly Welles was a bit of a find. She wasn't much
of a cop, actually, and even less of a lady. She cursed
like an out-of-work Teamster and could match any of the
male cops beer for beer. She was not a shrinking violet.
She was crazy about Michael Dowd. She especially liked
him when he was high, which was most of the time. They
were the future of police corruption in the NYPD.

Kimberly Welles took Joe Trimboli's investigations to
a lot of different places. She drove a brand-new white
Grand Am, an easy car to follow. On one occasion,
Trimboli saw her coming out of her house in the company of a white male he knew to have once been a cop in
the 75th precinct. Only now the cop had moved on. Now
he worked in Brooklyn North Narcotics. If this guy was
dirty it was really serious. He was around drugs all the
time. Joe figured this was extremely noteworthy because
Kimberly Welles was fresh from a vacation with a corrupt
cop and his Dominican drug dealer.

On another occasion, Kimberly Welles led Joe on a
trip out to Long Island and the house of a fellow named
Hernandez. He was a drug dealer who worked for Chelo,
and he was putting up Walter Yurkiw for a week. The
circle of intrigue was ever widening. On that trip Kimberly did not drive her own car. She was driving a car
belonging to a cop named Mandig. He worked in Brooklyn North Narcotics. Joe Trimboli was getting tired of
all the circles. While there was no evidence Mandig did
anything wrong, her circle of acquaintances did include

a lot of cops. At a meeting with IAD Trimboli gave investigators all of these names.

At one point Kimberly Welles got a little bit paranoid. She hired a lawyer. She called up IAD and said she was going to sue them for harassing her. She said she had caught whoever was tailing her. Joe's boss came to him the same day.

"You know," the captain said, "IAD wants you to make out a subject card for Kimberly Welles."

Welles was not investigated for any specific indiscretion. She was being followed because Trimboli suspected she was dirty. There was one allegation that a blonde cop was protecting a place at 57 Crescent Street, which was across the street from Auto Sound City. Joe thought this could be Welles. So he filled out a subject card on her. Welles claimed she was upset because she had caught someone tailing her while she was taking her kid to school.

"You know you have been made by her," the captain said.

"What are you talking about?" Trimboli said. "I have a news bulletin for you. I never followed Kimberly when she was taking her kid to school."

"Well, who the fuck was it then?"

"I have no idea," Joe said. "It wasn't me."

Welles may have made Trimboli tailing her some other time, but he had never followed her to school. He chalked it up to that phantom parallel investigation again. Who were those guys? Trimboli wondered.

She was in a car accident that year and injured her head. They said Michael Dowd was driving. She suffered some sort of neurological injury. For a while they put her in the rubber gun squad. It might have been what saved her from ultimate exposure.

One day in 1989 Kimberly Welles called the paper and identified herself as a cop in trouble that wanted to talk to me about police corruption. I had done a lot of work on the 77th precinct case. That trial was over. But sometimes corrupt cops still called. I was tired of being a priest to them. Once a cop from the 77th precinct named Brian O'Regan called me in the newspaper office, and invited me to meet him in an isolated diner in Rockaway. The cop admitted to everything he was going to be charged with in the morning. Then he got in his car and drove away, but the cop did not surrender, as ordered, the next day. He waited until the newspaper appeared with his story, put his police uniform in a garbage bag at the foot of the bed, then laid down in a rented bed and blew his brain across the room.

I never got over that. I think about the last desperate night with Brian O'Regan all the time, and never hang up the phone on cops who want to talk anymore.

"Don't worry," Kimberly Welles said. "I'm not another Brian O'Regan."

We met in a bar called Maguire's that night. She was a pretty raw character, loud and tacky. Actually, she scared some of my friends, the paper's sports columnist and the hunting writer.

"I may be nuts," Kimberly Welles said. "But I'm not crazy." She told us all about Michael Dowd. She seemed to have just broken up with him. He was no longer working in the Whitestone Pound, although she knew all about that.

"How do you know about the Dominican trip?" she was asked.

"I was with him," Kimberly Welles said.

Then she talked a lot about having made the trip to the Dominican Republic. She thought they were being watched by the DEA. She talked about Dowd and his drug use. She said it was only a matter of time before the 75th precinct blew up like the 77th precinct.

"I'm in the rubber gun squad now," Kimberly Welles said. "I was in a car accident with Michael." Then Michael was on wooden barrier detail at the UN, she said. He got drunk on duty during some parade detail with

President George Bush. So Dowd was not cured after his visit to the Farm. She talked a lot about her father. She said her old man was disappointed in her.

"My father hates that I swear so much," she said. She talked about her kid and boyfriends.

She left the bar quite late and called me again the next day. She wanted to talk more. I said I would look into the story, but it seemed kind of old to me. Besides, the DEA knew all about the case. Or so the cop said. I made some calls, and obviously I made a mistake in not pursuing the issue of Michael Dowd's corruption. But I did tell police officials about Dowd, not about my meeting with Kimberly Welles. Just that I talked to a cop who knew Dowd extremely well. I specifically called Daniel Sullivan, the Internal Affairs chief, who I knew slightly from the O'Regan incident, thinking I could trust the chief to do the right thing. Frankly I was worried that Kimberly Welles would cause herself harm.

"Oh, we know all about Michael Dowd and his little trip to the Dominican Republic," Sullivan said. "He is well known to us. We're all over him."

This was half of what I considered fair warning. I also called someone at the 75th precinct who I liked and trusted and gave the boss a heads-up on Michael Dowd and his pal Kimberly. But the boss seemed to know everything about Michael Dowd already. I hung up and moved on, as we do, to the next story. Kimberly Welles called a couple of times after that, but we never met again. Years later I would curse myself for not writing about Michael Dowd earlier, when the story had fallen into my lap.

QUITTERS

*T*hey needed to find a way to get me off the case. The 75th precinct was going to blow up and ruin a lot of careers. You have to understand that the real corruption in this case is not money. The ultimate corruption is power. On one level you have these dirtbags who will steal anything out in front of them. They were being watched by these bosses who will do anything to avoid losing their power in the wake of a corruption scandal. Which leaves you with dueling agendas.

The chief of Patrol in Brooklyn North during the Dowd years was Thomas Gallagher. He was a big, likeable guy who stood six foot four with a huge pair of mitts. I'm sure he had no trouble palming a basketball. And I remember the first time I met him in the chief's office. I wondered, given his size and demeanor, what this guy was like as a rookie cop walking a beat in the 1950s, fifteen years before the Knapp Commission. That guy must have been one hell of a foot cop. That was my first impression of Gallagher. Gallagher said he had something very important on his mind that he wanted to discuss, and I went down there with Captain Stephen Friedland. It was just the three of us. Gallagher told me that he had received information from a number of individuals who said there was a 77th precinct–type scandal

that was about to blow up in the 79th precinct. He wanted
me to handle this matter for him. But the manner in
which Gallagher did this was shocking. I walk into the
room, and he just collapses into the huge chair behind
his desk. "This is career threatening," the chief said.
"And you have got to help me with this." Captain Friedland was standing right next to me. I look at the captain,
and he was just nodding at the chief. So Gallagher tells me
that he has information that these specialized units within
the 79th precinct are trafficking drugs. He would never tell
us who gave him the information, but we think he heard it
at a police bosses' party. He was very explicit about the
fact that it was drug trafficking. During subsequent conversations he will tell us that most of our observations are of
drug locations. Gallagher hears that cops are using sledgehammers to knock down doors and steal drugs. This is
what he wants us to look out for. And we do a great deal
of watching. We can even watch for corruption in this precinct on weekends. I made $4,000 in overtime working
weekends on this case and nothing on Dowd after the one
weekend we saw him with Yurkiw.

In theory, it is all right for a chief to have his own
special detectives. The guy has to be able to protect his
city and his units. He can even do spying. But it is
against department policy to tell investigators to go out
into a precinct and look for drug dealing when you
haven't reported it to IAD. Those guys had nothing on
the 79th. Gallagher got around the rules with the cover
that we were looking into racial trouble in the precinct.
We were out there looking for corrupt cops swinging
sledgehammers.

We already had a version of this in the 75th precinct.
On the one hand Gallagher was telling me to shitcan that
investigation, and on the other to dig into the 79th. Captain Friedland took me for a walk around the park after
our meeting with Gallagher. "You heard the chief," he
said. "This is career threatening. We will spare no end
while looking into this matter for the chief. You will do

whatever you have to do, you will work weekends, you will work twelve-hour shifts doing observations." I am looking at this man in disbelief. He has rejected every single attempt I have made to do a weekend observation on Michael Dowd. Anyway we go back to our office and work out a schedule where we are going to devote twelve hours a day to watching these people, monitor their radio chatter and park outside their homes. Which is how an investigator has to do his job. Which is how a team of us should have done it with Michael Dowd.

And, of course, needless to say this was one humongous wild-goose chase. It was done, I always felt, to keep us out of the 75th precinct. Look at what Gallagher tells us. A corruption scandal is career threatening. Well, we all agree on that. But that isn't why the chief wants us in the 79th and out of the 75th. Michael Dowd could end the career of Chief Thomas Gallagher. Although questioned by Commission investigators, Gallagher was never called before the cameras of the Mollen Commission, probably because he was also around during the Crown Heights riot. Mayor David Dinkins was embarrassed by Crown Heights. The specter and remembrance of a race riot was career threatening for a black mayor in an election year, and no one could look at Gallagher without thinking of Crown Heights. So they never called him. In fact, after Dowd's arrest, he quietly resigned when the new police commissioner, William Bratton, came to town.

One day I was sitting with another investigator, Roscoe Smalls. I was off duty and working on the 75th precinct. Even when they ordered me to, I wouldn't give it up. Career threatening? Michael Dowd was life threatening. Smalls says, "Look, we both know this is bullshit. But if the bosses want to pay us to sit watching nothing, fuck them. Let them do it." I thought it was bad to sit and charge overtime when you knew there wasn't a case. It was obvious the bosses wanted me in the 79th precinct and not in the 75th. The secret investigation lasted six *weeks. By the time I got back to the 75th, Michael Dowd had moved on again. My investigation never really recovered from the lost time; it was the beginning of the end. I never recovered.*

———

At about the same time Kimberly Welles was trying to share her secrets about Michael Dowd with me, Joe Trimboli did a very stupid thing. He wanted to get a look at what was going on inside of Auto Sound City on Atlantic Avenue. So he foolishly came up with a plan to get inside. It was a simple plan really—simpleminded, that is. Joe put his hair into his best ponytail and borrowed Tony Vecchi's car. It had a vanity plate: LOUBABE—short for the nicknames of the owners—Lieutenant (Lou) and Babe (Alice Vecchi). It was the vanity car of all times. As he got out of the car, Joe noticed they had their names TONY and ALICE engraved on the floor mats.

Joe drove up to Auto Sound City and beeped his horn. The metal garage door rolled up. So the sergeant drove up to the gate and parked the car. No one came out to greet him. Curious, Joe Trimboli got out of the car. There was a door he noticed behind the counter. Joe did a stupid cop thing. He walked up to the door and opened it. There was a room inside. Joe didn't see anybody, so he just walked into the room. There was another door at the back of this room. What the hell, Joe thought, I've come this far. He strode into the second back room. He just opened the door and walked right in.

Technically, it was time to die. Sergeant Joseph Trimboli should have been shot on sight. Brooklyn etiquette demanded as much. Joe Trimboli's instincts told him he had just walked in on the middle of a drug deal. Joe looked around for the gunman. There had to be one in there, he realized. Actually, there were two gunmen in the back of the room. They had automatic weapons under their coats. One of the guys, Trimboli immediately recognized, was Adam Diaz. The surprised dealer slipped a hand inside his black leather jacket.

"What you want, mister?" Adam Diaz asked.

"What kind of place is this?" Joe Trimboli asked. "I need my car fixed. What is going on here?"

If anyone made a move, Joe was dead. The cop knew that. He couldn't do anything against automatic weapons. The cop was up against superior firepower. If they searched Trimboli for weapons—which is customary when a white guy walks into the middle of a drug deal—Trimboli would also be dead. The only smart thing he did was to leave his badge at home.

Suddenly Baron Perez was behind him. "What is your problem?" Baron asked. He put his arm around Joe and walked him outside. Baron needed this guy out of the room. And Joe wanted to be gone.

"There is static on the radio," Joe said.

They were both outside now. Baron had walked him out of the room. Adam Diaz and the woman made Joe for a loudmouthed dolt. Trimboli didn't think his problems were over; he did not want to die here. He thought he was about to be stabbed by Baron. Amazingly, they exchanged small talk about stereos. Joe knew nothing about sound systems. Luckily Baron knew even less.

"Can you leave the car?" Baron suggested. Whoever this guy was, the dealers figured they could find out if they kept the car.

"I can come back," Joe said. The dealers were still in the other room with their guns. Joe said a quiet good-bye.

"How is Alice?" Baron Perez asked. The guy had already searched the car. He saw the monogram on the floor mat.

"Alice is always breaking my balls," Joe said. "She screeches louder than the radio."

Baron Perez was pretty slick, Trimboli realized. He read the name on the floor and threw it back at him. Luckily the name "Alice" now meant something to Joe

Trimboli. It was a nice, quiet identification check. Joe waved and screeched away from Auto Sound City.

"I'll be back tomorrow," Joe said.

He was the first working New York City police officer not being paid by drug dealers ever to set foot in the place. Joe was flush with excitement and life as he rushed down Atlantic Avenue. It had been a stupid but wonderful caper. Joe Trimboli went into the place with no backup. He carried no radio. No one in the department knew that Joe Trimboli was even in the place. The bad guys could have killed him and thrown him and the car into a compactor. No one would ever have known. Incredibly Joe had stumbled upon a buy. But he had also stumbled upon huge street information.

"My sources, which are unimpeachable, tell me that the dealer named Adam Diaz is alive and well, and back in East New York," Sergeant Trimboli reported to his captain. "They tell me Adam is with Baron Perez at Auto Sound City."

Later that month, Joe called Landes to ask about Adam Diaz. Trimboli knew that Landes could get the federal prosecutors on the phone. They would talk to each other about cases. They would share secrets. Joe needed to have a sit-down discussion with Adam Diaz. Landes promised to get back to Trimboli, and this time he did. Landes said he had talked to the Feds. "They told me Adam is presently in the Dominican Republic and won't be coming back," Landes said. Joe wanted to know if Landes had thought to ask the Feds Adam's last name. Landes sounded surprised by the question. "You know," he said again. "I didn't think it was important so I didn't ask."

So Adam Diaz was working for the federal government, Trimboli now knew. He felt a little better. The feeling did not last long. On the morning of March 6, 1989, Captain Friedland walked up to Trimboli in the hallway. "They want to see you tomorrow," Friedland said. "They want to review your case."

"They" meant IAD. Friedland and Trimboli met at ten o'clock the next morning. They drove over in the captain's car to IAD headquarters on Poplar Street in Brooklyn Heights. They went up to the second floor. Friedland was waved into a room. Trimboli was made to sit in the hallway. He noticed the secretaries stopped typing. They just stared at him, as if he were on display. About five minutes later the door opened, and a gentleman stepped into the hallway and waved Trimboli in. There were nine people at the round, wooden table. Internal Affairs Chief John Moran was there, surrounded by Captain Callahan, Nacokivz, Johnson, and Friedland. Joe assumed the one vacant chair was for him. As he started to sit down, one of the guys remarked, "And by the way, Sergeant, you seem to be doing pretty well for yourself. How many trips have you made to South America?"

"What the fuck are you talking about?" Trimboli asked.

The man pointed to Trimboli's wrist.

"Well," he said, "I see you are wearing a Rolex."

Trimboli turned back to face the people at the table. They were all asses, he realized. This moment was about to become part of police department folklore. By now all the bosses were looking at Trimboli. He had just been accused of corruption by the IAD bosses.

"Well, Sergeant," Moran said.

Trimboli held up his watch.

"I just want you to know, gentlemen, that this is a thirty-nine-dollar bogus watch. It is a cheap imitation . . . And who the fuck is this asshole?"

Now Chief Moran leaned forward. He knew cheap imitations. Some people accused Moran of being one. "That will be enough of that, Sergeant," he said. "That man happens to be Inspector Pietrunti."

Trimboli was about to put the arrogant-looking police inspector through a wall, but restrained himself. Incredibly, a boss at IAD had just accused Joe Trimboli of corruption. The only cop on the police force to make a career of trying to put Michael Dowd in jail had just been called a thief by IAD. Years later when word of this meeting reached the public, Inspector Pietrunti would be called in and dressed down by Police Commissioner Ray Kelly. He later quietly resigned. Now he just took his seat.

Then the real harassment started. The IAD bosses were not going to review his work now. They had spent two years ignoring and denying his findings. No, they had a different agenda.

"Sergeant, how long have you been on this investigation?"

"Two and a half years," Trimboli said.

"You know, Sergeant," Pietrunti continued, "you come in here and you give us a lot of names. But you never give us anything criminal. You've never once come up with anything criminal the entire time you've been on this investigation."

Someone in the back of the room mumbled, "What are we paying him for, anyway?"

They were banging away at Joe Trimboli pretty good. His captain, Stephen Friedland, said nothing. The captain knew everything Trimboli had done to try and prove the department's case against Dowd. He knew the only thing standing between Dowd and handcuffs was IAD. It was the professional disinterest and even incompetence of IAD that kept Dowd on the police force. But the captain said nothing. Trimboli understood Friedland was no doubt worried about his own career.

So Joe listened patiently to the ranting of idiots. He wasn't going to argue with them or apologize for his investigation. If they wanted him to slink away, Joe would make it even harder to ignore him. Joe Trimboli knew exactly what he was going to do.

Finally, Moran asked, "Sergeant, do you have anything else to say?"

"Yes," Joe Trimboli said. He reached into his folder

for two new work sheets. "As long as I got you all here paying attention, I have two more names for you. These are the names."

The IAD cops were furious. But they took out their pens, and Joe gave them the names of the cops in the narcotics unit he had seen with Dowd's girlfriend Kimberly Welles. Now it was Trimboli's turn for a speaking part. "Anything else?" he wanted to know.

No one in the room dared to ask a question.

"No, Sergeant, step outside," Moran said finally.

———

Those pieces of shit. They had called me corrupt. They had accused me of being a drug dealer who wanted to go to the Dominican Republic too. It was incredible, but maybe this was how absurd and twisted they had become at Internal Affairs: Sergeant Trimboli was only chasing Police Officer Dowd because he was trying to frame an innocent cop. To them, I was just some lazy fanatic, or worse, a counterspy trying to hide my own corruption behind a corruption investigation. They were all lost souls. If the head of IAD can't tell when a watch is fake, how is he going to tell a real cop from a phony. This last meeting with IAD scared me more than anything that happened in my investigation of Michael Dowd. These slugs weren't just not going to miss catching Michael Dowd; they were never, ever, going to catch a corrupt cop again. They thought the good cop was the bad cop. They thought we were somehow misidentified. I made them all unsettled. Years later, when word of this meeting reached Police Commissioner Ray Kelly, he ran most of them out of the department.

———

On April 13, 1989, there was more bad news. The sergeant's sense of abandonment and isolation continued with one final call from Dan Landes. Joe wrote about the heartbreak in his own work sheet for case number 88-966. It was titled Conferral with SPO. It took the Watcher twenty-five minutes to type: ''The End.''

IO received a telephone call from Mr. Dan Landes of the Special Prosecutor's Office. Mr. Landes indicated that during an unrelated conversation with federal authorities the name ADAM came up. The Feds told Mr. Landes that ADAM was now in the Dominican Republic and that it was unlikely that he would return to the country. . . . Additionally Mr. Landes stated that since ADAM was no longer in the country, it would negate any value that Mr. Adonis would serve in this investigation. In conclusion Mr. Landes stated that since it now appeared that nothing criminal was going to come out of this investigation, IO could proceed administratively only if IO could come up with anything on any of the players in this investigation. Mr. Landes stated he was removing himself from the matter and relegating the case to a subordinate. Mr. Landes stated he would contact the lawyer for Mr. Adonis and tell him that he would not need his client for any covert operation.

Kenny Eurell had made the decision to get out. He knew everything there was to know about Michael Dowd. Dowd didn't make a move without Eurell. In fact on the day Dowd showed up high on crack in the precinct threatening to shoot a sergeant, Kenny Eurell had spoken to Dowd on the phone. Then he called in sick to avoid the scene. Kenny Eurell was not going to lose his pension over Michael Dowd. He had worked too hard to steal the money.

When Dowd went into the drunk tank, Eurell got scared the whole thing was going to come crashing in on him. Dowd was obviously out of control. He could flame out at any time and take his partner with him. Eurell asked to be put on a foot post by himself. He walked the streets planning his next move. He needed some sort of injury if he was ever going to retire. When no one was looking, he practiced falling down. On a lot of other nights he was assigned to guard hospital rooms. Sick prisoners could not cause Eurell any kind of injury. So there was nothing in that job for him. However, Kenny Eurell regularly worked guarding the cells in the precinct. All of the guys in the station house knew that Eurell was looking to suffer a minor injury and retire with three-quarters of his pension, tax free. They taunted the prisoners in his presence.

"Go ahead and punch him," the other cops said to the prisoners about Eurell. "He wants you to hit him."

The prisoners were kind of frightened at the invitation to punch a cop in his own precinct. They all refused. Eurell was, ahem, crestfallen. But at least the cop could say he had fallen.

Eurell had to get out, fast. Anything could happen to a cop who worked alone. Once Kenny Eurell was standing on the corner of Riverdale and Sheffield, minding his own business. The cop gave some dirtbag in a passing car some shit. The guy became angry at how he was treated. Later, the guy called the precinct and reported anonymously that Officer Eurell had taken money from him. True, Eurell had grabbed a couple of dollars' "tax" before letting him go home. But with no partner to defend Eurell's honesty, it took a year for IAD to clear his name. That was the kind of stuff IAD investigated.

"I'm getting out of the job before the job gets me," Kenny Eurell told his pals around the locker room.

A lot of nights Eurell worked at the switchboard. He was pushing his hand into the board when he suddenly screamed, "My hand! My hand!" There was nothing wrong with his hand. And actually Eurell didn't want anything to be wrong with his hand. He just needed people to think he had suffered a hand injury. What Eurell really needed was out of the police department. And now he had a medical disability. Just to be sure, he banged the hand on a sink in the locker room on his way out to see the department surgeon.

"Look, it's red," Kenny Eurell yelled, waving his hand. He couldn't have been happier.

Eurell knew the pension rules. He was counting on them. Once a cop retires and gets his pension, the money is his for life. You can kill somebody and go to jail. The NYPD will send checks to you in the big house. Eurell's lawyer argued that a ligament in his hand had been damaged, and the cop could no longer squeeze a trigger.

Still the cop was a little frightened. He had to pass an exit interview with Sergeant Joseph Trimboli.

Someone from IAD named Hannigan called Trimboli on April 19, 1989, to share some news with him. As part of a new service being offered by IAD, Hannigan was calling to advise Trimboli that Eurell had filed for a medical disability from the department. If the retiring cop wanted to get his pension, he would have to answer every question Trimboli put to him. The Watcher's own hands, both of them good, shook when he hung up. Trimboli was going to get his shot at Kenny Eurell, and Michael Dowd, after all.

———

When I found out that Kenny Eurell has put in his retirement papers for a medical disability, I was ecstatic. Well, I don't give a shit about his tax-free salary or anything else, but what I do care about is losing Kenny Eurell. Once he retires, I lose him. I have no more leverage with Kenny Eurell whatsoever. He can spit in my face on the street. So, I go to my boss and I tell him that I want to do a GO (general order) 15 on Eurell. A GO is similar to what I did with Michael Dowd and Walter Yurkiw way back when. I call him in, he brings an attorney, I sit him down, and I question him.

So I go to James Hegarty, and say, "I want to do this

GO 15. Kenny Eurell is ready to retire." I am going to hammer Eurell. I make my current boss, Captain Hegarty, very aware of that fact. I tell him, "Cap, this is our last shot. We've got leverage. He's looking for his pension. He's looking to go. We can really hang him out to dry at this point. We can use the pension against him at this point." That's the way I want to approach it. I have no intention of letting Kenny Eurell walk away with a tax-free pension. I am going to yell, "Stop, thief!" as loud as I can. I want everything Kenny knows before I let him go off the job.

Well, naturally Hegarty has to inform IAD. On the day the GO is scheduled, Kenny walks in with a lawyer. His knees were fucking knocking and his feet were dancing around. He knows that we know. I walk out, I let him see me, and he gets even more nervous. Now he realizes that I am the guy he had caught sitting outside his house in North Babylon. I have been watching him water his lawn for years. When I should have been home with my kid I was watching him with his kid. I literally have my life invested in this guy. I go back into my office and see Granville Davis sitting there. And I say, "Granville, I got him, he's dead. I am going to nail his ass to the cross." I have four hundred pages of work sheets in front of me. I am practicing my speech in my head. "Kenny, I know what you and Michael are doing out there. I want him, not you. I have Joe Adonis. I know about Adam Diaz and Auto Sound City. I am going to lock you up tonight. Your wife is not even going to see you. You are going to wear a wire for me tonight if you want to save your ass and you are going to give me Michael Dowd." This is going to be my approach with him.

Hegarty called me into his office about five minutes before the GO was supposed to start. He says to me, "Let him sit out and sweat a little bit." I said, "He's sweating pretty good right now." Hegarty says, "Well, let him sweat a little more." It gets quiet in the captain's office for a minute. Then he announces, "Joe, I am not *going to allow you to question him." I said, "What are you talking about, Captain? Why would I schedule a GO and not question him?" He says, "I am ordering you not to question him about anything involving your investigation." Well, what the fuck am I going to question him about then? And he gives me some bullshit about an allegation concerning him and his wife dealing drugs out on Long Island, which is small-time. But Hegarty is not going to let me question him about Michael Dowd or anything else. He won't tell me why. He says, "You are not going to question him. And to make sure you don't question him about that, I am going to sit in on your GO."*

Now you gotta understand something. I have had a lieutenant, on occasion, sit in on a GO. Never a captain. Never. Captain Hegarty sat in on this one. Why? I was sure at this point the Feds had an investigation of their own going. The captain was being cute by not telling me outright. It was a game. And a funny thing happened as soon as we sat down with Eurell. Something happened that showed me how the interrogation would have gone. Kenny was so scared. And he doesn't know I have just been called off. So as soon as I turned on the tape, before I even asked a question, Kenny Eurell said, "Nine two four Blake Avenue."

My eyes are wide open. I'm ready to jump him. This is the address of Joe Adonis's place.

Eurell says, "Listen, I know you guys know about it. I used to go to nine two four Blake Avenue." He is putting himself right there. Adam. Adonis. Eurell is putting himself with these people. "I only used to go there and have soda, sit down and bullshit with the old man, José. I don't know nothing else. At one time his son Joe used to come around. I knew him, too. He used to be good; he'd give us a robbery suspect once in a while."

It is all bullshit, but this Eurell believes we are interested in talking about this. He has given us an alibi even before we ask about the crime. Eurell starts with Joe

Adonis. It is how I wanted to start too. Eurell is showing us his fear. He just comes in and blurts this out, no questions asked. Obviously this guy is dying to rat people out. Whatever Kenny Eurell had to do to keep that pension alive, he's willing to do. He knows we are coming for him, so he admits knowing our main guy. He's trying to come up with a legitimate reason for knowing Joe Adonis. And I got him. I'm going to nail him to a cross.

And my captain jumps right in. He cuts me right off and shoves a piece of paper in front of me. "Joe, talk to him about this here." It is about sick days or something equally innocuous. And Kenny looks at the captain, and he looks at me. And he fucking realizes it is over. They're not going to let me get him.

So he sits back in his chair and his whole demeanor changes. And he listens to my questions, but now he has a smirk on his face. Because I am not coming for him. This is nothing like what he expected the day to be. This is cake. Kenny's lawyer is as happy as a pig in shit. And when the GO is over, I hit the fucking button and stopped the tape. Captain Hegarty just gets up and walks out. Eurell left with his lawyer. I was disgusted; I was the last person to leave the room. I walked into the hallway. Kenny was standing there. He'd just taken a sip of water out of the fountain. I thought he was already gone. His head comes up and he is looking right at me. Kenny Eurell says, "Sarge, you ain't going to try and take my pension, are you?" The pension was all that ever mattered to Police Officer Kenny Eurell. I looked at him and said, "Kenny, get the fuck out of my sight." I walked back into my office and sat at my desk. Gus Mulrain came over and said, "I know what they just did to you. They're a bunch of scumbags. Don't take it personally. What you are talking about here is a police department hindering a fucking investigation. They just allowed the guy to steal a pension, no questions asked. They should all be arrested."

Captain Hegarty was an honorable man. I have never

known him *to do anything contrary. He was ordered to
make sure I didn't ask Eurell about being a drug dealer.
If I got Eurell, I would have got the whole precinct, and
they didn't want me to have anybody. The commissioner, Ben Ward, had given a specific order. No more
scandals. Guys were jumping through hoops to follow
his orders.*

*The next time I saw Kenny Eurell he was on the front
page of the newspaper in handcuffs. He had just been
arrested out on Long Island with Michael Dowd and all
the other New York City cops. Kenny Eurell was a weak
man, and the prosecutors out there immediately turned
him. The Suffolk County district attorney turned him
over to the U.S. attorney in the Southern District. Eurell
ratted out Michael Dowd and other cops, including
his nephew, who ratted out two more precincts. The
scandals in the 73rd precinct—the so-called Morgue
Boys—and the 30th precinct—the so-called Dirty Thirty
gang—both broke after Eurell started to rat out other
cops. He literally taught investigators in the Mollen
Commission and the U.S. attorney's office how to trap
dozens of dirty cops. And I was never allowed to question him.*

———

There was still one cop out there that was even luckier
than Michael Dowd—his younger brother Robert. A lot
of cops—too many for Joe Trimboli's taste—still wanted
to believe the union's position, that drug dealers were
trying to get back at Dowd. Michael Dowd was a card-
carrying member of the PBA. So what if Dowd
"loaned" the PBA identification to an armed robber—
that was only an allegation. It had never been proven.
The armed robber was probably trying to frame Michael
Dowd with the drug dealers. It was all a plot, union delegates told their members. It is Us against Them. When
someone then tried to say something terrible about Robert Dowd, the union really howled.

"That is guilt by association," the PBA delegates would scream. "You can't ruin Michael Dowd, so you want to besmirch his brother's stellar reputation."

The accusations against Police Officer Robert Dowd started as soon as Joe Adonis walked on the set in September 1988. Adonis didn't know the guy's name, but he had been introduced to the guy by Michael Dowd as his brother. Adonis had seen the cop's badge and gun. He also saw him snort coke in Bailey's Bar. Lots of coke, he claimed. Lots of times. But the first cop to interview Adonis didn't believe he was for real. Kenny Carlson believed Adonis was driving around with baby powder hidden under his seat; so what if it turned out to be a real kilo of cocaine. Still, Carlson had to make calls. He personally made the call to IAD to report Robert Dowd.

His call was taken by the now infamous Deputy Inspector Michael Pietrunti, the same boss that would later accuse Trimboli of being corrupt. Pietrunti did nothing to put all these pieces together. Later, Robert Dowd was found to have a new roommate—Walter Yurkiw. Eventually, when Michael Dowd was still at the Whitestone Pound, Yurkiw drove Robert Dowd up to the Farm. Robert Dowd couldn't pass a drug test either. Like his brother's, Robert Dowd's job was saved by alcohol. But he got away with it. Robert Dowd was never investigated again. He was the luckiest Dowd of them all. He got a free ride because he was Michael Dowd's brother.

———

They gave me a job to do. It just wasn't my nature to look the other way. It still isn't. I won't quit, ever. Maybe it's a Brooklyn thing. Maybe it's an Italian thing. For me it became a cop thing. I was the last guy you wanted looking at you. Because I wasn't going to stop. I was just going to keep going until I proved or disproved what happened. I couldn't let Michael Dowd remain out there. Once, a long time ago, they took this badge away from me. I lost it for three years. And every night when I went to bed I would see that badge. I could remember every dent and scratch. That badge meant something to me, and it pissed me off that it meant nothing to scum like Dowd.

The hardest thing I ever did was shut down the Dowd investigation, in the fall of 1990. I was told that all of my investigations into the 75th precinct were being shut down. I went to IAD with my captain and sat with a guy named Donnelly who told me, "You've had your investigations long enough. They haven't been fruitful. There is nothing there, and we are going to close them." They told me to write up a preliminary closing, and I did. My version included some pretty hard words about IAD and their lack of assistance in this investigation. The closing report per se is available. It is not the one I wrote. I turned mine in with a lot of venom. And of course they completely cut it up on the computer system. They changed it to strengthen their own fiction. It was the tale they felt more comfortable with. And of course the bottom line for the bosses was their comfort. After all, they said, it's the captain's name that has to appear on the final report, not yours, Sergeant.

They have taken Adonis away. The office of the special state prosecutor for corruption has been closed down by the governor. The U.S. attorney is not helping me. Hynes is now the Brooklyn DA. He stands in the hallway when I come around. No one is going to help us. And so we went back and I wrote the closing. My version included a closing paragraph attacking IAD for its lack of assistance and everything else. I wrote, "This investigation was never attacked the way it should have been. No assistance was provided. No automobiles and no surveillance equipment. No manpower of any type was given. No weekend observations were allowed. No overtime of any kind was approved. We did not avail ourselves of informants. We never conducted integrity tests on the suspected officers. We never did any wiretap surveillance. Therefore this case has been marked Unsubstantiated. Not proven or disproved because of a lack of assistance from Internal Affairs." And of course that paragraph and others were immediately stricken from the closing report. The opus was rewritten into happy horseshit and forwarded to IAD. The report was immediately approved by Internal Affairs. They weren't even questioned; the reports were done deals.

Unknown to me at the time, I later learned that more cases against Dowd were coming in. There were a couple of them after 1990. And the Mollen Commission investigators asked me, "Did they come and tell you more cases were coming in?" No. "Did any investigator come to you and say 'Joe, you are the expert on Michael Dowd. What could you tell me about the guy, just on background?' " Again, no. IAD investigators were forbidden by their investigators even to tell me about the new allegations. They were told, "Don't go near Trimboli. Don't tell him nothing about a new Dowd investigation. We don't want him to start up again." And I would have started up again. Because I never closed the case on my guy, anyway.

Later on, after the Dowd case broke and he got locked up out in Suffolk County, IAD called me in. It was NYPD damage control, big-time. Guys were sitting at their desks trying to rewrite work sheets and department history. When the chiefs were done with me, IAD to review my memory. And the first person to greet me in IAD was Captain Donnelly. Two years before this he booted me off the case and said, "By the way, you know there is nothing there." So now he looks me in the eye and asks, "Do I know you from somewhere?" And I thought that was incredible. And I looked at him and said, "You better fucking know me. You're the guy that told me to close the Dowd case." And his eyes got really wide and he walked away.

———

The first of the last three closing reports on Trimboli's investigations were filed by Captain Bruce Hollenbeck on February 13, 1990. Like the last two that were filed on October 15, 1990, this one was addressed to Thomas Gallagher, the commanding officer of Patrol Borough Brooklyn North. The subject was marked "Investigation of Corruption Case. C# 87/2712, PBBN, FIAU #87/424."

1. Matter investigated by Sergeant Joseph Trimboli, shield number 2608, Patrol Borough Brooklyn North, Field Internal Affairs Unit, under the supervision of Lieutenant Ludwick Hakl and Captain Bruce Hollenbeck, commanding officer, Brooklyn North Field Internal Affairs Unit.

2. Allegation received at the Internal Affairs Division on November 16, 1987, from an anonymous male complainant who stated, Police Officer Michael Dowd, shield number 22310, and Police Officer Kenneth Eurell, shield number 10482, both assigned to the 75th precinct, are being paid off by drug dealers at a grocery store located at New Lots Avenue and Vermont Street. The complainant further alleges that the officers are shaking down drug dealers and giving the proceeds to a friend who runs a car stereo shop on Atlantic Avenue and Crescent Street.

3. A check of department records indicate police officers Dowd and Eurell are partners and are both assigned to uniform-patrol the fifth squad in the 75th precinct. A check of records of central personnel index indicates that 1. P.O. Dowd has five allegations of misconduct on his record. Two of the above involve allegations of

illegal drug activity and were found to be unsubstantiated. 2. P.O. Eurell has three allegations of misconduct. One of the aforementioned allegations is of illegal drug activity. Background checks conducted on both Police)fficer Dowd and Police Officer Eurell do not eveal any unusual possessions that might suggest access to large sums of money. The Organized Crime Control Bureau was contacted and its records indicate there are two locations at New Lots Avenue and Vermont Street for which drug complaints have been received.

4. The investigator conducted seventeen observations averaging one hour in duration at 44 New Lots Avenue and 924 Blake. No known or identifiable members of the service were observed at the location. Further no apparent drug activity was noted at either location. None of the license plates on automobiles at the scene were identified as members of this department.

5. The investigator conducted twenty-one observations averaging one hour in length at Auto Sound City. During each observation, the license plates of automobiles in the vicinity were checked. None were identified as members of this department.

6. The investigator conferred with Inspector Carney, Internal Affairs Division, who recommended that this office attempt to procure financial statements for both officers. Inspector Carney indicated that he would monitor this investigation. All work sheets should be forwarded to his office.

7. Captain Stephen H. Friedland, former commanding officer, PBBN/FIAU, accompanied the investigator to the office of the New York State special prosecutor's office and conferred with Special Assistant Attorney General Dennis

Hawkins. Mr. Hawkins reviewed the allegations against Police Officer Dowd and Police Officer Eurell and indicated he would obtain financial background information on both officers. Mr. Hawkins was subsequently contacted and stated he was unable to procure the financial information.

8. Ten observations were conducted of Michael Dowd when he was assigned limited capacity duty at the Central Repair Shop Motor Transport division (April 14, 1988) and the Whitestone Pound (October 24, 1988).

9. Ten off-duty observations averaging one hour in duration were conducted of P.O. Dowd. During the course of these observations the officer did not visit any known drug locations nor did he engage in any apparent acts of misconduct.

10. Nine observations of P.O. Eurell were conducted at his residence while he was off duty. He did not visit any known drug locations or engage in any apparent acts of misconduct.

11. Police Officer Eurell was transferred to the applicant processing unit in February of 1989. Officer Eurell always appeared fit for duty and did not engage in any acts of misconduct.

12. Police Officer Eurell was interviewed under the provisions of patrol guide procedure 118.9 and stated: He has no knowledge of illegal drug activity involving any members of the service. He further stated he never used narcotics and has never been in the company of any member of the department who did.

13. On September 29, 1989, P.O. Kenneth Eurell was approved by the article 11 pension board for a disability pension. P.O. Eurell has since retired from the department.

14. During the course of this investigation two other investigations alleged similar acts of mis-

conduct on the part of the aforementioned officers. Though the allegations were drug related, the locations differ. Those investigations pertaining to the misconduct of P.O. Dowd are continuing under FIAU case number 88-027 and FIAU S.G. number 88-966.

15. Investigation into the above matter did not develop evidence to support the allegations of the anonymous complainant. Therefore, the disposition in this matter is marked UNSUBSTANTIATED for file.

Bruce A. Hollenbeck
Captain

The gangly and nervous acting chief of Brooklyn North, Thomas Gallagher, must have been relieved. Trimboli closed three more Dowd probes before the fall ended. Three major cases were closed on October 15, 1990. The Yurkiw investigation that led to the self-generated case, an investigation into Dowd's homes, and an allegation that the cop had been seen snorting coke in Auto Sound City all died a quick, premature death. Still, Hollenbeck was no dope. He no doubt believed that this thing would blow up one day. If that happened, Hollenbeck would need a place to land. So after Trimboli had left the investigation he wrote an addendum to the closing report, which was really a trap door. "Although the dispositions in these cases were Unsubstantiated, it is the opinion of the investigators that there was some substance to the allegations." *What?* Someone has alleged that an NYPD cop is a drug dealer, and there is "some substance" to the accusation. Police Commissioner Ray Kelly went crazy when he finally saw this report two years later.

Chief Gallagher was saved, at least momentarily. Either by design or ineptitude, Gallagher had avoided bringing a huge corruption scandal to Brooklyn. But it was only a scandal deferred. Michael Dowd was no longer a "career-threatening" situation. Gallagher endorsed the wonderful closing report with a short letter of his own. The whole affair was filed and forgotten.

Clearly, Michael Dowd put the lives of police officers in jeopardy. It was just blind luck that Police Officer Michael Dowd never got a cop killed. Not that he would have cared, mind you.

One officer who worked alongside Dowd in the 75th precinct was named Joel Goldberg. He was a veteran cop who had no time for Dowd and his nonsense. On October 31, 1990, Police Officer Goldberg was ordered to an address to handle reports of a "domestic dispute."

It was an argument about drugs in a known drug location. Goldberg, an innocent, didn't know Chelo and his gang from the Hole in the Wall Gang. As he entered the stash house, the cop was hit with a shotgun blast at point-blank range. He lost part of his arm. By then Michael Dowd, ever the self-promoting creep, was working in Queens. But he sent his condolences to Goldberg.

Two 75th precinct homicide detectives were sitting in a surveillance van in 1991. One of them, Joe Hall, had walked in to see his boss, Captain George Duke, that year. Hall had a stack of homicide folders under his arm, all drug related. A Dominican gang has taken over East New York, Hall reported, and he had heard about this guy called "Chelo." Duke gave Hall permission to start a task force. (Ultimately Hall and Hank Mathes got into an argument with Joe Borelli, the department's chief of detectives. They quit and became federal agents, taking the Chelo case with them.)

Suddenly Hall saw the bad guys surrounding his van. He started up and began to drive away. The bad guys got into their own car. They followed Hall and started firing shots at his van. Hall grabbed his radio and called in "1013 shots fired." Then he gave a brief description of the other vehicle. The police dispatcher radioed him right back.

"What is the description of the car you are pursuing?" the police dispatcher asked, calmly.

"I'm not chasing anyone," the exasperated detective screamed. "They're chasing me."

And that, in a nutshell, is how things had changed in East New York. Now the bad guys chased the good guys around. Luckily, Hall wasn't hurt. But he never forgot that night or Michael Dowd, the cop who used to try and read names off his desk.

On March 5, 1991, their boss, Captain George Duke, called IAD to report some news. Hall and Mathes had turned in an informant in the Chelo case and taken him to see David Fein, a federal prosecutor in Manhattan. The informant said he ran four spots for Chelo between 1987 and 1989. He said he had attended a meeting between Chelo and Eurell and Dowd, who were being paid $10,000 a week. This went on for a year, he said, until the cops wanted a raise. Then Chelo moved the operation. All of this information was given to IAD, which turned it over to Lieutenant Sino, who got nowhere with the leads. Later, those same informants would be used to nail Dowd with the same information. It was nice to know IAD consistently screwed up, and blew a golden opportunity with Trimboli and Hall's informants.

Now IAD knew about Joe Hall. They also knew about Joe Trimboli. But Hall and Trimboli never knew the other one existed until after Michael Dowd had been caught in Suffolk County. Hall, a traditionalist, may have been reluctant to talk to IAD cops himself, but he certainly disliked Dowd enough to talk to Trimboli. If the department had made one guy aware of the other in 1991 and brought them together, Dowd wouldn't have lasted a week on the street.

The federal racketeering indictment against thirteen main survivors of La Compania was filed on March 26, 1991. It covered a dozen murders. The gang used to make $1 million a week on two Brooklyn street corners.

They would sell their product, police investigations not-withstanding, twenty-four hours a day. The massive amounts of cocaine distributed by Chelo were packaged in Washington Heights and driven to Brooklyn in cars with especially equipped hidden compartments.

Members of La Compania, including Chelo, made it a practice to beat their employees. Intimidation kept the organization spineless. La Compania had a squad of kill-ers that murdered competitors and laborers who ran afoul of the corporation. Chelo protected his base of operations in San Francisco de Macorís—riches, hideouts, and re-cruiting efforts—by buying politicians in the Dominican Republic.

The incestuous nature of drugs and Dominican orga-nized crime in East New York was remarkable. Everyone indicted in the case pleaded guilty, so there was never a public airing of the corruption charges involving Police Officer Michael Dowd. Again, he got lucky. One of the first murders solved by the federal investigators was com-mitted on May 7, 1990. Ramon Diaz was killed by one of the Lugo brothers. Homicide investigators were certainly familiar with the Dominican surnames Diaz and Lugo by then. In 1988, Police Officer Walter Yurkiw robbed the Lugo family bodega at 923 Livonia. He took Braulio Lugo as hostage. Ramon Diaz was also pretty well known. He was related to Adam Diaz. It was a very small world.

Actually, a lot of what was about to become the brief Lugo family history in New York centered on their activ-ity in one Brooklyn home at 672 Jamaica Avenue. The Lugo brothers tried to rob the place, Chelo's stash house, in early 1990. That was extremely stupid. Chelo prom-ised revenge. The first Lugo brother, Robert, was killed as he stood at the corner of Belmont Avenue and Line Street on February 24. The drive-by shooting lasted thirty seconds. Lugo's remaining brothers, Francisco and Rafael, as well as a friend named Esmeraldo Reye were killed on November 7, 1990. Tactically, this shooting was more interesting. All of the dead men thought they were going to a sit-down to make peace with Chelo. Peace was not being offered, however. The three men got out of their car unarmed. The secret compartments were opened when they got out. Guns popped out. The unarmed men were neatly murdered. Chelo was very proud of that killing. But it was the set of murders that put Detective Joe Hall on Chelo's tail.

Before the killings, Chelo's subordinates in the stash house became nervous. They were worried about being robbed again. Officer Goldberg, a seasoned thirteen-year master, was called to the scene. The only cop the dealers had ever seen in the place before was Police Officer Michael Dowd. He always had his hand out. Goldberg had his gun out. So the dealers fired on the cop. The dealer who shot him, who was from San Francisco de Macorís, never made it home alive. The cops called to the scene correctly shot him dead.

Chelo told some cops that he actually approved of the killing. Shooting a cop, he said, was bad for business. It meant more to a drug dealer, apparently, than to Michael Dowd to be even partly responsible for the shooting of a New York City police officer. By then Chelo had stopped paying Michael Dowd. By then he had threatened to hit the cop.

"Mike the Cop wants too much," Chelo was heard to say. "Most of the time he is wrong. He should die."

There was a lot of dying in East New York during the winter of 1991. Two swollen corpses had just been discovered in the marsh out by Jamaica Bay. Actually, they were found near the Pool, where Dowd and his Crew used to play. The message was as clear as the winter sky. You had two informants facedown in a wildlife sanctuary. There is no safe haven for the mob canary, not even in a bird sanctuary.

One of the Dominicans discovered there in handcuffs, blindfolded with duct tape and shot in the head, was

Rogelio Lopez Doran, forty-two. He was the former mayor of San Francisco de Macorís. His family had advised the NYPD of his disappearance in early January. The politician was already two weeks missing by then. The kidnappers made one phone call demanding a ransom payment of cocaine and money. They never called again and they were never apprehended. And then, on August 5, 1991, a fisherman from Queens searching for worms made the gruesome discovery. FBI agents found the case fascinating, if only because it is not every day that you find a former mayor murdered in Queens. They thought they saw Chelo's hand at work here. He gave thousands to politicians at home. The mayor couldn't have been killed without Chelo's knowledge, agents said privately. The FBI further identified Doran as a close friend of two Dominican presidents. He had headed President Joaquin Balaguer's election committee and served as former President Salvador Jorge Blanco's envoy to Colombia.

The second murder victim was Angel Morantin, thirty-two. A Washington Heights drug dealer, Morantin had masqueraded as a travel agent. So drugs and Dominican politics were all over the case. But there wasn't much mystery about the killer's pedigree. A piece of cardboard was wedged between the bodies. It read: "From the San Francisco de Macorís drug cartel."

The cartel was about to take a very large hit. Chelo was about to die of the ultimate American heart disease: greed. He had pretty much lost his love for killing people and drug dealing as Valentine's Day approached. Chelo, much like his former employee Police Officer Kenny Eurell, told associates he was getting out, retiring. The nuts-and-bolts street dealing was handled by a couple of his subordinates, Ramon and Humberto. Chelo only cared about the good life now. He wanted to surround himself with women and retire to San Francisco de Macorís. He decided, however, to raise the $15,000-a-week rent he was charging his subordinates for the right to sell cocaine on the two Brooklyn corners. The new guys were smart. They had ambition and guns. They also realized that all an entrepreneur needed in New York was a little patch of pavement. One corner had been the secret to Chelo. Now he was renting sidewalks to them. Ten days after the former mayor of San Francisco de Macorís was murdered in the bird sanctuary, two assassins waited outside the Bronx home of the town's unofficial mayor. They got out of their car and shot Chelo as he came down the stairs. Chelo died in a bloody cloud of mink. He bled to death as his limo idled nearby.

Hall and Mathes were driving to work on the Southern State Parkway when they heard the news about Chelo. They were about to name him as the kingpin in a huge, multihomicide racketeering indictment. They were kind of defeated, actually. The investigators switched their attention to Michael Dowd and Adam Diaz. Michael Dowd, meanwhile, just changed teams. The dirty cop moved closer to Adam Diaz, his new boy. The Feds switched targets. They moved from Chelo to Dowd.

Within two months after Chelo was murdered, federal investigators were confident they knew what they were talking about. They had a new informant by then. His name was Adam Diaz. Eventually, the Feds also wound up with Joe Adonis. Michael Dowd was over.

10

CAPTURE

Michael Dowd needed a fresh stomping ground. He had been granted a new beginning by the police department, so he needed a new precinct. In the eyes of the NYPD, the cop was pure again. The one investigator who knew better, Joe Trimboli, had been ordered to drop all of his investigations. After he had finished guarding parked cars in the Whitestone Pound, Michael Dowd's new home in Port Jefferson Station became forbidden territory. No one from the NYPD could go there and watch anymore. The cop had been freed from suspicion with no probation. Dowd was still getting high whenever possible, but he stopped drinking as much in public. At least in uniform, anyway. A lot of the old Crew was gone. No one went to Bailey's anymore. Walter Yurkiw was in jail. So was Joe Adonis. Kenny Eurell was home in North Babylon lounging by the pool. Michael Dowd was ready to move on to the next scheme. But first he had to find new turf and a new partner in crime.

One morning in February 1990, Michael Dowd walked into the 94th precinct in Greenpoint, Brooklyn. It was a low-crime precinct that was being used by the NYPD as a dumping ground for troubled cops. The place was a marvel of debauchery. Indeed if Michael Dowd were allowed to design a police station, he would have sketched up the 94th precinct. On his first day there, Dowd needed to see how far he could go with his new bosses. Everything with Dowd was a stress test, and he needed to know the limits. The old deceptions were new again. The first allegation against Dowd in the 75th precinct was that he stole money from dead bodies. In Greenpoint, Dowd didn't even wait for a dead body. He was sent with three officers to a dead man's apartment. The man's family needed a suit for his funeral. On the way into the apartment, Dowd jabbed a sergeant in the ribs.

"There might be something for us inside," Michael Dowd said. "We could get lucky."

This supervisor told the officer to stop fooling around. The PBA ran this precinct. Certain union delegates spent a lot of time drinking, on and off duty. They supervised what they called Monte Carlo Gambling Nights—an evening of drinking and gambling in the precinct basement. Sort of like teaching arsonists how to light gasoline in a firehouse. In the street, in the locker room, in his patrol car, and during Monte Carlo nights, Officer Dowd was always talking drug money. He was always bragging about his homes and his cars. Though most of the 116 cops in the precinct did their jobs well and honestly, the station lacked supervision, discipline, and order, once again allowing Dowd to operate by his own rules.

Dowd loved to be seen as a renegade and continued to report to work drunk. He drank and snorted lines of coke in his patrol car. Although he had been sent away to the Farm and was known to be a crackhead, no one ever ordered him to take a drug test. And when they did finally give Dowd a urine test, he switched the vials, giving investigators "clean" piss.

On October 3, 1991, someone called to say that someone from the Ship's Mast Bar had placed a case of liquor in police car 4247. The complaint was given to Granville Davis. It took Officer Methodical two months just to figure out the caller had transposed the identification number. Car 4247 was out on Staten Island. Car 4742 belonged to Michael Dowd. Not that anyone could find Dowd's car anyway. Dowd and his new pals disappeared for hours. It was impossible for a dispatcher even to raise them on the radio. When they tracked him down he was usually at a bodega, socializing with drug dealers.

Dowd couldn't have been happier. There were no rules. He kept cocaine in his locker. His drug problem was so bad that one cop, William Carlson, refused to work with him anymore.

"You're no fun since you stopped drinking," Dowd complained.

Dowd gravitated to the worst corner in the precinct. The same cop who once felt comfortable hanging out on the corner of Fulton and Norwood in East New York was now hanging out at the corner of Kingston Avenue and Jackson Street. People saw him carrying packages out of a corner bodega all the time.

"You have a gun, you have a shield, and you belong to the biggest street gang in the city," said Carlson, who told *Newsday* he happily retired rather than work with Dowd. "You can take on an attitude that nobody can stop you."

That was Michael Dowd. Eventually, the NYPD police officer nicknamed Most Corrupt Cop Ever wound up with the Cop with the Biggest Grudge Ever. Thomas Mascia was once a good cop. He was very gung ho, brave, and sometimes quite violent. On January 30, 1988, Mascia and two other cops were called to a Brooklyn apartment house. Juan Rodriguez, who was emotionally disturbed, was breaking windows in his own house. The cops handcuffed the guy while he was lying in the fetal position in his own bed. When Rodriguez pushed Mascia, the prosecutor charged, the cop hit him in the head with his portable radio. Rodriguez died on the way to the hospital. Mascia, who bought new batteries at the corner store to replace the blood-soaked ones in his radio, denied crushing the victim's skull. All three cops were charged in the police custody death. They went to a nonjury trial. Hynes was then the Brooklyn district attorney. The prosecution, handled by one of his assistants, was fairly weak. Hispanic and Latino activists in the city all screamed. They held demonstrations. But on March 22, 1990, Officer Mascia was acquitted of assault charges in the police custody death. He was ready to return to work.

But where, and with whom? The cop had a very bad attitude. Mascia hated judges and prosecutors equally. He hated the law, period. That made life difficult for the would-be lawman. He believed everyone was against him, except the PBA. Thomas Mascia was the perfect partner for a rejuvenated and rested Michael Dowd. The extra bonus was that he had no problem with cocaine. His sister, Julie, had just become a transit cop. Then they gave her a drug test, which she failed miserably. His girlfriend was also about to be run off the force. Now Mascia even hated the police department.

In the meantime Joe Trimboli was getting on with his life. On July 11, 1990, he had filed his last investigative work sheet in any of his Michael Dowd case files. He was now assigned to make the rounds of the precincts and give advice to Integrity Control officers. He was marking time until he got out of FIAU and returned to a precinct detective squad. Michael Dowd was a bad memory. He tried not to think about the guy but couldn't help himself. Late in 1990 he wound up at the 94th precinct. In theory, Trimboli went there to talk to the ICO. In actuality, he went there to check on Michael Dowd. Joe never lost sight of the cop. Sometimes—more times than he liked to admit—he would drive by the cop's house just to check on how things were going. Once he changed a tire right in front of Dowd's home so he could sit in the cul-de-sac and watch. Dowd was hung over, passed out in a lawn chair. Trimboli was still slightly obsessed with the case; he was still looking for that lucky break.

Trimboli was amazed when he met the precinct ICO. The cop said he had been watching Dowd very closely.

"Michael Dowd has become a model cop," the ICO claimed. "He has completely turned around his life. The department should be very proud of him."

Trimboli grabbed his own head with both hands rather than attack this guy and cursed.

"Open your eyes, pal," Trimboli said. "You have to watch this guy all the time. If you don't, Michael Dowd will be the end of your career too."

The ICO saw that Police Officer Michael Dowd was given a Highly Competent rating that year. That was Dowd's best mark ever. It was also his last mark.

One afternoon in late 1991 at borough headquarters in the 90th precinct, Trimboli spotted Michael Dowd, who had come there for a training session. Dowd was standing over the water fountain getting a drink. It was the same fountain Kenny Eurell had stopped at on his way out of the police department. As Sergeant Trimboli approached, Michael Dowd caught sight of him out of the corner of his eye. He straightened up and stiffened. It was the cop who Dowd had seen outside his home all of those times. The cop who caught him off post all those years ago with Walter Yurkiw. It was the enemy. The two men stared at each other. Trimboli would not look away. After exchanging the dead stare, Dowd turned around. The Watcher also turned around and started to walk away. But then he heard Dowd stop walking behind him. Trimboli continued down the stairs. He reached the bottom stair and looked up. There was Michael Dowd, watching him. There was nobody in between them. They stared at each other for about thirty seconds. Neither man would break. Finally Dowd coughed and looked away. Trimboli shook his head and continued down the stairs.

This was Suffolk County, circa 1992. And in the supposed hinterlands of western Long Island, the line between good cops and bad guys had not grayed. It hadn't even yellowed.

They were looking to bust drug dealers. The narcotics cops who worked out of a fortress in Yaphank, Long Island, had developed a snitch. In the middle of a cocaine conspiracy case, an informant promised the narcotics squad that he could connect the cops with a lot of people. He never mentioned police, because the only cops he knew put him in handcuffs.

"I can put you in with this guy Harry Vahjean," the informant said. "He's just a kid, but he seems to be moving a lot of product."

So the case began. It wasn't really a case actually. It was just an outing by the narcotics unit. The informant and an undercover had no problem getting close to Harry Vahjean, who lived by himself in a small house in East Islip. Cops would sit on the house and watch. They did the first buy that day, and built from there.

The cops went to Robert Ewald, the chief of the narcotics bureau in Suffolk County. The assistant district attorney was a raillike man who was determined to stand, fortresslike, against the entry of drugs into Suffolk County. There were two young assistants in his office, Tracy Hoffman and Jenny Butow. The assistants were less experienced than Ewald but equally ardent. All that followed—the Suffolk arrests, the federal and state cases, the commissioner's destruction of the Internal Affairs Division, the Mollen Commission hearings, and the eventual collapse of half a dozen city police stations—is all a result of their work. Along with Ewald, they were the Mothers of Invention, so to speak. Amazingly, they would never be thanked publicly by any of the state or federal prosecutors who feasted on their evidence.

The narcotics detectives were going by the book. Their investigation was classic because it was so ordinary. Michael Dowd could easily have been caught by using the principles taught in Sleuth 101. The first guy had been arrested and turned. Then they used the informant to introduce their undercover to the drug dealers. The next stop was to get a wiretap order, which Ewald gladly signed. The case was starting to look mildly interesting, but only mildly.

On February 24, 1992, the undercover walked into Harry Vahjean's house and saw a blond guy in his early thirties. The guy said his name was Kenny. The guy didn't talk much; he seemed a little nervous. The undercover left the apartment. No cocaine was exchanged, but they agreed to talk more. Kenny watched the undercover leave and get in a car and then wrote down the license plate.

"Can I use your phone?" Kenny asked Harry. "I want to check on this guy."

Kenny picked up a phone and dialed a number in Brooklyn. He asked to speak to Danny Eurell. When someone asked who was calling, the investigators heard Kenny say, "Eurell from the seven five." The man on the other end of the phone recognized Kenny's voice. "Sure, pal," he replied. In another second, Danny Eurell got on the phone.

"I need you to run a plate for me," Kenny said to his cousin. "I'll come over and get it tonight. We need to know who we are dealing with." Kenny read off to Danny the license plate number of the undercover cop's car. Using a police department computer, Danny Eurell did the plate check at ten-thirty that night. Though it was a phony, set up to look legitimate by the Suffolk cops, no one, not even a computer whiz working in the Department of Motor Vehicles, could trace the license plate back to narcotics cops. During two monitored phone calls that day, Kenny and Danny made small talk about what they called "the job." It wasn't much really, just two drug dealers talking shop.

In the unmarked Suffolk County Police Department's surveillance van, parked nearby, two narcotics cops listened in on the phone conversation. They were not privy to any conversation inside the house. One of them, the more experienced detective in the unmarked van, was struck by an odd sensation. He was listening to an odd version of himself.

"That's a cop talking," the detective said. "This guy just called a New York City police precinct and asked someone to run a check on a plate for him. The bad guys are cops."

An hour later, they knew Kenny Eurell had called Brooklyn's 73rd precinct from a phone in a drug dealer's house. Police Officer Danny Eurell ran the plate for his retired cousin. Somewhere in New York, someone had just lit a crack pipe and a bomb.

Then the cops ran a plate check on Kenny Eurell's car. They now know he lives on Westchester Avenue in North Babylon. One of the case detectives checked with the NYPD. Kenny Eurell retired with a hand disability in 1989. Danny Eurell was an active cop with a clean record who lived in North Babylon. On March 2, IAD opened a new file, based on the Suffolk County inquiry. P.O. Daniel Eurell was supplying police department information to his cousin Kenneth Eurell. A wiretap order for Kenny Eurell's house was signed by a judge the next day, and Danny's phone was also tapped. Now Suffolk detectives were up on both lines, listening to Kenny and Danny at home. And the case was beginning to take off. The next day, Michael Dowd called.

"Hello, Loser," Michael Dowd said.

"Hello, Loser," Kenny Eurell answered.

The meaning of this conversation was not lost on Robert Ewald, who admitted to being something of a cop buff. That day he named the case Operation Loser. Luckily, this was never an NYPD Internal Affairs case. This was a cocaine case in Suffolk County. They all said that "out here" it still means something to be a cop. So the cops out there went after Dowd with a vengeance.

Suffolk County was scared of letting IAD know too much, too soon. On March 20, 1992, Lieutenant Thomas Dowd called Suffolk County to inquire about the case.

They hung up and called to inquire about Thomas Dowd. Michael Dowd had just become a subject. Was Thomas Dowd a relative? The DA thought the Dowds might be related. It was just coincidence. There is no relationship between the two. But now, on April 2, IAD knew that Dowd was also a subject out in Suffolk.

On April 15, 1992, electronic eavesdropping equipment was installed on Michael Dowd's home telephone line. Suffolk just needed to identify the players. In all, there were about fifty guys involved in the conspiracy. Actually, there were two branches of criminals. On one side you had the white guys, cops mostly. They were known as the Loser's Club. It was funny, but these guys only trusted white folk. On the other side you had your more traditional drug dealers—stickup men and connivers with long rap sheets. They were known as the Losers, period. Neither group seemed to know that the other group existed. Everything went through Harry Vahjean. Oddly enough, to the Suffolk cops he was a minor player at first. They believed he was slow and stupid, something of a dolt. There was a quick reevaluation.

By late April, investigators knew that Dowd was an active New York City cop with ties to Kenny Eurell. They once had been partners in Brooklyn's most notorious precinct, but NYPD Internal Affairs would not give the Suffolk cops any information. So the Suffolk cops didn't know about the drug allegations and IAD's reluctance to nail the cops. IAD seemed embarrassed to talk about Dowd and Eurell.

Steadily, more cops began to talk their way into the web being spun by the Suffolk police. Danny Eurell started to get calls from his partner, Phil Carlucci. One cop from the 73rd precinct led investigators to another cop, and then another. Police Officer Kevin Hembury was calling his partner regularly, looking to be made part of a drug scheme. Another cop from the precinct was overheard selling steroids to them. The corrupt cops wanted to look like Superman when they came busting into an apartment. Eventually, when Hembury and Carlucci started talking, a whole precinct would fall. These two cops told federal prosecutors about the Morgue Boys—a blue gang in the 73rd precinct. The Morgue Boys used to meet at an old factory in the neighborhood that built refrigeration units for medical examiners.

Through all of this, in every conversation reviewed by assistant district attorneys Hoffman and Butow there was one constant. His name was Michael Dowd. He was the soundtrack of corruption.

In total, investigators identified six cops and one former cop. But, over the next two years, before the whole thing was over, those six cops would lead investigators to another sixty corrupt cops. Not to mention a couple of wives. Carlucci's wife helped the cops move money and stolen checks. Kenny Eurell's wife helped them move cash and packages.

The Loser's Club existed for a year before narcotics discovered it. By the time examiners uncovered the ring, Kenny Eurell was turning his share of the business over to Vahjean.

"I'm not going to touch the stuff anymore," Eurell said. "Harry is going to do that now and I'm going to charge him."

So, Kenny Eurell had farmed out his franchise. There were several combinations that made the business go. One of the easiest involved Dowd. He would drive to Brooklyn and either buy or steal a dealer's coke. Then he would drive the coke out to Suffolk County and hand it to Eurell, who would give it to Vahjean.

In the end, Kenny Eurell was kind of like an adviser. He had created the cocaine pipeline and hired the workers. Now he could relax. He sat around his house and played with the kids at pool parties. He had no job. But he did have drugs and the pension money, not to mention a Corvette. As a precaution, he kept a black pit bull in his backyard.

Twenty-eight wiretap orders were issued. Rather than

hide their identities as police officers, the corrupt cops traded on their badges. Dowd boasted as loudly in Suffolk County as he did in Brooklyn. In the city, Dowd bragged to cops that he was a drug dealer. In the country he bragged to drug dealers that he was a cop.

Traditionally, the further along you get in an investigation, the closer you get to your target. The cops tried to stay away from obvious drug terminology. They didn't talk about coke on the phone, particularly on the 73rd precinct phones. Still, Kenny Eurell wasn't very inventive. Instead of coke, he talked about suits and Sheetrock. The words were in the news then. They were being used by every gangster caught on a phone tap. This was a terrible comment on the lack of originality in the ring. But by then they probably figured they could say anything and get away with it. Everyone who heard the cops on tape knew they were making a coke deal. A lot of the tricks the cops had been taught by real drug dealers came in handy. They used the same numbers, 911 and 24, on beepers.

With Vahjean doing the actual transactions, the cops were free to move on to other matters. And here the details of the drug trades got more interesting. The cops would all "pool their money" and then buy cocaine from a dealer named Ramon, Dowd said. The cocaine would then be driven back to Long Island and sold. Back in 1987, this is precisely the way Joe Adonis told IAD that Police Officer Michael Dowd was doing business. Joe Trimboli had been right about Dowd then and, as Suffolk County investigators learned, he was right today.

The investigators were surprised and disappointed. Kenny Eurell, they discovered, was the ultimate manipulator. He sold cocaine out of a house with a FOR SALE sign out in front of it. He wrote a letter to a newspaper, *Suffolk Life,* complaining about taxes. "I am leaving," Kenny Eurell wrote. "Taxes are driving me out of Suffolk County."

The arrogance was incredible, the investigators said. Eurell wasn't paying taxes on coke money. He was also stealing a pension from the city tax coffers. Even worse, detectives were being paid by Suffolk County taxes to follow this dirtbag around day and night. The Letters of Outrage, as Kenny Eurell liked to brag about them in his neighborhood, may have been the ultimate outrage.

"He's really complaining that his cocaine business isn't making enough to pay his taxes on Long Island," said Tracy Hoffman, the assistant on the case.

The letter was the final insult to the diligent detectives assigned to Operation Loser. In the end, Eurell was as lazy a drug dealer as he had been a cop. At first, he sold coke and distributed it himself. It was a thriving business. But then Eurell told Harry Vahjean, "I'll give you my customers and suppliers. All I ask is my cut in return."

On one occasion members of the Loser's Club pooled a total of $100,000. At first, investigators couldn't understand how cops could have so much cash on hand. Then they learned the cops were robbing drug dealers in the city. They would then pool the stolen money and buy cocaine, which they turned around and sold. The cops were doubling the value of every dollar they stole. It was great work if you could get it.

Michael Dowd came up with $17,550 in late April. He kept that much money kicking around his new house in Port Jefferson Station. By then even his new partner, Thomas Mascia, was interested in dealing coke. Mascia didn't give Dowd any money to buy drugs, but he didn't tell him to take a hike either.

"I fell into it there in the end," Mascia would later say.

Eventually the corrupt cops realized they could make an even more monstrous profit if they sold their coke in a better market.

"We can triple our investment if we sell the coke in Atlantic City," Kenny Eurell said. It fell to Dowd to make the arrangements, and he did so happily and quickly.

The Suffolk cops had all of these conversations on tape. Robert Ewald began to wonder in late April how deeply into the city the corrupt cops would take him. Ewald would go anywhere the case took him. The Suffolk County District Attorney, James Catterson, would not back down. Catterson didn't care about borders any more than he cared about jurisdictions. If these cops were drug dealers, Catterson gave Ewald explicit orders to ferret them out.

IAD was only vaguely interested. They were surprised Dowd and Eurell had talked on the phone. But it was still a thing that happened "out there." By now, however, Ewald believed the cops were driving the shipments in and out of the city themselves. A couple of dealers, including the troubled son of a brilliant detective boss in Queens, were driving into the city to run coke back out to the suburbs. Ewald had to send narcotics investigators with them. He wasn't shy, either, about stepping on the toes of feet that had backed away from arresting Michael Dowd and Kenny Eurell years ago.

Still, he invited IAD into the case. He wasn't going to tweak them. Even the city investigators admitted privately that IAD had screwed Joe Trimboli and a dozen Dowd cases. Some of them were happy to have what was now either the sixteenth or seventeenth chance to nail him.

"Can you arrange to get it?" they heard a frantic Kenny Eurell ask Dowd when he was talking about a dealer he knew in the city. "Can you make it happen for me?"

"You got it, Loser," Dowd replied.

The next day Michael Dowd went to a bodega and picked up some cocaine. He drove it back to Long Island. Kenny Eurell couldn't have been happier. Neither could the police tracking the case.

The Suffolk cops drove into the city with video cameras. IAD even managed to set up the equipment. It was really quite easy and incredible. Even the New York City cops were amazed. No one had ever made tapes like this before. CNN was going to go crazy when they got a load of these cops.

While Los Angeles was erupting over the Rodney King verdict, back in New York City Michael Dowd drove in to work. The cop was ten times the criminal and twice the drunk as anyone ever accused Rodney King of being. And yet, Michael Dowd bragged to his drug-dealing friends that night, "If I had jacked Rodney King, the bastard never would have gotten up." It was amazing, everyone agreed, that after the Rodney King verdict there was no riot or violence in New York City. Everyone said that was a victory for Mayor David Dinkins and his police department. On the very night Dinkins slept peacefully in Gracie Mansion and the New York City Police Department was being credited with saving the city, Suffolk County cops recorded Dowd on videotape doing a drug deal. It would be two years before anyone saw the tape publicly, but it was worth watching. At one point, the dealer is seen outside the car. Then you see him giving uniformed cops the package; it is a four-ounce sale. On the tape, Michael Dowd is seen smiling. He had a lot to laugh about.

On the night of the arrest, May 6, 1992, the Suffolk cops followed four men into and then out of New York City to make the pickup Dowd had set up. They went straight to Vahjean's house. A case that had started with a phone call from this same address ended with cops rushing in to arrest Kenny Eurell. When they struck, Eurell was doing a sniff test on the coke and was very surprised to see them. He asked permission to go puke in the bathroom.

They grabbed Michael Dowd the same night too. The investigators drove to the 94th precinct with the same temerity they would have approached a crack house. Dowd and Mascia were on patrol. A detective put a red light on the roof of his car and hit the switch and pulled over Dowd. He was in uniform with a noseful of cocaine. After all those years of investigations, Police Officer Michael Dowd was fired from the police department for being high on cocaine.

On the way back out to Long Island, Dowd tried to be funny. But he wasn't some dope walking down a bus aisle half-naked anymore. He was finally under arrest. Laughs from cops would be tough to come by.

"Hey, can we pull over and get a six-pack?" Michael Dowd asked. And then Michael Dowd offered the NYPD his immortal, lasting slight. "The NYPD couldn't get me," he bragged. "It took Suffolk County to catch me."

They were all taken to the DWI facility in the Dennison Building. Dot Eurell, Kenny's wife, was very happy to see her husband. She never liked him being a drug dealer. She always told her husband that she believed having a drug dealer for a dad presented the wrong image for their kids.

"I told you this would happen," she told her husband. He turned in his chair to avoid the domestic argument. Fifty people were arrested that night. They took $20,000 in cash and a 9 millimeter pistol out of Dowd's house. The serial number had been filed off. They also found two phone numbers in his bureau. One listed a number in Santo Domingo with the handwritten notation "Adam Diaz." The second listed a number in Brooklyn at Auto Sound City and the notation "Adam Diaz." In addition to three of Dowd's cars, authorities also confiscated a 1986 Buick from Carlucci, a 1987 Bronco from Danny Eurell, and a 1989 Lincoln, 1987 Corvette, and 1990 Chevrolet from the happy pensioner, Kenny Eurell.

Michael Dowd was one of the last prisoners to arrive. He said to the Suffolk cops, "Hey, how about a little professional courtesy? We're all cops here." They wanted to smack him. Kenny was actually surprised to see Michael. He raised an eyebrow.

"Hello, Loser," he said.

"Hello, Scummer," Michael Dowd said. "What are the losers in the world doing tonight?"

The story was big for a day or two. If the NYPD had to live with corruption stories, this one wasn't bad. The dirty cops did their bad business out on Long Island. It wasn't, the department spokesman said, a replay of the 77th precinct scandal. The most intelligent statements in the Dowd matter were being offered by Suffolk cops.

"If they're in fact involved with cocaine, they don't belong on a police force, they belong in jail," said Lieutenant Robert Muller. "It's an embarrassment. The fact that it's a different department doesn't relieve us of any embarrassment."

The questions about IAD were obvious, though, even absent any facts. Why did it take Suffolk County authorities to make the case against Dowd and his Crew? They sold their drugs on Long Island but got them on the job, everyone agreed. Where was IAD? Did they just miss one? IAD said yes. They wanted the entire country to believe they had been outsmarted by a crafty crew and its monstrous genius.

"We did look at him, but we couldn't tag him," said IAD Chief Robert Beatty. "Sometimes you have to marshal all of your forces finally to succeed. With guys like Michael Dowd, sometimes that is what it takes. They are extremely bright and know law enforcement."

This was incredibly insulting to the guys who had tried, guys like Trimboli. All of them knew that cops like Beatty were the problem. It was apparently their love of career and advancement that kept investigators from ending Dowd's career. And now they had to protect their careers by saying that Dowd had never been an IAD problem.

True, one of the system's chief anticorruption safeguards had been imprudently removed in 1990 when Governor Mario Cuomo abolished the offices of the special prosecutor. But that was only half of the problem. The Dowd case had been well known to the SPO, and they were as guilty as IAD in allowing Dowd to flourish. Internal Affairs had simply abandoned the police corruption business. In 1987 there was a total of 112 police officers charged with corruption or police misconduct. By 1990, two years before Dowd was arrested, there were no corruption arrests in the NYPD.

"These were individuals acting on their own," Beatty said. By then, the IAD chief looked and sounded like a Michael Dowd apologist. Still, by the end of the second week in May, the story of the so-called cocaine cops was dying on an inside news page. New York City didn't care about a drug problem on Long Island. Off-duty cops moonlighting as drug dealers was a boring story. It couldn't approach the 77th precinct scandal for local interest, and there was no national interest in routine police corruption.

Even Michael Dowd was bored with all the attention. When police officers arrived at his door later that spring with a copy of departmental charges, the corrupt cop simply ordered them off his property. They rang the doorbell again, and Dowd started screaming for the cops to leave what had already been correctly identified on the front page of the *New York Post* as THE HOUSE THAT COKE BUILT.

The suspended cop, now facing a life sentence, said, "Get the fuck out of here."

11

COVER-UP

The cop story was over. In the city of New York, which has a limited attention span, this Long Island story of police corruption had come and gone in a week. The police commissioner, Lee Brown, had taken a helicopter out to Suffolk County and announced the bad cops slipped through the cracks. The PC had ten more cops assigned to his helicopter detail that day than had even been assigned to try and catch Michael Dowd. Commissioner Brown, a smart fellow who just never made sense in New York, actually called Michael Dowd and Kenny Eurell "a Suffolk County problem." Then he jumped back in the helicopter to avoid traffic on the Long Island Expressway. The IAD chief, Beatty, said something equally moronic about the cops being risk takers. But the police reporters wrote it and walked away. They were sick of corruption too.

My son was born the night of the riots in Los Angeles. So I was on vacation when the cops were arrested in Suffolk County. The story was over, thankfully. I was not that excited about the story because I had done it before. I spent most of two years writing for *New York Newsday* about the 77th precinct scandal and most of a year with Henry Winter, the cop who brought down a precinct. I always believed that Winter was a good cop who went bad. Unlike Dowd, who became a cop to steal, the corrupt cops in the 77th precinct had no such sinister mission. Winter came to a rough precinct and did terrible things. But though he was a corrupt cop, I always believed he was a follower. He didn't steal out of frustration or greed. Winter stole because he wanted to be accepted by the Club. And at the 77th precinct the most popular group was a gang of thieves.

But other parts of that story made it wearisome too. Police Officer Brian O'Regan had killed himself after I went out to meet him and take notes for his obituary. He even waited until the newspaper came out with the story in it. Suicide is a pretty severe review.

I wrote a book on post-Knapp police corruption, which in the context of this madness is really kind of funny. Dowd later said that he had studied *Buddy Boys* as a police corruption "how-to" manual. Anyone else who read the book could have predicted the collapse of IAD and the destructive ambition of Hynes. It took me a long time after that to like cops again. It took the cops even longer to trust me. I liked detectives, though. The rank-and-file cops on patrol seemed to be loud yahoos—almost like a bowling team full of hockey fans. The PBA encouraged them to be loud and stupid. So I preferred detectives. It was amusing, I always told young reporters, but something wonderfully decent seemed to happen each time a policeman earned a detective's gold shield. If you have five good detectives, say one in each borough, a columnist can cover the entire city. Detectives were the best friends you could have in the newspaper business. God invented them for slow days in the newspaper office.

At that time Pete Hamill also wrote for the *New York Post*. He was very giving with advice and guidance. He asked me, "Where have you been on this cop thing? You should weigh in on this story." He was always decent with advice like that in the newsroom. I was out on Long Island that weekend but looked at a map and realized most of these corrupt cops lived nearby. At around 9 P.M.

on a Saturday night I got in the car and went to take a look. The first house I went to belonged to Danny Eurell. It was a small thing, a minor place really, and I could see kids in the window. I went to the door and knocked but then thought better of bothering these people. All the cops were still in jail, trying to raise bail. I wasn't even sure I liked the story. I went to the next house on the list. It was in North Babylon and belonged to Kenny Eurell. No one was home, which made sense. Eurell and his wife were both in jail. It was custom-built on an acre and included an indoor pool. The cop was retired a couple years now; even I knew that much then. Maybe the ex-cop had been lucky with investments or something.

I drove up to Port Jefferson Station next. Michael Dowd lived at the end of a cul-de-sac in a towering yellow Colonial on a knoll. As my car approached, a set of motion detectors ignited a domino string of harsh lights along the block. Unless Michael Dowd was driving, it would be impossible for crime to sneak up on this block. The paint on the renovated house was new and almost wet to the touch. The place had the crisp, clean smell of money. The grass on the one-acre lot was as neatly cropped as the hair on a police cadet's head. It would have been nice to sit there outside the $350,000 home on a spring afternoon and daydream. Kids roller-skated and played street hockey in the cul-de-sac. There were half a dozen cars in Dowd's driveway. One thing was obvious: No cop making $40,000 a year could possibly afford all of this. Obviously, if IAD ever sent a surveillance team out here, Michael Dowd would have been indicted on the house alone. They would have at least gotten the police officer's financial reports. That was step one. It was the step the SPO would never help Joe Trimboli make.

There were a couple more homes to look at in Stony Brook. One belonged to a cop from the 73rd precinct named Kevin Hembury. It had been recently renovated. A new fence surrounded the whole property, and a new four-wheel-drive truck was in the driveway. It was too much house for an honest cop. Philip Carlucci used to drive into work with Hembury at the 73rd precinct. Carlucci's house was even more impressive than Hembury's. He was at the end of a dreamy lane too. The cops had gone to the academy together. I went back the next day to see if the houses looked as impressive in the daylight. They did. Michael Dowd's wife was holding a young baby in the window. She was young and I felt bad for her.

"Who the fuck are you?" Mrs. Dowd wanted to know. "Are you one of those motherfucking IAD shitheads?" I told her my name and said her husband would know it. I did not feel so bad anymore about violating the woman's sense of space.

The next day, May 13, 1992, the *New York Post* ran photographs of the cops' homes. Michael Dowd's residence was pictured on the front page under the headline THE HOUSE THAT COKE BUILT. It was obvious to everyone who saw the photographs that these cops were making money illegally. The cops' homes shouted the word *scandal,* but no one from IAD had ever been out to look at the homes. The story took off.

I began to hear stories about this guy named Joseph Trimboli. Anonymous men, obviously cops, would call me at the *Post* and say, "You have to find Joe Trimboli. He is the key to this whole thing." I wasn't sure where to find him. But then another person called and said, "He is the sergeant at the 61st precinct in Brooklyn." I wasn't sure what story Trimboli had to say, but I gave our police reporter, Anne Murray, his phone number. She knew about Dowd and had once interviewed Yurkiw. She got Trimboli on the phone.

Now that I knew Joseph Trimboli existed, I got busy with the story. The people in Suffolk County were very good. I learned all about their videotapes and taped phone conversations. The case had been made by talented Long Island cops. People forgot that and credited Internal Affairs. But the case was made by narcotics cops interested in arresting drug dealers. It was a classic investigation. They built and built and built. And when they heard cops in the conversation, no one flinched. It didn't matter what these guys did in New York City. They were drug dealers in Suffolk County, Long Island, and simply had to be arrested. There was even a sense of rivalry here. The Suffolk County cops were better paid, and they felt more honest. The case fit their jingoistic argument perfectly. The videotape story about the so-called Loser's Club also made the front page. I knew a lot of people at the 75th precinct. They were telling me about Joseph Trimboli too. I couldn't use their names but I knew them well. These were trusted people who, I learned, had met Trimboli.

"You have to get Trimboli to tell you what happened," said one boss. "If he tells you what happened, the story will take down the whole department."

The investigators who created the Chelo case were my friends. Joe Hall was a wonderful detective, obviously a world-class investigator. I had known Hank Mathes and Mike Race from the 77th precinct days. Along with Jerry Holly and Frank Shields, they taught me how to cover cops. I drove out to Hall's house. All of the sleuths were there, sitting in the kitchen. I was amazed at the story they told about Dowd and the drug dealers. But mostly I was shocked to learn about IAD's slipshod investigation. They were equally shocked.

"I told them," Joe Hall said. "We even gave them the informant."

In a way, it fit their stereotype of IAD. Cops believe that IAD cops are stumblebums. These detectives gave IAD a case and a witness. IAD could do nothing. Mike Race obviously enjoyed turning the tables on IAD by talking about their foul-ups. They all agreed that I had to find Trimboli. The *Post* ran a front-page story the next day. It detailed the story of the kidnapping attempt. It

featured a mug shot of Michael Dowd and was headlined, THE DIRTIEST COP EVER.

I called Joe Trimboli two days later. The sergeant, who
now ran a Brooklyn detective squad, agreed to meet with
me in front of the precinct. I drove out, parked in front
of the place, and called Trimboli a couple of times on a
cellular phone, but they said the sergeant was gone for
the day. Trimboli stood me up. But as I drove away that
day I noticed a guy in a phone booth and was struck by
an odd feeling. I felt I was being observed. And I was.
The Watcher was studying me from across the street.

After being given the runaround, I was even more determined to meet Joe Trimboli. I didn't know what the
sergeant could tell me, but I knew Trimboli was the real
Michael Dowd story. Everyone was telling me that the
department should have known about Dowd years ago.
Trimboli made the guy his career, they said, and no one
would listen.

At this point, Trimboli's name had not appeared in any
newspaper. The city did not know he belonged to this
story—whatever the Dowd story was. I ran the sergeant's name in the computer. I was looking for an address in New York City or Long Island. There were half
a dozen Joseph Trimbolis in Brooklyn and Queens. None
were the right age. Four cars were registered to a Joseph
Trimboli dating back to 1979. All of the cars were traced
back to Seaford, Long Island. The license also listed
Seaford as his home address. There was one car registered to the same Joseph Trimboli in Rockville Centre.
But the telephone company said there was no telephone
for Joseph Trimboli, listed or unlisted, at that address. I
was frustrated. But then my wife looked at the list and
figured it out.

"He must be going through a divorce," she said. "He
must be staying with a girlfriend in Rockville Centre."

Then I got out the reverse directory—a phone book
where numbers give you names. The people in the house
had been living there for twenty years. Maybe relatives,

I thought, and called. An elderly woman answered. When I asked for Joe Trimboli she said, "He's not in yet. He's still at work. He will be home at midnight."

Bingo. Trimboli was working a four-to-twelve tour.

I drove out and sat on the house. I stayed parked there until 5 A.M., well after every last call in every bar had been offered. Nothing. Finally, I went home. Trimboli called early the next morning, laughing.

"If I had two guys like you helping me with Michael Dowd," Joe Trimboli said, "I would have got the bum five years ago. My aunt made you waiting outside, sitting in your car, and called me in the precinct. I ran the plate, and there you were. But you are pretty good. All the other schmucks are looking for me up in Seaford."

We made plans to meet on Sunday night in a Starrett City parking lot, just off of the Belt Parkway. I hadn't been there for years. Trimboli, the former Starrett City security guard, knew every inch of the place. There was no guarantee that the sergeant would even talk to me about the case. We agreed to meet, nothing more.

"I will find you," Trimboli said.

Obviously, I was the first one there. I got there at about nine in the evening. I made a right off of Pennsylvania Avenue and drove past some sort of community center. I parked on the main road in back of a black car and stayed there for an hour, waiting. There was a steady stream of traffic, but no one stopped or looked suspicious. Suddenly, two cars parked across the street, about a hundred yards away. They were facing each other— driver's window to driver's window. The operators were talking. They each had a male passenger. I looked closer and spotted one extra but tiny antenna on the back of each vehicle. Detectives. They were anticrime cops from the 75th precinct. I got nervous because I didn't want the cops to recognize me or spot me talking to Joe Trimboli. Whatever happened down the road, I knew then, we would need the meeting to be deniable.

Quickly, the cars screeched off, burning rubber. I relaxed and hit the window button. I gazed to my right and saw a man with grayish hair positioned there. The Watcher had been standing there for half an hour.

"They're just from the precinct," Joe Trimboli said. "Don't worry about them."

I got out and came around. The man studied me and backpedaled slowly into the parking lot.

"You alone?" he asked.

I nodded. We stood there looking at each other nervously. We moved around each other, measuring each other like two fighters. We were each looking for a weakness. Trimboli noticed that I was not carrying a pencil or notebook.

"You wired?" Trimboli asked.

"No." And I wasn't, either.

We were unsure what to do with our hands, so we reached for cigarettes and shared a match. It was the first thing we ever did together.

"I will lose my job," Trimboli said. "If I tell you what happened, they will fire me. They are already trying to make me the scapegoat."

I knew that. Police Commissioner Lee Brown and his Internal Affairs chief, Robert Beatty, were out there doing major-league damage control. They had the city convinced that Michael Dowd was an aberration. He dealt cocaine at home in Suffolk County. As far as the NYPD was admitting, Police Officer Michael Dowd was guilty of moonlighting as a drug dealer.

"You are going to have to trust me," I said. "No one will ever know we talked."

Trimboli was anxious and confused. He loved the New York City Police Department. They had screwed him, sure, but he was still one of them. He didn't know this newspaper guy from Adam. Why tell me about Adam Diaz? I wasn't even a retired cop. Trimboli reasoned that if he talked he would be betraying his police department. He didn't need revenge on IAD that badly. Joe Trimboli commanded a precinct detective squad in Brooklyn now, which is all he ever wanted anyway. It is the reason he went into the Field Internal Affairs Unit. The chase was over. Michael Dowd was gone, arrested out in Suffolk County. The story could die with Joe Trimboli.

"I'm leaving now," Trimboli said. I reached for another cigarette. We were both watching the parking lot entrance. Trimboli was shaking with a case of the skitters. His eyes were shy and even vague. The sergeant had never even talked to a reporter before. He was certain a photographer would jump out of the bushes any moment and snap his picture. He would be on the front page, destroyed.

"I knew Brian O'Regan," Trimboli said.

I was ready to go now. But the sergeant didn't leave. I was a little spooked by the reference to the dead cop. Most people believe that reporters will do anything for a story. It is the fable of infamy that newspaper people have to live with. It is an untruth, and the good ones can work around the stereotype. Sure, everyone who is any good in the newspaper business wants a good story. But the truth is that good stories last for a week. They are not permanent. When reporters are young they make stupid mistakes. Hopefully you learn some pace and manners as you move through stories.

Eventually, the good people will argue, the only person who matters in a tale is the onlooker. The columnist is the constant. He develops a voice. If the voice isn't shrill or silly, you can trust his sound. So I wasn't going to hurt Joe Trimboli, or even use him. I actually had a plan that could help the scared cop.

"If I tell your story correctly none of the bosses will be able to come near you," I said. "We never quote you in the story. We are just omnipotent. We know your story and it is a grand tale of one man against the police department."

"I don't want to be a hero," Trimboli said. "Shit, they wouldn't let me catch the guy."

The sergeant was still obviously stung by his memory of Michael Dowd, who had been arrested a month earlier, and no one had mentioned Joe Trimboli publicly yet. The department did not want him to exist. He was one man standing in the middle of a deserted parking lot in East New York. I thought the cop looked shaken and even teary. But it might have been cigarette smoke in Sergeant Trimboli's eye. The sergeant looked away before I could be sure.

"Are you sure you are not wired?" Trimboli said. "If anyone in the department saw me with you I would be fired."

I took off my jacket and held my arms out so he could search me. The sergeant did not search me.

Just then, a car drove into the lot, and we both flinched. We had been there for an hour now. Mostly we chain-smoked and shuffled nervously.

"So if I talk, I will become an untouchable," Joe Trimboli said.

"One way or the other," I replied. We both laughed and I walked back to my car. As I left, I looked in my rearview mirror. The Watcher was standing in the middle of the sidewalk, staring.

We met a couple of days later on Long Island in a hospital parking lot just off the Southern State Parkway. We got into Trimboli's car. The sergeant drove around several housing developments. I had no idea where we were. Occasionally we would park. The sergeant drove and talked. Chasing Michael Dowd was an incredible tale of ineptitude, indifference, and incompetence. Once it was known, it would mean the end of Internal Affairs. The head of IAD would have to resign. The special prosecutor would be disgraced. It was a huge tale of cover-up and disgrace.

The story appeared on June 15, 1992, on the front page of the *New York Post*. It featured a front-page photograph of Sergeant Joseph Trimboli as he stepped into a car outside the 61st precinct. It was headlined: THE NEW SERPICO. The story detailed Trimboli's story without directly quoting him. The rest of the papers wanted to know if the story was true. The police department knew it was true. But IAD had hidden Trimboli's story from the police commissioner. Lee Brown wanted to know if Trimboli had spoken to me himself. He assigned Ray Kelly, his first deputy commissioner, to find out. It was amazing, but police department brass didn't want to know why Trimboli hadn't been allowed to catch Michael Dowd. The department's first instinct was to find out if the lonely sergeant they never wanted to hear from again had talked to a reporter. It wouldn't have mattered, incidentally. As soon as his story became known, Joseph Trimboli became a hero to the city. The department couldn't touch him. Joe Trimboli was Sergeant Untouchable.

By noon of that day Lee Brown appeared frantic. The police commissioner, who had never worked as a cop in the city before becoming boss of the department, was notoriously slow to do anything. But the Trimboli matter was serious. It made his police department look absurd. No one had even told him what was going on in this investigation. And now the whole county was talking about corrupt cops and Frank Serpico again. He issued a press release that day. He also faced the television cameras to make a statement.

"Today's *New York Post* contains a number of very serious allegations concerning the police department's investigation into the Michael Dowd case, and other issues related to the performance of our Internal Affairs Division," Brown said. "Because of the Dowd case, I had already directed that the chief of inspectional services look at our existing system of internal investigations, including IAD, the Field Internal Affairs Units, and any other relevant systems, to determine how and why these officers were not stopped sooner. From my initial review of this case, there is no reason that Officer Dowd should not have been terminated long ago."

From there, the commissioner went on to order a special report. At the time, Brown was considered the national expert on community policing. Out-of-Town Brown, as he was affectionately known, never considered it important, until this precise moment, to assign sharper cops to investigate the community of police he was sending out to police those communities. He continued: "However, today's *Post* raises issues of such concern to me that I am designating the first deputy commissioner, Raymond W. Kelly, to oversee an examination of every allegation made by the *Post* and any other related issues. . . . I want to make it clear that illegal activities by any members of this department are totally unacceptable. They will be rooted out and crushed. For the past twenty years, this department has stood as an example of integrity to every police agency in this country. I will not permit the reputation achieved by our demanding standards and low expectation to be clouded by the performances of a few."

Ray Kelly wanted me to come see him. I had a lawyer who used to be Kelly's partner, and he said I could trust him. Kelly was the first deputy commissioner at the time. I got a call from his office saying he wanted to see me the next day, and they would call me at the time they wanted to see me. They called me at about five after nine the next morning and said, "Okay, he will see you at ten o'clock." I said, "Okay, I'll be there." I was about to hang up when they said, "Wait a minute, Sergeant, we're going to tell you where to meet him." I said, "What do you mean, I'm meeting him at One Police Plaza." They said, "Oh no you're not. You've got to go to One World Trade Center and take the elevator to the 102nd floor. Get off, step to your left, and go all the way down the hall. You are going to come to a door with no number on it. Knock on that door three times."

These are my instructions, believe it or not. Beautiful. I am going to meet the first dep in an unmarked office. I can't believe this. But I go and knock on the door three times. This huge black guy answers the door. Kelly has never asked to see me until the newspaper article appears. Once I'm on the front page of the Post, suddenly the First Deputy Commissioner wants to see me. Anyway, the guy says, "Are you Trimboli?" And I tell him, "No, who the fuck do you think I am?" He tells me that he is a lieutenant, so I clean up my language. And he says, "Come on in." And I walk in and it is a totally gutted apartment. There is no floor or ceilings, no walls, no lighting, nothing. He points to the back room and says, "He's in the back there." So I walk toward the back and I see him at a table facing me. Ray Kelly is sitting on a folding chair, and he's apparently been reading the New York Times. He's looking out the window when I come in. He shakes my hand and says, "I brought you a cup of coffee." I said, "Nah, I don't drink coffee, I brought myself a juice." So I sat down and I looked at him, and the first thing Ray Kelly, Times reader, does is push a copy of the New York Post at me. He puts it right in front of me and says, "Are you responsible for this shit, for this pack of lies?"

Now I know what the deal is. Ray Kelly doesn't want me to help him investigate why his department didn't catch Michael Dowd. He doesn't want to investigate the story of how they allowed this corruption to go on, and on, and on. He wants to investigate how a story about Joe Trimboli and IAD got into a newspaper. So that limits my next move considerably. I denied it. I said, "I don't know what you are talking about, Boss." He says, "You didn't do this? You didn't provide this pack of lies?" I said, "Boss, you know I can't talk to a newspaper." He yells, "Well, how did it get there? I want you to tell me right now who did it." And I turned and said, "Wait a minute, Boss, I don't think we are going to be talking anymore." He said, "What are you talking about? I'm the first deputy commissioner." I said, "I want a lawyer. Because I was told I was coming up here to assist you in an investigation. And all you are doing is sitting here and talking about a newspaper article that I have already denied any knowledge of." I lit a cigarette. And he said, "You know, Sergeant, there's no ashtrays here." I said, "You know something, there's no floor here either. This place doesn't exist." And I kept smoking.

So we had a very bad two hours. And every fifteen minutes, he'd come back to the fucking newspaper. Again and again, he would push it in front of me. He wanted an admission from me that I'm the guy who spoke to the newspaper and besmirched the character and the integrity of the NYPD. In fact he asked me specific questions. "Well, what about this, is this true, that Chief Gallagher did this?" And I said, "Gee, I don't know." And I denied half the shit. Because this guy is trying to back me into a corner. My union told me to go talk to this man without an attorney, and now he's looking to whack me out. Now I know I am going to be suspended. The minute that I admit that I have any knowledge of this newspaper article I am getting suspended. So I can't admit to anything. I deny the whole fucking thing.

And I realize at that point that Ray Kelly isn't interested in truth. Ray Kelly is interested in damage control. His view of the police department is totally obstructed by his time and devotion to those people who have been implicated in this article. And I realize that, so I am not giving him shit. He went through a point-by-point questioning on the major aspects, how IAD had hindered the investigation. He kept saying, "That isn't true, is it, Sergeant?" And I would say, "Well, I don't know, I didn't write the article, I don't know where he got this stuff." Or, he'd say, "Well, it doesn't sound true to you?" "No, Boss, it doesn't sound true, you're right." "The thing with Kenny Eurell and the captain, that's not true. Couldn't it have been something else?" "Well yes, Boss, *it could have been that the captain didn't want to give up any information on an ongoing investigation." And this is the way it went. He didn't want me to talk to him. He was letting me know what kind of answers he wanted from me and what kind of answers he needed to hear from me in order to let me walk out that door without getting suspended.*

It was unknown to Kelly at this point, but every chief in the department had been dragging me in front of them. They were getting ready to cover their asses and lie to Kelly if they had to. Kelly wants to know about the newspaper. In fact, he does say one thing that shocks me. He looks me straight in the eye and says, "Sergeant, you were doing observations on your own, weren't you?" Only two or three people knew that. And Ray Kelly has spoken to them. That meant he had to know the truth about the whole freaking investigation. Why go through this charade then? I'll tell you why. Ray Kelly was pissed because he felt that I had hurt the police department. I thought he would lay off me then, maybe have some pity. Maybe he would feel bad for a guy who had so little life that he would watch Michael Dowd on his own time. But fuck no. This man was coming after me, and the minute I sat down, I knew he was coming after me. And I wouldn't cooperate with him. Fuck no. He taped the whole meeting. I later found out because there's a reporter who he gave the tapes to, and he said, "To show you how full of shit Trimboli is why don't you listen to these fucking tapes and see the difference between what he told me and how much he remembered when he spoke to the Mollen Commission." The next day he called the reporter back and said, "You know what? You're not really supposed to see those tapes. Give them back to me." And the reporter gave them back to him. A year later, when I heard about Ray Kelly's tapes for the first time, Judge Mollen was sitting right next to me.

Later I had my official meeting with Ray Kelly; it was the GO 15. We went through a lot of the old stuff. It was

*about two years after I closed my Dowd investigation,
and I was a little shaky. Kelly let me look at some of
the work sheets but not all of them. His big thing was
Gallagher. For some reason he wanted to protect Gallagher. By that point, I didn't care. The truth was the
truth, and it was never going to change. There was so
much politics going on in the end, it was absurd. People
said, "It's politics. Who gives a fuck?" But I gave a
fuck. I thought Ray Kelly was going to be the savior; that
is what I had been told, that's the way it had been presented to me. And he humiliated me with those tapes.
That incensed me. Maybe Lee Brown put him up to all
this. I want to believe Kelly is a good guy. He was a
strong figure and a good PC. But the old-school boys lied
to him about Dowd. Kelly was a product of the old
school. He was not going to kill fifty friends when he
could just shoot Joseph Trimboli, some two-bit sergeant.
Later, after he became commissioner, Kelly was always
quite decent to me. I think, in the end, even Kelly realized the bosses had lied to him. But what was Ray Kelly
really supposed to do? Lee Brown gave Kelly an order—
"shut it down." I can understand that. In this police department you follow orders. They told me to lay off
Dowd. I didn't want to, but I had to. You follow orders.
Maybe this was one Kelly had to follow.*

*Not too long after Kelly questioned me for the second
time I got a call from Tony Vecchi. He was my friend
and former lieutenant from FIAU. He was retired now,
living in Florida. So he calls me and says, "Hey, Joe,
guess who is coming down to see me tonight?" I said,
"Who?" He says, "Ray Kelly." I says, "What?" And
Tony says, "Yeah, Ray Kelly is flying in at eleven tonight. I am picking him up at the airport and he is coming
straight to my house." I figured Tony was breaking my
balls, but he said, "No, he's really coming." They sit at
Tony's kitchen table all fucking night. Ray Kelly with a
jacket and tie, Tony wearing shorts. Ray Kelly said, "Do
you think Joe Trimboli is responsible for those newspa-*

per articles?'' Tony says, ''No, Joe is a team player. He wouldn't do something like that.'' Kelly asked Tony a lot of other questions about FIAU and IAD. Finally Kelly said, ''Thank you, good night.'' It was maybe 3 A.M. Kelly wanted to go right to the airport and wait for his 5 A.M. flight. Tony said he finally got Kelly to lie down for an hour and then drove him to the airport. It was unbelievable though. Ray Kelly flew all the way to ask Tony, among other things, ''Do you think Joe did the newspaper thing?'' Ray Kelly could have suspended me right there if he had proof. And that was the point of it, to besmirch my character, and ruin my fucking name.

———

As soon as Joe Trimboli's story was published, it became obvious the mayor would have to investigate police corruption. I suggested the formation of a Knapp-like commission. Eventually, all of the newspapers joined in the call. Mayor Dinkins was concerned. He was facing a stiff reelection fight against Rudy Giuliani, who was unquestionably procop. Rudy was also something of a historical revisionist. As a federal prosecutor in Manhattan, he made his name putting corrupt cops in jail. The Prince of the City case belonged to Giuliani. In an earlier life, as a federal prosecutor, Rudy wanted everyone to believe in his star informant, a corrupt police officer named Bob Leuci. This led to a couple of cops committing suicide, and many more went to jail. Rudy, all the cops said, made a deal with a dirty rat bastard. He freed a bum, they said, who put cops in jail. To some, that made Rudy as bad as the rat. That year, cops hated him. Publicly, Rudy never mentioned the scandal; he wanted cops to like him and forget about it. Rudy claimed that whenever the movie *The Prince of the City* came on TV he changed the station. It was as if that part of his past never happened.

Eventually, Rudy became the darling of the cops

again. Now Rudy Giuliani spoke loudly at police union rallies. The number-one issue on voters' minds was crime. So, politically, Rudy stood for cops, cops, and more cops. Dinkins had a different core of constituents. Many of his supporters were suspicious of the NYPD. They didn't trust cops. The precinct in the mayor's strongest district—the 30th precinct in Harlem—was about to blow sky-high with an enormous corruption scandal. One of the worst cops who were stealing drugs and robbing people in that scandal would be a Dominican-York named Compres who moved to New York City from San Francisco de Macorís. Deputy Mayor Bill Lynch lived in the same precinct. The mayor may have had his difficulties, but they did not include Lynch. He was an able organizer. I could talk to him, and called him at City Hall after meeting Trimboli.

"You should form a commission to investigate this matter," I said. "You can't have a police department where this kind of corruption is allowed to go on."

We were on the same page, and Lynch quickly agreed. Lynch asked if I had any specific ideas about who could head such a mayoral commission. For some reason I thought of Milt Mollen. The former judge was old, but everyone seemed to believe he was fairly competent, and even earnest. He had just investigated a stampede during a rock concert at City College. Half a dozen people had been crushed to death. Mollen did not spare the police department.

"How about Mollen?" I suggested without giving the choice much thought. Frankly, I was surprised to be asked. "But surround him with strong investigators," I said. "Mollen can be like Knapp, a figurehead."

"That sounds right," Lynch said. "Give us a day or two to work out the details and set this up."

I suggested that a commission be formed in a column the next day and recommended that Judge Milt Mollen be put in charge. Two days later, on June 19, Lynch kept his promise. Mayor David Dinkins appointed a "special eounsel'' with broad powers to probe police misconduct and review the police department's internal-monitoring system. The mayor told Lee Brown about the move at the last second. Rudy Giuliani, Republican mayoral candidate, called the Mollen Commission an exercise in political damage control.

The old cop had been out in the garden, tending vegetables. During the summer and fall of 1992, he was living on a farm in upstate New York. The telephone rang a dozen times before he answered it.

"Have you been calling long?" the most famous cop in the modern history of the New York City Police Department wanted to know. By then I had been trying to reach Frank Serpico for a week. He is deaf in one ear; the last thing he heard in that ear was the sound of gunfire.

A police car passed outside my window at the *Post.* The car shot up FDR Drive, lights flashing and siren wailing, on the way to some unknown misfortune in the city of anonymous mishaps.

"That sounds familiar; I still like that sound," Serpico said, finally. He listened to the police siren from a hundred miles away until the noise vanished.

There was another alarm ringing out over the city that summer. Frank Serpico had heard that one too. A couple of weeks before, Serpico had walked into a diner. Someone handed the recluse a newspaper. The headline screamed THE NEW SERPICO and detailed the frustration of a police sergeant, Joseph Trimboli, to get anyone in a position of authority to act upon evidence of corruption in the NYPD. It was an old story, and Frank Serpico had lived it once. The Old Serpico, as he called himself now, recognized the comparison with the New Serpico.

"Did they try and discredit Trimboli yet?" Serpico wanted to know.

"The commissioner has ordered the first deputy to conduct an official investigation of Trimboli's claims," Serpico was told. "I'm hearing that they're going to try and blame Trimboli for their own oversights."

"Of course they are," Serpico said. "That's how it works. They don't want you to fuck up their system. So they sit around and say, 'How much does he know? How badly can he hurt us?' They investigate you and not what you're saying."

"Well, it's happening again," he was told. By then, Kelly had met with Joe in the World Trade Center. The department was greasing the skids.

"Maybe Trimboli will do better than me," Serpico said. "But his story is verbatim to what happened to me. No one wants to hear. No one wants to know. All I can say to Trimboli is, 'Welcome to the fucking leper colony.' "

"What would you do with Trimboli?" I asked.

"If Lee Brown really wants to get rid of corruption, here is what he does," Serpico said. "He calls a big fucking press conference tomorrow and appoints Joe Trimboli to the fucking NYPD Hall of Fame. There won't be any change in the police department until the crooked cops fear the honest ones and not the other way around.

"If you really want change in the department, you have to protect Trimboli," Serpico continued. "Recognize him as the hero that he is. I've been thinking about the guy a lot. I remember on the day I retired, I was walking out of Police Plaza and some boss said, 'Frank, it will take us twenty years to fully appreciate the results of your work.' Here we are twenty years later. And what's the result? The result is Trimboli. The department doesn't even listen to the guys they're paying to find corruption. It's sickening."

Frank Serpico was fifty-six years old. He lived with a woman in a white farmhouse on a hill overlooking a field with horses. Other than his companion, Serpico doesn't talk to human beings much anymore, preferring the company of animals. Serpico became, to many people's way of thinking, a little wacky. He beat the system on his own terms and was a rugged individualist, but then he became a sort of woolly hermit and stereotypical peacenik; in fact, he now lives near Woodstock. On those days when he's not working in the garden, he busies himself digging through Indian ruins for arrowheads. He is forever a bewildered man lost in some mislaid time.

"I don't know if I'm a recluse," Serpico said. "What do you call someone who doesn't like people and only talks to animals?"

"A recluse," I answered.

Serpico said he got a letter in the mail in early 1992 inviting him to the twenty-year reunion of the Knapp Commission, sponsored in part by the *New York Times*. Frank Serpico's testimony before the Knapp Commission investigating payoffs to the NYPD made him a national hero—and an outcast. Embittered by the consequences of his exceptional personal campaign against police corruption, and incapable of enduring the resulting fame he neither sought nor wanted, Serpico disappeared. He lived for a decade in self-imposed European exile. The eccentric former cop has survived his odyssey. But Frank Serpico did not attend the reunion.

"I got a letter from the boys in the band," Serpico said. "It read: 'You've got to come to our reunion. This all started with you.' They really think they've got something to celebrate? What was accomplished? I mean I read the stories in the *Times* about what a fucking lovely time was had by all. But what did Knapp accomplish? Michael Dowd has a whole crew of corrupt cops working for him. Dowd is worse than any of the guys I worked with. If it weren't for the Suffolk County cops, Michael Dowd would still be working. And people are celebrating? Did someone stand up and say, 'Congratulations, folks. Frank Serpico got shot in the head. Drinks all around.' That's the only Knapp legacy—the bullet in my fucking head."

Serpico may have been overstating his case. But the department always overstated the value of his testimony. The Knapp Commission did not end police corruption, it changed it. The organized pad of the Knapp infamy became obsolete. Where every cop was putting money in his pocket during Frank's career, you now had pockets of corruption. Pads were too dangerous. One-time scores were the future. At the very least Frank Serpico seems to have a better understanding of language nuance than the current brass, who kept saying that a Long Island drug dealer named Dowd just happened to be a cop.

"Any way you say it, they still got fucking corruption," Serpico said. "Am I surprised that Michael Dowd could kidnap some dealer off the street and turn him over to a bad guy? Would I be surprised if some cop could shoot a kid in Washington Heights and then drop a gun on him? Hey, the cops I worked with set me up to be killed. I remember this guy I worked with, Cooper, he told me after I got shot, 'Yeah. I remember the night we had our meet to discuss getting rid of you.' And I said, 'What? We're talking about another cop here.' And he said, 'No, Frank. We're talking about our money here.' "

He wanted to know more about the Next One, as he called Trimboli. He wanted to know his physical build. He wanted to talk about the cop's carriage and composure. Frank Serpico said he was scared for Joe Trimboli.

"I know what he went through and what he will go through," Serpico said. "You end up going from one guy to the next, and you don't know who is corrupt. It can make you border on the psychotic. What you go through . . . it really takes its toll."

He talked then about the brotherhood of lies. "It is a system in which the cops lie for each other, right from the start, right out of the academy. You lie for them, they lie for you. And if you rat them out, they can rat you out. It's a trap." As Serpico said this, the conversation suddenly died. I thought he had hung up the phone.

"Frank?"

"Yeah. Just a second."

And then Frank Serpico started to cry. He explained that he was remembering a young woman who had died of cancer. The excuse did not fit with the conversation. We had been talking about cops and corruption. As he remembered, Frank Serpico cried. He still cries after all these years. He cries for the cop he wanted to be and maybe for a police department that has never been.

"Fucking cops," Frank Serpico said. "Fucking cops will break your heart every time."

Serpico wanted to speak to Trimboli, and I got them together. They became quite friendly, forming an odd little club actually. Serpico was very helpful to Trimboli during this time. He used to call Trimboli in the middle of the night with advice; it was all very strange. Sometimes Serpico would get stuck talking to the sergeant's answering machine.

"Joe, this is Frank Serpico. I was just thinking about you hoping you are okay. Don't let the bastards get you down. I'm pulling for you. If you win, you win for both of us."

It turned out that Joe Trimboli was right about Kenny Eurell. The retired cop couldn't wait to rat out his "colleagues." James Catterson didn't have to work very hard on him. The Feds called and inquired about using Eurell as a witness against Michael Dowd in their La Compania case. Catterson said he would think about it. He turned over Eurell to the Feds that week. By the middle of the summer Eurell was working for them full-time. He even wore a wire on Dowd and volunteered to help federal agents nail down corruption in the 73rd precinct.

Eurell and his wife finally moved out of their house in North Babylon. Taxes were no longer a problem for the federal prisoner. They had actually found a buyer: the government. The day that this blond, muscular ex-cop, clad only in a sweatshirt and jeans, walked back into the 75th precinct with federal authorities, the cops in the precinct grabbed their chests. It was as if they had seen a ghost. Actually they had seen a rat. Eurell was going to give the Feds Michael Dowd. It was the trump card he had been holding the whole time. Kenny Eurell always knew that he could give up his partner in a pinch. As he walked back into his old precinct, Eurell smirked. He led the investigators down into the locker room and removed items from his locker. Later the Feds came back to Dowd's locker with bolt cutters. They took his old memo book and personal items that could be used to corroborate his tale of deceit.

"See you later," Eurell said on his way out of the precinct. He was never seen again by anyone in the NYPD. He wound up in the witness protection program, living, as they say, "somewhere in America." That is a comforting thought. Kenny Eurell is not your friendly neighborhood cop anymore. But he could be your neighbor.

Michael Dowd was arrested on federal racketeering charges on July 30, 1992. He was charged with accepting tens of thousands of dollars a week as bribes from two cocaine rings between 1986 and 1989. The federal charges accused Dowd of taking from between $5,000 and $10,000 a week in exchange for inside information that helped drug gangs avoid detection by police and DEA agents. According to confidential informants, Mike the Cop would give guns, badges, and police radios to a Dominican gang called La Compania. Also arrested that day was Baron Perez. Adam Diaz had told the whole story to police. What Diaz didn't know, Kenny Eurell filled in, and he also wore a wire on Michael Dowd after their arrests. Diaz and Eurell were named as unindicted coconspirators, partners to the end.

When Joe Trimboli picked up the newspaper and read an account of Dowd's arrest on federal charges, he threw the paper against the wall.

12

REDEMPTION

Raymond Kelly took six months to complete the investigation that Commissioner Lee Brown had ordered after reading the story about Trimboli in the *New York Post*. By then, Ray Kelly was the police commissioner. Lee Brown had left town, citing his wife's grave illness, but he was equally sick of the NYPD by then.

"On June 15, 1992, a *New York Post* article leveled serious charges of impropriety in the police department's handling of earlier investigations of Police Officer Michael Dowd," Police Commissioner Kelly wrote. "In response, former Police Commissioner Lee Brown directed then First Deputy Commissioner Raymond Kelly to undertake a thorough investigation to determine if the department's internal affairs apparatus was flawed and if there had been any cover-up of police corruption. . . . This report is a product of this investigation. It illustrates a series of missed opportunities, a failure of coordination, and the shortcomings on an internal investigative structure built on overlapping responsibility and bifurcated authority."

In a 161-page report, Kelly and his fellow investigator, Assistant Commissioner Michael Farrell, found the department's corruption-fighting procedures in a pitiful state.

"Frankly," Commissioner Kelly admitted, "if it weren't for those stories that appeared in the *Post*, nobody would have looked at the system."

Still the report was a hedge bet, issued to submarine the Mollen Commission. Instead of firing bosses who had mishandled Trimboli's investigation, Kelly simply pointed out their mistakes and moved on. These superiors, the report said, were not motivated by the classic form of corruption—money. Yet none of them was willing to take responsibility for the probe and the scandal it might uncover. The report admitted that the police department began getting tips about Dowd's corruption in 1985—seven years before his arrest. Since then, there were seventeen Dowd-related cases, Kelly said, and virtually no action was taken against the rogue cop. And while superficial investigations were being conducted, evidence was mounting that Dowd was on the take, selling drugs, and abusing both alcohol and drugs.

Kelly said there was no indication that the investigation had been interfered with or intentionally undermined. It could have happened, Kelly was admitting, but we can't prove it. Kelly singled out the special prosecutor's office for a lot of abuse, but they were no more guilty of institutional blindness than Internal Affairs. Kelly promised to dismantle the Field Internal Affairs Units and replace IAD with an Internal Affairs Bureau, which would have sole responsibility for all police corruption complaints. "There are no heroes in this report," Kelly said, but he did praise Trimboli as a "hardworking investigator."

"He was working on his own, and the system did not support him," Kelly allowed, and that was all the new police commissioner would admit. He wasn't ready yet to recognize Joe Trimboli as a hero. To do so then would be to admit that the bosses should have been fired, and Ray Kelly was not about to start shooting Good Old Boys out of a cannon.

"This is the type of thing that happens in a bureaucracy when there has been no monitoring of a system for twenty years," Kelly said.

No, Trimboli didn't catch Michael Dowd. But he caught IAD. And that was the biggest police collar ever. As it happened, two of the cops arrested with Michael Dowd were sentenced to jail that day. No one knew it yet, but Kevin Hembury and Phil Carlucci were working with federal investigators working the 73rd precinct. Danny Eurell, Kenny's cousin, had also turned. All these cops had been questioned by Robert Ewald, the Suffolk County prosecutor. Danny Eurell told Ewald all there was to know about the Morgue Boys. He was quite specific too. He mentioned the names of cops no one suspected of being thieves. IAD had no idea that there was a scandal waiting to happen in the Brownsville precinct. James Catterson, the Suffolk County DA, turned Danny Eurell over to the Brooklyn DA, Charles Hynes, who turned him over to the U.S. attorney. They made a dozen cases with him.

Back in Suffolk County, on sentencing day, the judge ridiculed the fired cops, Hembury and Carlucci.

"You are a complete hypocrite, a Judas, really," Judge George McInerney told Kevin Hembury, twenty-eight. "Get out of my sight."

Speaking before the judge, Hembury said, "I am sorry. My only crime is not having the integrity to come forward in this situation." By then Hembury had already made the decision to rat out the cops in his precinct. He got two years. Carlucci, who also pled guilty to a stolen-check scheme, got three years. As part of Carlucci's agreement, his wife was allowed to walk. Given their cooperation with the Morgue Boys case, odds are that they both will serve no prison time.

The old judge Milt Mollen was getting ahead of himself. He surely wanted to be remembered; he wanted a legacy. No one could remember anything Knapp had ever done as a judge. He had served well but would always be remembered for the Knapp Commission. It was an immutable title; a commission was permanent. It was forever. But how was Mollen going to assure himself of a lasting reputation? The answer was twofold: Joseph Trimboli and Michael Dowd. The judge would give the city both of them. He would sit the good cop and the bad cop at one table. He would allow a television camera to be pointed at them. Their pictures would be flashed across the country. Michael Dowd would cry for "60 Minutes"; Joe Trimboli would chat it up with Larry King. Before any of that could happen—and it all happened—the retired judge needed people to associate one name with fighting New York City police corruption—not Joseph Trimboli, but Milt Mollen.

However, once blinded by the television lights, the judge lost sight of his mission. One of his people called Michael Dowd's lawyer, who was delighted to hear from them. In exchange for his testimony, Milt Mollen would write a letter, at sentencing, to Michael Dowd's judge. The lawyer was surprised, but ecstatic. No one had offered Dowd a deal before, and here was the commission offering to write a letter to the judge on his behalf. Dowd wouldn't have to name names, he wouldn't have to give money back. He would just show up in a hearing room one day and tell a story in front of a television camera. The corrupt cop, a world-class liar, wouldn't even be under oath. You don't have to swear to tell the truth, the whole truth, and nothing but the truth when you testify. No one could check out the story. It was a freebie.

"Done," said the lawyer.

Milt Mollen had one of his people call the *New York Times* to announce there was a deal with Michael Dowd in exchange for his cooperation. The paper knew even less about Dowd, apparently, than the judge, so they ran the story.

"We have an agreement," Mollen said. "If appropriate, he will testify at the hearings."

This was Saturday, April 3, 1993. Joe Trimboli was spending a lot of time with Mollen Commission investigators that week. He trusted them to tell his story, and then he reads about a back-room deal with Michael Dowd. Frankly, he was amazed; it was treachery, he told them. Of all the crap that Trimboli had to put up with, this was one of the most insulting blows in all his dealings with Dowd. The federal racketeering case still existed, but Mollen seemed to forget that Michael Dowd was also facing life out in Suffolk County.

The Suffolk County DA, meanwhile, had never been asked about a deal with Dowd. It was James Catterson, in Suffolk County, remember, who finally caught Michael Dowd, and he was not going to just disappear. Dowd was still facing life in Suffolk County, no matter what Mollen promised. Michael Dowd could not believe his luck, but his luck was just about to run out, courtesy of Catterson. Difficult to corner and impossible to trust, Dowd had just agreed to a twelve-year federal prison sentence. Even worse, Dowd was facing life in Catterson's jurisdiction. Unable to cut a cooperation deal with the Feds, Dowd needed one last patsy. And that is when Milt Mollen stumbled upon the crime scene, as it were.

"If you cooperate with this commission fully," he told Dowd, "I will write a letter to the judge outlining your cooperation." When Catterson heard about this, he was confused and couldn't understand what Mollen was doing. Was the old coot just absentminded? "No one has talked to us about where we stand on a deal with him," Catterson said. "He is still facing a trial out here. We haven't been asked to become part of any deal. Twelve years isn't enough time. This guy, Dowd, is a woeful human being. That is where we stand."

Incredibly, a week after reaching a cooperation agreement with Michael Dowd, Mollen still didn't know the status of the Long Island case.

"Let's see, the Suffolk County matter," Mollen said when I called to ask about his "deal" with Dowd. "Wasn't that case dismissed?"

"Absolutely not," I told him. "They're looking to jail Dowd for life out there."

"Gee," Mollen said, "I didn't know that."

It was one thing for Mollen to sign up Dowd for fancy public hearings. It was quite another for a former judge to be making a deal with a felon that could compromise another case he had simply forgotten about. At that point, the Mollen Commission simply existed to write a manifesto, a book report for the mayor, nothing more.

"We heard the Suffolk County case was over," said Joe Armao, the Mollen Commission's crack investigator.

"Who told you that?" he was asked.

"Michael Dowd's lawyer."

Michael Dowd must have loved seeing these guys coming. He used to tell his wife, "If and when I get caught, I'll just rat out some other cops."

Mollen's deal with Dowd strained the commission's credibility. Joe Trimboli had met with the commission twice that month and balked at another meeting. The commitment of the Mollen Commission people reminded Trimboli of IAD people.

"I don't know if I can even talk to them anymore," Joe Trimboli said when the story broke. "What are they trying to do, get Dowd off the hook? At this stage, I'm not even sure who I'm talking to anymore, Milt Mollen or Michael Dowd."

There was going to be a public viewing of Michael Dowd the next day at Manhattan Federal Courthouse in Foley Square. Ten years ago, in January 1982, Michael Francis Dowd, the son of a retired New York City fireman, seemed the perfect police candidate. He was both sturdy and smart, and as Trimboli knew only too well, conniving. No one, having looked at Michael Dowd's record, could have predicted the infamy he would bring to the New York Police Department. As part of his plea bargain he was going to agree to a jail term. He would be there for a very long time, but it would have been a lot less time if Milt Mollen had had his way. Thank God for Jim Catterson. As per the new agreement, three years were tacked on, so Michael Dowd had to serve a minimum of fifteen and a half years before being eligible for parole.

I called Joe Trimboli on the night before the sentencing to see if he wanted to attend.

"Only if Dowd can see me," Joe said. Trimboli began to think back to the days when the Dowd file belonged only to him. He kept a personal copy of the file and thumbed through it that night.

On the night before he pled guilty, one piece of paper in Michael Dowd's personnel folder stood out. Joe held it in his hands.

"I, Michael Dowd, do solemnly swear that I will support the Constitution of the United States and the Constitution of the State of New York, and that I will faithfully discharge the duties of the office of police officer in the Police Department of the City of New York according to the best of my ability."

The oath. It made everything that followed a lie.

After a year in which the name Michael Dowd became synonymous with deceit and corruption, the dirtiest cop in the modern history of the department would plead guilty to racketeering charges in Manhattan federal court. Dowd deserved all of his fifteen years and more.

Trimboli was one of the people who would have preferred Dowd to be exposed in public, at the expense of IAD and the New York Police Department. He wanted to see Dowd sweat on the witness stand. There was still the videotape out there in Suffolk County showing Michael Dowd in uniform, making a drug deal out of his patrol car. The city should see that tape—every cop should see it—but it would take another five months to come to air. Because just as Michael Dowd followed the cops in the 77th precinct, there are cops in Brooklyn even now who think they are too smart to get caught stealing drugs. So the trial would have been good, Trimboli thought. It would have been the great cathartic event of policing in the 1990s. Unfortunately, Dowd's guilty pleas would be his one and only court appearance.

It was funny that night, Trimboli realized, to look back at the old evaluation reports written by Dowd's supervisors. The first one, written in June 1983, rated Dowd as an "above standard" cop. It read, in part, "Officer is an energetic individual, makes excellent decisions based on the facts on hand. Officer handles a variety of jobs very well." "This officer possesses qualities that are an inspiration to some of the newer members of this command," a boss wrote of him in 1984.

By then, informants were telling Internal Affairs investigators that Dowd and his former partner, Gerald DuBois, were stealing money from drug dealers.

Dowd fooled too many people for too long a time. Even as late as 1988, at a time when half of the Western World was looking to put Officer Dowd in jail, his old boss in the 75th precinct, Paul Sanderson, was signing on to a report that read, "good career potential." The question was, What kind of career?

Trimboli was going to see Michael Dowd again and hear him plead guilty and be sentenced to jail. His next status report, Trimboli laughed, will be written by a prison warden. At least someone caught the guy. But that was not good enough for Joseph Trimboli. It would never be good enough for him. There was a certain satisfaction, but the people who failed to catch Dowd were still out there, and there was no reason to believe it would be any different the next time.

Joe Trimboli stepped out of the courthouse elevator looking grim and tentative. His heart pounded. There was a line of sweat on his brow.

"Is Dowd here yet?" Trimboli wanted to know.

"Probably still with the marshals, downstairs, in the lockup," he was told.

"Jesus," the cop said. "Isn't there any air-conditioning in this building?"

He wanted a cigarette then but fought back the urge. There was a day, way back when, the Watcher remembered, that the undercover detective would sit outside of Dowd's house chain-smoking Marlboros. Trimboli hadn't smoked a cigarette since he sat with Ray Kelly and talked about Michael Dowd in an unmarked room with no ashtray. "I'd like one now though," Trimboli said. "Jesus, it is hot in here. I can't breathe."

When it came to being in a room with Michael Dowd, Joe Trimboli operated at a different room temperature than most people. If he wanted to, the sergeant could still smell Michael Dowd's cologne. Try as he could, he could never imagine keeping up with Dowd's red Corvette on the Belt Parkway. Michael Dowd's wife was standing across from him in the hallway. Looking at her reminded Trimboli of all the time he had lost with his own daughter while eating Sunday dinner in his car, watching her husband.

In truth, Trimboli became a zealot. The case cost him his marriage. It would cost him his place in the police department. Even then, while standing in the hallway waiting, he remembered the names of all the incompetent and disinterested bosses who told him to quit the case. Those bosses cost the NYPD this scandal. They all loved the department less than he did. Yet despite it all, Trimboli felt vindicated. The rat really was in the trap.

"It will be worth it to see Michael Dowd admit his guilt," the cop said. "I wonder what he looks like now. I wonder how it will feel to look at him."

One of the rogue cop's brothers, looking puffy and pale, passed the narrow hallway outside Justice Kimba Wood's federal courtroom. By then, the judge was quite famous. She could have been United States attorney general, but the Nannygate scandal did her in. Dowd was allowed to deal drugs, steal, report to work stoned, and jeopardize his fellow officers, but because she didn't properly pay taxes for a nanny . . . What a system, Joe thought. But it was even worse. Lee Brown could have caught Michael Dowd. Now the former police commissioner works in President Bill Clinton's cabinet as something called "drug czar." Kimba Wood didn't have that opportunity, she wasn't good enough, but Lee Brown, apparently, never had any nanny problems.

Trimboli wondered what Judge Wood would do in the face of genuine evil and corruption. Dowd's brother was carrying a gray garment bag that included a starched white shirt, black suit, and severely polished black shoes. Michael Dowd, apparently, wanted to look pretty in confession. Even at the end, Trimboli said to himself, this bastard cop is driven by ego and vanity.

"Hold on to the clothes," a federal marshal said. When Michael Dowd entered the courtroom, he turned to face his family and saw instead Joe Trimboli in the front row. The prisoner bucked as he met the detective's stare. Trimboli flashed back to 1986 and remembered the first time he saw Michael Dowd . . . Perp Fever; his instincts had never been sharper. Dowd broke off the stare with an impish schoolboy grin.

"He's still trying to be cocky," Trimboli whispered. "But he looks dead. Pale. Dramatic weight loss. No muscle tone. I wouldn't have even known him on the street."

All of the people who actually helped catch Dowd were in the courtroom. David Fein, the federal prosecutor, who turned witnesses Trimboli was forbidden to question, was in the back row. So was Joe Hall, the former detective who discovered Chelo's and Michael Dowd's ties to San Francisco de Macorís. He looked absolutely triumphant.

Catterson, the Suffolk DA who hung the wires that strangled Michael Dowd and his Loser's Club, sat at the prosecution table. He measured the defendant with a look of disgust. No one from the Mollen Commission was there, nor should they have been. They were a product of this insanity. The Mollen Commission was the final act in this comedy of errors. Yes, they showed us Dowd and his corrupt gang, but once again no one in the justice system was held accountable.

Joe smiled at Hall, who was once shot at by a member of a gang that Dowd was being paid to protect.

"How is Adam Diaz doing?" Trimboli asked.

"Fine," Hall said. "But he kept us busy. I can't believe we were out there the whole time, looking at the same thing, and we never met each other," Hall told Trimboli. "Nice to finally meet you."

"Nice to know you exist," Trimboli said. "I was afraid I was alone."

Hall motioned to Dowd. "He don't look like much now," Hall said.

"He isn't much," Trimboli said.

Without his suit, Michael Dowd was forced to wear a light blue shirt and dark blue pants with white socks and slip-on shoes. Michael Dowd's prison uniform, everyone could see, was cop blue.

"I can't stand to see him in that color," Sergeant Trimboli said. "It's funny after all this time, what bothers you."

Joe wanted to get out of the courtroom into the fresh air, but he needed to see this through. Trimboli desperately wanted closure. The final act made him feel weak and angry. When he swallowed, Joe tasted sweetness and bile. The whole day was a confusing contradiction. He heard Dowd enter his plea to racketeering and drug conspiracy charges. Steadily, Dowd admitted to a set of crimes that Joe had filed with Internal Affairs.

"I did aid and abet a drug organization by giving them information," Dowd admitted. "Most of it was bogus. . . . It was just a way to gain their confidence. Not that some of the information wasn't good. It was a way to fleece them for money."

Judge Kimba Wood would have none of Dowd's ridiculous waffling. Joe Trimboli liked her already. He already suspected that Wood believed a fifteen-year sentence was insufficient punishment for Michael Dowd. When the judge warned Michael Dowd's lawyer that she might be forced to add more years to the agreement,

Dowd began to shake. This wasn't some scheme after all. Finally there might be justice.

When Wood demanded more specifics from the defendant, Dowd dared to smile. He thought his cuteness would get him through again. Then he touched his head and said, "I'm a little brain-locked right now."

Wood lowered her gaze. Then she closed her eyes and shook her head.

"I told them to shut down for a day," Dowd said of his deal with Adam Diaz. "So, what the heck, they didn't get arrested that day. So they paid me."

Steadily, the prisoner began to shrink. The prosecutor stood up and said there was no deal. David Fein said that a letter from the Mollen Commission meant nothing to him and evidently didn't have much impact on Kimba Wood. Catterson never moved. Dowd looked again to his lawyer. They were both scared now.

"At the time you did this, you knew you were breaking the law?" the judge asked him.

"Yes, I did," Dowd replied, softly. The cop turned and spotted Trimboli again. He shook, quivered actually, and looked back to the judge.

I think I love her, Joe Trimboli thought. She shouldn't settle for attorney general. She should be fucking president.

Dowd jerked his head. He was twitching uncontrollably. Mostly he looked bewildered. His hands trembled one second, then balled into fists. When Wood talked about the public trust, Dowd shook his head and said, "Oh, man." At times he admitted ample guilt. As he was let out in his cop-blue uniform, his wife blew him a kiss.

Joe Trimboli's own shirt was soaked with sweat by the time he reached the street. He walked away, smiling, having fought off the urge to smoke a cigarette. He had finally quit his two bad habits of the 1980s: cigarettes and surveillance. Make that three, if you count Michael Dowd.

"It's just a matter of discipline," the Watcher said, as he stood there, watching him go.

The Mollen Commission hearings opened on September 27, 1993, with Michael Dowd center stage, not just a corrupt cop anymore but a television star with a nice neat haircut. Joe watched Dowd's entirely rehearsed testimony on television, none of it surprising, or even interesting. It was kind of like watching a guy kill himself in slow motion. He just went on and on. By then, anyone with even a passing interest in Michael Dowd knew his story. With eyes downcast, a subdued Dowd explained how corruption had worked and even been encouraged by his supervisors.

"It's us against them," Dowd explained, reciting the PBA mantra that allowed him to survive so long. " 'Us' were the cops and 'them' were the public."

He spoke for four hours. It was as if TV cameras were eavesdropping on a group therapy session in a drug rehab unit. Michael Dowd's testimony consisted mostly of what he thought the commission wanted to hear. It was delivered without emotion or remorse. He was saying the department was an enabler. "I would not have robbed people," Michael Dowd was saying, "if they ordered me to stop robbing people." At one point Dowd said he had joined the force "to help people." If he regularly assaulted people it was not because he liked beating them up but because they were disrespectful. Michael Dowd never gave another cop up; he confessed to corruption in generalities. At least the testimony was entertaining, dramatic, and beat the daily soaps, Trimboli thought. The corrupt cop confessed to every single allegation Joe had ever filed with IAD. At the end of the day, Joe switched off the television set. The Watcher was officially done watching Michael Dowd.

Even at the very end, Trimboli was still following Dowd. They called him the next day, and he was ready to name all of the people who had stopped him throughout the years. The public had just finished meeting Michael Dowd, Trimboli said, why not give them the names of the bosses who refused to let him catch Michael Dowd? But after all this time, the commission did not want to be weighed down by specifics. Trimboli couldn't understand why the commission wasn't interested in finding out why Michael Dowd had been able to prosper and linger. There was too much politics in the room.

Most investigators only wanted Trimboli and others to testify about how to better the system so it wouldn't happen again, what they called "a permanent oversight monitor." All the Mollen Commission investigators really wanted, in the end, was more jobs. He could hang a "hire me" sign on the whole gathering. So Trimboli talked mostly in generic terms about how cops couldn't be trusted to police cops.

"Instead of reviewing my cases, they started to berate me," Trimboli said. "They told me I had been unable to gather one iota of criminal evidence. Nobody made mention that I was the only one investigating this drug conspiracy."

During the lunch break, the chief counsel for the commission, Joe Armao, came to see Trimboli.

"Will you play ball?" Armao asked.

"What?" Trimboli wanted to know.

"Will you say that we need a permanent outside monitor?" Armao said.

Trimboli was shaken, but agreed. He had wanted to go into the details of the cover-up. The city needed to know details. He felt the NYPD needed to fire people or rebut him. An outside monitor had been in place when Michael Dowd happened and his name was Charles Hynes, special prosecutor, and that permanent outside monitor never even bothered with Michael Dowd. What were people talking about? And why didn't they call more people from the special prosecutor's office? That was a dream; it was never going to happen. So he would settle for what he could get.

The commission didn't bother to call Lee Brown. He was now working for the president. The mayor didn't need Brown around to remind voters of the Crown Heights riot again. City Hall did not, at that precarious time, need to embarrass President Bill Clinton by reminding the country that a police force under the direction of his new drug czar tolerated cops selling drugs in New York, among other offenses. Besides, Dinkins needed Clinton that month; the president and his wife were pulling out all campaign stops for the mayor, even suggesting that white people who wouldn't vote for a black mayor were racist. Crime was the nation's biggest issue. Cops were good, not bad, was the White House mantra.

Ray Kelly came, but by that time he had said all a police commissioner needed to say about Michael Dowd. Mostly Ray Kelly talked about Joe Trimboli. He had decided by then that he was wrong about Trimboli. He didn't want people to come away from the Mollen Commission hearings with a lasting memory of Michael Dowd. He wanted them to remember the good cop's perseverance rather than the bad cop's corruption. The police commissioner wanted people to remember Joe Trimboli rather than Michael Dowd. He wanted to put a positive spin on the entire affair.

"We are sending a message to all other police officers that Sergeant Trimboli is our definition of a good cop," Kelly said, reading from a ten-page statement.

Reached at his precinct later that day, Joe Trimboli told reporters that he was stunned.

"I'm really gratified he feels this way about me," Trimboli said, and as a result he would even reconsider retirement plans.

The commission hearings, although good television fodder, were very short on plot. No bosses were called on the carpet. Robert Beatty, the IAD chief, skated. Ben Ward, the commissioner who basically outlawed corruption investigations, wasn't asked tough questions. The hearings were largely an exercise in self-promotion. They had no lasting purpose, effect, or conclusion.

The former head of IAD, the legendary John Guido, seemed to put things in perspective. Guido spent forty years keeping cops scared straight. He was a legend, and not a silent one.

Guido, then sixty-eight, dismissed suggestions that a flawed bureaucracy allowed corruption to flourish.

"Bullshit," said the former chief, who put more police officers in jail than any other cop. "Everyone missed the point. There was a breakdown in leadership. It all comes down to the same thing . . . leadership. And the biggest deterrent to corruption is the certainty of being punished."

It was the ultimate Halloween surprise. Everywhere, Joseph Trimboli saw faces that he no longer recognized. People who always wore frowns were suddenly smiling. Cops who looked angry when he walked in a room now smiled and greeted him warmly. It was like the department had gone through an amazing, overnight metamorphosis. All the masks had been changed. The myth of the "bad cop" in police legend had been reversed, for the time being. The Watcher was now the "good cop."

The commissioner, Ray Kelly, was now his friend. Their first meeting and Trimboli's harassment had been swept under the carpet. This time Ray Kelly wanted Joe Trimboli to come to One Police Plaza along with the media to a very public promotion ceremony on October 29, 1993. It was an exculpation for the cop who stood alone—the one the newspapers were now calling The Lone Ranger. Trimboli was being publicly exalted by the New York Police Department.

As he put on his blue uniform and a pair of white gloves, Joe remembered that morning last year when the commissioner had questioned Joe Trimboli's worth as an investigator. He wondered if Kelly gave it a second thought or if he was too busy covering his butt.

Trimboli was promoted to detective squad supervisor. This was the reason he entered FIAU in the first place. It took a little longer and turned out to be more than he bargained for, but ultimately he got his gold shield. After years of being set up for a fall, Trimboli stood up for applause. It washed over him, his face reddened, and he fought back tears. The applause increased, as did Joe's embarrassment. Applause was a simple reward, but it was the only recognition Trimboli wanted or expected from his department.

On that day, Trimboli could hardly remember the bad years. He forgot the harassment, the times his car was broken into or when his mail was left opened on his desk or cut to pieces. Having reached a point where he trusted no one, Trimboli was standing in the middle of a room with seven hundred applauding cops. It was like Sally Field's famous line, "You like me, you really like me."

"This is not the police department of Michael Dowd," the police commissioner said. "It is the department of Joe Trimboli. He has put respect for the law, pride in the law department, and the steadfast faith in what is right before all else."

Joe stepped forward, his chest swelling.

"In promoting Sergeant Trimboli," Kelly said, "we are recognizing that faith."

The applause from a department that abandoned him washed over him. The bogeyman was exorcised; Trimboli's work had been vindicated.

That night Joe Trimboli went home and called Frank Serpico. The Old Serpico was proud the New Serpico had been publicly sainted. They had developed an odd kinship. Joe Trimboli went to bed as a recognized NYPD hero, a long overdue tribute. That night, Joe dreamt about his first meeting with Dowd. It was 1986 all over again and he was standing in the parking lot outside the 75th precinct. The dream was a recurring one, but this time it ended differently. This time Joseph Trimboli arrested Michael Dowd.

As Joe put handcuffs on Dowd, the surprised cop demanded, "Who are you, anyway?"

"They call me the Watcher," Joe Trimboli said.

At that point Joe awakened. It was a dream, sure. It would always be a dream. But Michael Dowd wasn't his nightmare anymore.

EPILOGUE

The Mollen people, as they affectionately became known, couldn't leak enough details about their good deeds to enough reporters. The reporters didn't know better than to listen. And so, for the better part of six months, different "working" drafts of the so-called Mollen Commission Report were being leaked to four different newspapers. It was dizzying. The real thing, when it came, was anticlimactic. *The New York Times,* which had not shown any signs of interest in a police corruption story since Frank Serpico went to the newspaper with his tale, was especially taken with Judge Milt Mollen. But the commission hearings were a televised farce built around the fundamental deceit and villainy of Michael Dowd.

Joe Trimboli quietly put in his retirement papers in November 1993. By then he had made peace with his one-time antagonist, Police Commissioner Ray Kelly. In the end, the two men came to respect and like each other. They are only at odds now in police folklore. The last time I saw them together, Kelly and Trimboli were standing together at my birthday party chatting. All the friction that had developed between them was forgotten. Six months later, on the night before Dowd was sentenced, Kelly laughed and said, "Trimboli is all right. Hey, you take your heroes as you get them."

The new police commissioner, William Bratton, liked Joe Trimboli. He also liked the message keeping him would have sent to the NYPD.

When a New York City civic association honored Trimboli in March 1993 as the Cop of the Year, Bratton stood up President Clinton to personally deliver the award. The sergeant was offered a job with Bratton's own special investigative unit. Although grateful, Trimboli simply felt his time had come and gone. There were too many old IAD warriors still in the department, buried like land mines throughout the city.

Trimboli got quite sick the next month; he collapsed at home and was rushed to a Brooklyn hospital. He nearly died of insulin shock. Doctors changed his diet and suggested Joe find a new job. Stress, they said, was killing him. Like a heat-seeking missile that had been pointed at Michael Dowd and locked on his exhaust for most of a decade, Trimboli simply ran out of fuel. He nearly crashed and burned.

His hair grayed and his eyesight worsened. That was enough for the Watcher. John Daly, a former New York City cop who now headed an investigation team working for the Queens district attorney, Richard Brown, offered Trimboli a job. He was quickly hired, in June 1994, as a senior investigator in a corruption investigation unit.

The Mollen Commission report was finally published on July 7, 1994. It was a distortion wrapped in a misrepresentation. Still, *The New York Times* ran the story across three columns on the front page with the banner 2-YEAR CORRUPTION INQUIRY FINDS A WILLFUL BLINDNESS IN NEW YORK'S POLICE DEPT. The companion piece on Michael Dowd was headlined, OFFICER FLAUNTED CORRUPTION, AND HIS SUPERIORS IGNORED IT. Amazingly, both stories ignored Joe Trimboli; talk about revisionist history. Still, in the *Times* scheme of the world and front-page history, this was Knapp Commission treatment.

It read, "A 'willful blindness' to corruption throughout the ranks of the New York City Police Department has allowed highly organized networks of rogue officers to deal in drugs and prey on black and Hispanic neighborhoods, according to the final report of the commission that investigated the department.

"The report by the Mollen Commission, based on a two-year investigation, is particularly powerful in its criticisms of sergeants and other commanders of the five precincts found to be riddled with corruption. And it takes to task the police union, the Patrolmen's Benevolent Association, and the department's own internal investigation apparatus for effectively curtailing anticorruption efforts."

It looked like a huge scandal, but a careful, educated reading of the 158-page report left a lot to be desired. The main tenet of the Mollen Commission's argument was a call for a permanent outside monitor to investigate police corruption.

There was little mention, however, of the permanent monitor that was in place during the Dowd years. Charles J. Hynes, the former State Special Prosecutor for corruption, was given a pass. Incredibly, the same prosecutor who turned a blind eye to Michael Dowd was never held accountable. Milt Mollen had a huge blind spot of his own named Charles J. Hynes. Mollen sanctioned the ineptitude of Hynes's office and refused to ridicule his work; Hynes was now the Brooklyn DA and campaigning for state attorney general. Mollen's own blindness was a match for that of any of the woeful Internal Affairs investigators and police officials who the judge mentioned in his report.

The city's police reporters, all desperate for inside information and access to the vacuous Mollen Commission investigation, were equally blind. Like Judge Mollen, they never went back to the beginning. It was all there, in police reports and court documents. No one wanted to know how Milt Mollen had been used by a corrupt cop who then used a commission to excuse the blind ambition of his friends. As soon as Michael Dowd was done testifying and duping the commission he wrote a letter to

Adam Diaz asking for a payoff. That same month, Judge Kimba Wood, of the federal court, received a letter from Milt Mollen pleading for her to go easy on his prize witness. Nothing had changed. Where Dowd once barged into a bodega on New Lots Avenue and demanded cash from Diaz, he now wrote a letter from jail. Like Milt Mollen's missive to a federal judge, the corrupt cop's letter was postmarked with gall.

Federal prosecutors, meanwhile, knew the absurd truth. But they just waited and took notes for their final sentencing report on Michael Dowd. Their report, when it became public, would embarrass the judge and all of his appointed jackals in the press.

Lee Brown, who was hired by Mayor Dinkins on the advice of Milt Mollen, was never questioned by any investigator. Incredibly, Brown's name was not even mentioned once in the final commission report. To do so would embarrass Dinkins and Brown's current boss, President Clinton. It appears that Judge Mollen's legacy was to protect his cronies, so he allowed Brown to walk away. Still, there was enough nice, bold writing in the report to keep the newspapers' editorial pages busy.

"What we found is that the problem of police corruption extends far beyond the corrupt cop," Mollen wrote in a rewrite of the twenty-year-old Knapp report. "It is a multi-faceted problem that has flourished in parts of our city not only because of opportunity and greed but because of a police culture that exalts loyalty over integrity; because of the silence of honest officers who fear the consequences of 'ratting' on another cop, no matter how grave the crime; because of the willfully blind supervisors who fear the consequences of a corruption scandal more than corruption itself; because of the demise of the principle of accountability that makes all commanders responsible for fighting corruption in their commands; because of a hostility and alienation between the police and community in certain precincts which breeds an 'Us vs. Them' mentality; and because for years the New York

City Police Department abandoned its responsibility to insure the integrity of its members.''

The commission recommendations were equally tired and windy. Mollen wanted formation of a permanent independent oversight body to fight corruption, improvement of screening and recruitment, stronger internal intelligence, more prevention and detection of drug abuse, and the support of the police union in fighting corruption.

Joe Trimboli felt betrayed. Mollen was as pathetic as any of the police commanders and special prosecutors who shut down his Dowd investigations. Specifically, Trimboli had been promised that commission oversights would be straightened out in the final commission report. Instead, they were ignored altogether. It was a whitewash. In many ways, it was the final fix. Clearly, the report was carefully constructed to protect Judge Mollen's dearest friends. Trimboli had told the Mollen Commission all about Hynes and they largely ignored him. The sergeant recalled one meeting with Dennis Hawkins (Joe Hynes's assistant) on the subject of Adonis and other prospective informants when the prosecutor kept getting up and leaving the room. He seemed to have kidney problems. Finally, Trimboli followed him out into the hall. There stood Hawkins speaking to Hynes, who was listening, hands behind his back. Even then, Hynes wanted the ability to deny. The special prosecutor for corruption was too busy with his own career to come in from the hallway.

"When I steered them to Hynes," Trimboli said after he read the report, "they just walked me in the other direction. The judge protected his golden boy. He didn't want to hear a word about Hynes."

In his own Dowd report (ordered by Lee Brown after Trimboli's story was publicized), former police commissioner Ray Kelly severely criticized Hynes. Hynes, then the Brooklyn DA, said he would not respond to Kelly's questions. He promised, however, to sit for the Mollen

Commission. During the spring of 1992, I went to see
Dennis Hawkins, who had prepared a report on the Michael Dowd cases. I read the report in his presence and
was amazed. It read like a bogus reconstruction created
by Hynes and his subordinates to excuse their mistakes.
It was just so much unconnected gibberish. Yet I still
thought Hynes would work closely with Mollen; but he
did nothing, and his mistakes were simply glossed over.
There was no detailed investigation into the SPO failures,
and no adequate explanation for Hynes. It was as if that
part of the Dowd investigation never happened. Mollen
had the audacity to actually thank Hynes in the acknowl-
edgments of his final report to the court.

So the final Mollen Commission report was a sham. It
was the last testament to the Michael Dowd cover-up.
But federal prosecutors were readying their own Michael
Dowd report, to be revealed at his sentencing. It was the
secret antidote to an overdose of Mollen Commission
fever.

UNITED STATES DISTRICT COURT
SOUTHERN DISTRICT OF NEW YORK
- - - - - - - - - - - - - - - - - X

UNITED STATES OF AMERICA,   :
               :
       - v -   :   S1 92 Cr. 792 (KMW)
               :
MICHAEL DOWD,   :
               :
          Defendant.   :
               :
- - - - - - - - - - - - - - - - - X

GOVERNMENT'S SENTENCING MEMORANDUM

            MARY JO WHITE
            United States Attorney for the
            Southern District of New York
            Attorney for the United States
                 of America

DAVID B. FEIN
ROBERT E. RICE
Assistant United States Attorney

     - Of Counsel -

UNITED STATES DISTRICT COURT
SOUTHERN DISTRICT OF NEW YORK
- - - - - - - - - - - - - - - - - - X
                                     :
UNITED STATES OF AMERICA   :
                                     :
        - v -   :
                                     :
MICHAEL DOWD,   :   S1 92 Cr. 792 (KMW)
                                     :
              Defendant.   :
                                     :
- - - - - - - - - - - - - - - - - - X

GOVERNMENT'S SENTENCING MEMORANDUM

The Government submits this memorandum in support of its application that Michael Dowd be sentenced at the high end of the applicable Sentencing Guidelines range. This Memorandum will provide the basis for that request, as well as the basis for the Government's opposition to Dowd receiving credit for his attempted cooperation with this Office or his cooperation with the Commission to Investigate Alleged Police Corruption (the ''Mollen Commission'').[1]

Specifically, this Memorandum will address: (1) Dowd's criminal activity and the resulting Sentencing Guidelines range; (2) Dowd's attempted cooperation with this Office; (3) Dowd's plea allocution before this Court; (4) Dowd's cooperation with the Mollen Commission; (5) the Pre-Sentence Investigation Report; (6) Dowd's appearance on the television program ''60 Minutes''; (7) two letters Dowd recently wrote to co-conspirator Adam Diaz; and (8) the inappropriateness of a downward departure.

Background

On July 30, 1992, Michael Dowd, a former officer with the New York City Police Department (the ''NYPD'' or the

---

[1] In a separate letter dated November 5, 1993, the Government responded to the Court's request that the parties furnish the Court with law and precedent on whether the two-point upward adjustment was sufficient to reflect the abuse of position of trust in this case. Prior to accepting Dowd's plea, the Court informed the parties that it would consider an upward departure beyond the two-point adjustment.

''Police Department''), was arrested by the Police
Department and the United States Drug Enforcement
Administration (the ''DEA'') pursuant to a federal
complaint charging him with conspiring to distribute
narcotics. The federal arrest came less than three months
after Dowd was arrested on charges of cocaine trafficking
by the Suffolk County District Attorney's Office. Dowd had
been released on bail from Suffolk County and continued to
engage in criminal activity until his federal arrest.

A federal grand jury returned an indictment against
Dowd and co-defendant Borrent Perez, a/k/a ''Baron,'' on
September 20, 1992, charging them with conspiring to
distribute and to aid and abet the distribution of cocaine
and heroin. On February 26, 1993, Perez pled guilty to the
one-count indictment. In separate cases, two of Dowd's
other co-conspirators—former police officers Kenneth
Eurell and Thomas Mascia—were charged federally and pled
guilty to racketeering and narcotics conspiracy,
respectively.

On June 10, 1993, Dowd entered into a plea agreement
with the Government, in which he agreed to plead guilty to
a two-count superseding information. (A copy of the plea
agreement is attached as Exhibit A.) Count One charged
Dowd with engaging in a pattern of racketeering activity
in violation of Title 18, United States Code, Sections
1961, et seq. (the Racketeer Influenced and Corrupt
Organizations Act or ''RICO''), and Count Two charged Dowd
with conspiracy to distribute and possess with intent to
distribute cocaine and heroin, in violation of Title 21,
United States Code, Section 846. On June 10, 1993, Dowd
pled guilty to both counts of the Information.

1. Dowd's Criminal Activity

By any standard, Michael Dowd's criminal activity as
an officer with the New York City Police Department was
heinous, both in the type and variety of crimes he
committed and in their unflagging repetition and duration.
This section will review Dowd's crimes, in particular: (a)
Dowd's work for major drug organizations in 1987 and 1988;
(b) Dowd's cocaine trafficking in and around Suffolk
County from 1989 until his May 6, 1992, arrest; (c) Dowd's
participation, while released on bail from Suffolk County,
in a scheme to rob and then abduct a woman; and (d) Dowd's
other crimes as a police officer.

a. Work for Major Drug Organizations

In or about June 1987, Michael Dowd and Borrent
Perez, a/k/a/ ''Baron,'' agreed that Perez would attempt
to identify drug trafficking organizations that would make

cash payments to Dowd and his partner Kenneth Eurell in
exchange for information and other assistance. Perez
initially made arrangements with the ''Company,'' a drug
organization involved in the weekly distribution of multi-
kilogram quantities of cocaine in Brooklyn.[2] In late June
or early July 1987, Perez met with Dowd and Eurell and gave
them the initial payment of approximately $7000 he had
received from the Company. Because that payment was
several hundred dollars ''short,'' the arrangement with
the Company ended after the initial payment. Prior to
ending their relationship with the Company, however, Dowd
and Eurell observed the Company's primary drug trafficking
location and gave advice as to how to conduct business in a
manner better designed to avoid police scrutiny.

In or about August 1987, Perez arranged for Dowd and
Eurell to meet Adam Diaz, the leader of another drug
organization involved in the weekly distribution of multi-
kilogram quantities of cocaine in Brooklyn (the ''Diaz
Organization'').[3] Diaz, who is cooperating with this
Office, wanted to have police officers on the Diaz
Organization's payroll. Thus, Dowd and Diaz agreed that
there would be an initial payment of $24,000, followed by
weekly payments of $8000.

Pursuant to the arrangement, Dowd and Eurell used
their positions as police officers to provide the Diaz
Organization with a variety of assistance, ranging from
information about the presence of narcotics officers and
raids in the vicinity of the organization's trafficking
locations to harassing or intimidating rival drug
organizations. In return, the Diaz Organization made
weekly payments of $8000, of which Dowd and Eurell each
kept $3500 and Perez received $1000.

One of the first ways in which Dowd and Eurell helped
the Diaz Organization's drug trafficking was to observe
the trafficking spot and to make specific recommendations
as to how to avoid police scrutiny. Subsequently, Dowd and
Eurell found new locations from which the Diaz

---

[2]This Office, along with the NYPD and the DEA,
investigated and prosecuted approximately twenty leaders
and ''hitmen'' of the Company on narcotics conspiracy,
racketeering, murder and firearms charges. See United
States v. Maximo Reyes, et al., 91 Cr. 348 (LBS). The
cooperation of certain defendants in that case led to this
Office's investigation of Dowd.

[3]The investigation and prosecution of members of the
Diaz Organization were conducted by the United States
Attorney's Office for the Eastern District of New York.

Organization would sell its cocaine. For example,
following arrests at one of the organization's locations
in the fall of 1987, Dowd and Eurell located a new
storefront, which the Diaz Organization acquired for
$60,000 and then used to continue its sale of cocaine. In
December 1987, Dowd and Eurell helped Diaz move his
business once again, on this occasion to a business
location controlled by Perez, where the Organization
continued its cocaine sales.

In January 1988, Dowd and Eurell dealt frequently
with a particular worker of the Diaz Organization (the
''Diaz Worker''), who is cooperating with this Office.
Dowd sometimes received money directly from him. The Diaz
Worker wanted to obtain a firearm, and Dowd gave the Diaz
Worker a .357 Magnum, which Dowd and Eurell had acquired
illegally several months earlier.

At around that same time, Dowd began obtaining ounce
quantities of cocaine from the Diaz Organization, which
Dowd then distributed. Dowd received the ounces of cocaine
from Adam Diaz himself, as well as from the Diaz Worker. On
one occasion, while on duty, Dowd and Eurell drove to a
government office where one of Dowd's brothers worked, and
Dowd sold a quantity of cocaine to his brother who was and
is a public safety employee (''Dowd Brother #1'').

Adam Diaz asked Dowd and Eurell to assist the
organization further by disrupting the drug business of a
competitor located nearby. Dowd and Eurell, along with
four other persons they solicited, including another
brother of Dowd's who was and is a law enforcement officer
(''Dowd Brother #2''), went to the competitor's location
as if they were all officers. In fact, only Dowd, Eurell
and Dowd Brother #2 were officers; the other three persons
impersonated officers by wearing badges and carrying
firearms. Dowd and Eurell waited outside, while the four
others entered the location, showed badges and pretended
they were conducting a raid. They did not fully carry out
the feigned raid.

On February 6, 1988, Dowd and Eurell responded to a
radio call at the Diaz Organization's primary trafficking
spot. They spoke to the Diaz Worker, who told them that he
had been robbed at gunpoint of many kilograms of cocaine by
a man named ''Franklin.'' Dowd and Eurell looked for
Franklin, finding him three days later, on February 9,
1988. They stopped Franklin in his car, and Dowd gave
Franklin a summons for numerous automobile violations,
which Dowd never filed with the Police Department. The
summons was recovered in a garbage dump in Suffolk County

several weeks after Dowd's arrest pursuant to the federal complaint.

The Diaz Organization's business was slowed by the February 6, 1988, robbery, as well as the subsequent arrest of the Diaz Worker and other important members of the organization on March 28, 1988. During this time, the payments to Dowd and Eurell became erratic, both in frequency and in amount. Dowd was reassigned out of the 75th Precinct in or about April 1988.

Even after Dowd left the 75th Precinct, he remained in contact with Adam Diaz, who continued to operate his drug business sporadically until his arrest in June 1989. Diaz continued to make payments to Dowd—on an inconsistent basis—in 1988 and 1989; in fact, Diaz made a payment to Dowd several days before Diaz's June 1989 arrest.

b. <u>Cocaine</u> <u>Trafficking</u> <u>in</u> <u>Suffolk</u> <u>County</u>

Following Dowd's reassignment out of the 75th Precinct, he increased his own trafficking in cocaine. Initially, Dowd used Perez to obtain cocaine, purchasing cocaine from him approximately six times over a four-month period in 1988. Those transactions ranged from one ounce (approximately 28 grams) on about five occasions to 125 grams on one occasion. Dowd sold Eurell one ounce (or approximately 28 grams) from the 125 gram transaction.

In late 1990 or early 1991, Eurell (who, by then, had retired from the NYPD) was approached by two police officers (now terminated) who wanted to know if they could buy cocaine from Dowd. Eurell found out that Dowd was still selling cocaine, and arranged for the two officers and himself to buy ounce quantities of cocaine from Dowd on a weekly basis. Eurell and the two officers purchased approximately four ounces of cocaine each month from Dowd for several months.

In mid-1991, Eurell purchased one ounce of cocaine from Dowd. Eurell sold portions of that ounce to Harry Vahjean, a civilian who distributed small amounts of cocaine in Suffolk County. In or about the fall of 1991, Eurell increased the amount he bought from Dowd to 125 grams. At that time, Dowd's supply was low, and Vahjean introduced Eurell to another seller, from whom Dowd and Eurell each purchased 125 grams of cocaine. Later in 1991, Dowd and Eurell together purchased 500 grams of cocaine from a partner of that seller for approximately $9000. Following that purchase, Dowd's supply increased again, and Eurell split one kilogram of cocaine with Dowd.

In December 1991, Dowd asked Thomas Mascia (who was Dowd's regular partner in the 94th Precinct) to invest in a

kilogram of cocaine. Dowd told Mascia that, as long as they
contributed the money toward the purchase of the kilogram,
they could share in the profit made from its resale without
being involved in its distribution. Dowd asked Mascia to
contribute half, or $8750, but Mascia declined at that
time.

In April 1992, Dowd made a similar offer to Eurell to
invest in kilograms of cocaine. Eurell and the two police
officers discussed above gave $17,500 to Dowd to invest,
and Dowd, along with Mascia, invested an additional
$17,500, all of which Dowd gave to a cocaine dealer named
''Ray,'' who had become Dowd's main source of supply. Ray
purchased and resold two kilograms of cocaine and returned
to Dowd the initial investment, plus some profit.[4]

On May 5, 1992, Dowd and Eurell introduced Vahjean to
''Renee,'' another cocaine dealer that Dowd knew, so that
Vahjean could purchase 125 grams of cocaine from Renee. On
May 6, 1992, Dowd, Eurell, the two police officers
referred to above, Vahjean, Renee and others were arrested
by the Suffolk County Police.

c. The Kidnapping Scheme

Following the arrests of Dowd, Eurell, Mascia and
others by Suffolk County on May 6, 1992, this Office, in
conjunction with the NYPD and the DEA, continued its
investigation of Dowd, which had begun in 1991 based on the
cooperation of certain members of the Company.

In July 1992, following the release of Dowd and
Eurell on bail in Suffolk County, Eurell decided to
cooperate with this Office. After lengthy proffer sessions
in which Eurell described not only the conduct the
Government was already aware of but also substantial
additional criminal activity committed by himself, Dowd
and others, this Office entered into a cooperation
agreement with Eurell.

In July 1992, Eurell informed the Government that
Dowd had told Eurell about the planned robbery of a Queens
''stash'' house with a drug dealer named ''Danny,'' who
had an active criminal case in Brooklyn and was renting a
portion of Dowd's house in Brentwood, New York. Dowd hoped
to make enough money from the robbery to fund his flight
from the jurisdiction to avoid prosecution on the Suffolk
County charges. Dowd planned to flee to Nicaragua with his

---

[4]At around this time, Ray offered Dowd $10,000 if he
would transport cocaine from Texas to New York City. Dowd
discussed this proposition separately with Mascia and
Eurell, but both declined.

family, Eurell and Eurell's family.[5] The Government
instructed Eurell to learn as much as he could about the
robbery plan and to provide information about it to the
Government. Meanwhile, the NYPD and the DEA conducted
surveillance and other investigation of Dowd's ongoing
crime.

On July 27, 1992, Eurell was invited to Dowd's
residence in Port Jefferson, New York, where he met with
Dowd, Danny and two of Danny's associates, ''Hector'' (who
had an active drug case in Louisiana and also lived in
Dowd's house) and ''Ray.'' Eurell learned that the planned
robbery of the stash house also contemplated the abduction
of the woman who lived at the house. Eurell also learned
that the now-deceased husband of the woman who lived in the
Queens house had taken ten kilograms of cocaine from Ray
without paying for them and Ray was being held responsible
for the debt by his Colombian suppliers. Ray had been
following the woman for weeks in order to learn her
routine. The five individuals drove from Dowd's house to
Queens to familiarize themselves with the neighborhood of
the stash house.

The five individuals agreed on the following plan:
Danny, Hector and Ray would enter and secure the woman's
house while Dowd and Eurell would remain outside,
monitoring police activity in the area. While inside,
Danny, Hector and Ray would take any cash or drugs, and
then abduct the woman in order to turn her over to the
Colombians for her execution to satisfy Ray's debt.[6] Dowd

---

[5]In a conversation with Dowd consensually recorded by
Eurell, Eurell said that Eurell's wife told him that
''she's (referring to Bonnie Dowd) not too excited about
going to Nicaragua, huh? I thought she wanted to go?'' Dowd
replied, ''In the beginning she did. I told her, 'you're
not the one doing the fucking time, I am.' ''
[6]In a consensually recorded conversation, Eurell
questioned why Dowd wanted to be there when the woman was
brought to the Colombians. Eurell suggested that the
Colombians ''might fucking do everybody, they don't want
no witnesses after they do this broad.'' Dowd said, ''fuck
them, I'll fucking kill them if they (unintelligible
(hereinafter ''U/I'')) my gun, they got money.'' Dowd
said, ''you got to realize, not that many people can kill
somebody, you understand?'' When Eurell said he did not
understand why Dowd ''wanted to be there when the broad was
fucking turned over,'' Dowd said, ''I didn't really.''
Dowd added, ''these fucking Colombians would love to have
us, what are you kidding me?'' Eurell adds, ''yeah, when we
were working, they would have loved to have us.''

and Eurell would each receive a share of whatever drugs or cash were recovered from the robbery.

Dowd and Eurell gave advice on how best to carry out the crime, recommending, among other things, point-to-point radios and a police scanner. It was decided that entry would be made during the day by Danny, Hector or Ray posing as a flower deliverer or electrician.[7]

The NYPD and the DEA had Eurell tape record his telephone conversations with Dowd and wear a body wire on the eve and day of the commission of the crime. While they drove to the Queens house on the day of the planned robbery and abduction, Dowd told Eurell about a conversation Dowd had had with his wife that morning:

> 'Well I'm going off to work,' that's what I told my wife. She goes, uh, 'I had plans today to do things,' (U/I), 'I'm going to work.' And she goes, 'robbing somebody is not going to work,' and I said, 'well it is this time.'

Dowd continued to describe the conversation with his wife, and said that she wanted to go out to exercise and to have him stay home with the children. Dowd told her:

> I said 'you exercise at home.' What pisses me off is, I said, (U/I) 'if I had a regular job to go to today, you couldn't do this, you'd have to get a babysitter.' 'But you don't have a regular job.' I said, 'yes I do, this is my regular job now.' . . . What was I going to say to her. I have to rational—explain, you know what I mean. Like she was planning on daddy being home, well I ain't. 'Now do something. I'll be home for your 4 o'clock fucking job. Other than that I got the whole day to myself.'

Dowd also told Eurell how he had thought about the robbery and abduction plan the previous night. Dowd said:

> I laid down. I didn't go to sleep right away but about twenty minutes after I laid down . . . I talked it over like three times, I said, 'that's enough. I'm just like them now, going (U/I) there blind. I don't give a fuck. They're the ones going in, I don't care, I'll leave, see ya.'

---

[7]Two days prior to the planned robbery, on July 28, 1992, a Queens woman was killed in an unrelated robbery in which the assailants coincidentally posed as flower deliverers. In a conversation consensually recorded by Eurell, Dowd said: ''the motherfucker beat us to the punch, that's what pissed me off,'' referring to the fact that someone else had already used the flower delivery pretense for a robbery.

Dowd added, ''I plan, but they don't listen to the plan.
They can go on their own. I'll still get money if they get
in.'' In describing the robbery, Dowd said: ''The real
worry is getting in her fucking door. After that, fuck
everything. Once you're in her door, man, it'll be like a
fucking picnic.''

The NYPD and the DEA located the woman and evacuated
her and others from the Queens house hours before the
attempted robbery and abduction. When Dowd and Eurell
arrived in Queens at the scheduled time, they heard over
Dowd's police scanner a report about law enforcement
surveillance being conducted at the target location. Dowd
said: ''I think that Colombian was setting us up. Either
that or Danny eh, to get his brother out of jail . . . Danny
. . . might not even know about it.'' Dowd drove out of the
area and returned home, after taking Eurell home.

Later, Dowd telephoned Eurell's residence and
learned that Eurell had gone to his lawyer's office. Dowd
immediately drove to Eurell's lawyer's office and
confronted Eurell with the possibility that Eurell was
cooperating against him. Eurell attempted to persuade Dowd
that he was not cooperating, and Dowd returned home, where
members of the NYPD and the DEA arrested him that afternoon
based on the federal arrest warrant.

    d. <u>Other</u> <u>Crimes</u>

In addition to the crimes described above, Dowd
committed numerous other crimes during his career as a
police officer. Those crimes are summarized briefly, and
are listed in three basic time periods: (i)
1983–1986—Dowd's early years as an officer in the 75th
Precinct, during which he committed crimes with his first
regular partner; (ii) 1987–Summer 1988—Dowd's return to
the 75th Precinct, during which he committed crimes with
his second regular partner, Kenneth Eurell; (iii) Fall
1988–May 6, 1992—Dowd's remaining years as a police
officer, during which he worked at the Whitestone Pound
and then the 94th Precinct, where he committed crimes with
his third regular partner, Thomas Mascia. The description
of these crimes is based on Dowd's public testimony before
the Mollen Commission, the Government's investigation or
both.

      i. 1983–1986

* Stealing one-half kilogram of cocaine from crime
  scene and subsequently selling it for $14,000
* Using excessive force against prisoners and
  civilians
* Using, possessing and selling firearms illegally
* Stealing drugs, cash and firearms from crime scenes,

including scenes with persons seriously injured and dead
* Illegally raiding drug locations; burglarizing and robbing drug dealers of drugs, cash and firearms, at a frequency of five times a day for an average gain of $200 a day ($500 a day during holiday season)
* Failing to arrest individuals in possession of drugs and firearms; allowing such individuals to remain in possession of some quantity of drugs
* Selling drugs
* Committing perjury in criminal cases
* Receiving gifts and gratuities from civilians and local business owners
* Receiving money from automobile drivers in exchange for not issuing summonses

ii.   1987–Summer 1988

* Stealing heroin and cocaine from a murder crime scene
* Stealing money from a burglary crime scene by having the victim identify where her mother kept money, which had not been stolen at initial burglary
* Using excessive force on prisoners and civilians
* Riding ''shotgun'' with drug trafficker to protect transportation of drugs or money
* Using cocaine and alcohol while on duty
* Purchasing and selling ounce to kilogram quantities of cocaine

iii.   Fall 1988–May 6, 1992

* Receiving kickbacks from tow truck companies for referrals
* Receiving kickbacks from automobile repair shops for referrals
* Making impounded vehicles inoperable and then receiving gratuities from owners for making vehicles operable
* Creating false police reports to allow civilians to collect insurance money fraudulently in exchange for money
* Providing drug trafficker with information from police vouchers, including other drug trafficker's name, date of birth, spouse's name, address and telephone number, in exchange for money
* Stealing money from person or home of ''dead on arrival'' victims
* Stealing money from drunks in the street
* Receiving money from drunk automobile drivers in exchange for not arresting them
* Taking from church quantities of food that had been provided by the federal government for the needy
* Failing to respond to call for help from supervisor because supervisor was strict in his supervision

* Engaging in acts of police brutality against
   criminals and non-criminals
* Threatening victims of police brutality with
   additional brutality if they reported his misconduct
* Using cocaine and alcohol while on duty

   e. Dowd's Sentencing Guidelines Range

   The Sentencing Guidelines range agreed upon by the
Government and Michael Dowd (in an agreement that is not
binding on the Court or the Probation Department) is 151 to
188 months. The Probation Department concurs in the range
agreed to by the parties.

   A significant portion of Dowd's charged criminal
conduct, indeed, all crimes above and beyond his
distribution of five kilograms of cocaine, have no effect
on his Guidelines range due to the grouping analysis
required in RICO cases. Dowd's base offense level would be
the same if he had only trafficked in five kilograms of
cocaine;[8] his other criminal activities are not accounted
for in the Guidelines range.

2. Dowd's Attempted Cooperation with This Office

   Dowd attempted to cooperate with this Office, but his
cooperation was rejected because he was found to be
untruthful and evasive. Following his arrest on federal
charges, Dowd met with representatives of this Office, the
NYPD and the DEA on several occasions to discuss his
possible cooperation.[9] This Office told Dowd repeatedly
that he had to be fully honest and candid, that he should
describe all criminal activity with which he was familiar,
and that this Office had the right to accept or reject his
proffered cooperation in its discretion.

   In the judgment of this Office, the NYPD and the DEA,
Dowd was untruthful and evasive, and this Office informed
him of that conclusion and of its decision not to offer him
a cooperation agreement. Examples of his lack of
truthfulness and candor are as follows:

   a. Dowd grossly minimized the assistance he provided to

   _____

   [8]Dowd's Suffolk County cocaine trafficking, which is
Racketeering Act 11 in Count One of the Information,
itself involved approximately five kilograms of cocaine;
accordingly, that conduct alone would have resulted in the
same Guidelines range as that which results from all of
Dowd's criminal conduct grouped together.
   [9]On most occasions in the proffer sessions when
discussing crimes that had occurred, Dowd refused to
identify himself, instead using the term ''another
person,'' apparently to protect his strategy if he decided
it was in his best interest to proceed to trial.

the Diaz Organization. Dowd claimed—and continues to claim—that he was involved with the Diaz Organization at most from August to late October or November 1987 and that he played a minor role for them.[10]

The evidence establishes that Dowd was involved with the Diaz Organization from August 1987 through March 1988, and then again prior to Diaz's arrest in June 1989. That evidence includes the statements of Eurell, Perez, Adam Diaz and the Diaz Organization Worker, as well as police reports and other documents that date certain pertinent events, such as the robbery of a Diaz location and Dowd's issuance of a summons to the robber in February 1988, well after November 1987.

b. Dowd did not describe the involvement of Dowd Brother #1 (a local public safety employee who bought cocaine that Dowd had received from the Diaz Organization), or Dowd Brother #2 (a local law enforcement officer) and a civilian friend, who had participated in one of Dowd's illegal raids on behalf of the Diaz Organization.[11]

c. Dowd did not acknowledge his intent to flee the jurisdiction after his release on bail on the Suffolk County charges or his participation in the robbery/ abduction scheme that was ongoing until his federal arrest. Later, Dowd claimed through his attorney that he was entrapped (or importuned and encouraged) by Eurell in the kidnapping scheme and that co-conspirators Danny, Hector and Ray were actually government informants.

To the contrary, the evidence demonstrates that it was Dowd who brought Eurell into the scheme, which, prior to Eurell's participation, already included Dowd and Dowd's drug trafficking associates who were

---

[10]In a February 1993 letter to the Court, Dowd maintained this position, indicating his belief that he deserved a two-point reduction in his Guidelines range for mitigating role, a contention belied by all of the facts known to the Government. Dowd repeated this claim at his plea in June 1993, see p. 20 infra, but took a contrary position during his public testimony in September 1993, see pp. 20–22 infra.

[11]Notably, Dowd does not contest the Government's description of his brothers' involvement in his crimes, which is contained in the PSR.

renting one of Dowd's houses.[12] Significantly, once
it became apparent to Dowd that law enforcement was
aware of the robbery/abduction plan, Dowd did not
fault Eurell for getting him into this scheme;
rather, Dowd suspected that the ''Colombians set it
all up.''[13]

Moreover, as a consequence of Dowd's failure to
cooperate promptly and fully, Dowd's co-
conspirators, drug traffickers who were renting one
of Dowd's homes, remain at large.

d. Dowd claimed—and continues to claim—that the only
gun involved in the racketeering offense was a .357
Magnum, and that Dowd did not give that gun to the
Diaz Organization Worker.

The evidence shows that there were numerous guns
involved in the offense, and that Dowd himself gave
the .357 Magnum to the Diaz Organization Worker. That
Dowd gave the gun to the Diaz Organization is based
on the statements of Eurell and the Diaz Organization
Worker, who were both present.

e. Despite being urged to describe all crimes about
which he was aware, Dowd revealed information
selectively, even withholding an allegation of
police misconduct (about which he was aware when he
was still an officer in the spring of 1992) until
December 1993, only after he had already given the
information to a major television network, which had
investigated the matter but stopped when they
discovered that the alleged victim had died in about
October 1993.

Moreover, even though Dowd did provide the

---

[12]In fact, Dowd himself described in a consensually
recorded conversation how he became involved in the
robbery/abduction scheme. Dowd said that Hector's sister,
Margie, ''called me up when she found out I was fucking in
trouble.'' Dowd said ''Margie spoke to me and said, 'Mike,
look, I know you're in trouble for what you've been (U/I),
my brothers are involved in that, if you want to do
something with them, they can help you, you can help
them.' ''
[13]After hearing that law enforcement was in the area,
Eurell said to Dowd: ''I said to you from the beginning
man, can you trust these fucking guys? How do you know
they're not trying to set us up.'' Dowd replied, ''Oh, how
do I know?'' Eurell said, ''No, (U/I) you know, that I
suggested that right away and you said no, you trusted
these guys.'' Dowd said: ''I trust them enough but I think
(U/I) Colombian set it all up.''

Government with some information believed to be truthful,
that information was not useful. Much of the verifiable
information Dowd provided we learned from other accomplice
witnesses who, based on their honesty and candor, were far
more suitable candidates for cooperation and would make
significantly more credible witnesses than would Dowd.
Further, most of the crimes Dowd described as to which he
had personal knowledge were less significant than his own.
Dowd's allegations of more significant police corruption
were often not based on personal knowledge, and the Police
Department's initial investigation into such crimes
generally proved fruitless.

3. Dowd Was Not Fully Truthful in His Plea Before This
Court

Dowd was not fully truthful to this Court in two
respects in his sworn allocution during his June 10, 1993
plea. First, at his plea, Dowd stated ''I accepted bribe
money from certain organizations involved in drug dealing
for information, most of it bogus information.'' (Plea Tr.
23). Dowd said that he gave them ''information on police
color vehicles or unmarked cars . . . and most of the stuff
was just to get their confidence, none of it—not that none
of it was good information, but much of it was basically to
fleece them for the money.'' (Plea Tr. 24). The Court
inquired, ''You get all this money just for identifying
unmarked cars?,'' and Dowd replied, ''For the most part,
yes, and not arresting them for what they were doing.''
(Plea Tr. 27).

The Government's investigation revealed that Dowd
violated his sworn duty as an NYPD officer by performing a
wide variety of services to assist the drug organizations,
well beyond ''identifying unmarked cars'' or ''not
arresting them for what they were doing.'' In exchange for
payments of thousands of dollars and ounces of cocaine,
Dowd provided the following assistance:

a.   Providing specific and general law enforcement
     information to drug organizations, including
     alerting drug organizations as to potential
     undercover or covert raids and advising them as to
     how to conduct their business without attracting
     police scrutiny;

b.   Using his position as a police officer to harass or
     intimidate drug dealers for the benefit of a rival
     drug organization, including illegal raids and
     recruiting of former officers and a civilian who
     impersonated officers with badges and firearms;

c. Riding ''shotgun'' with drug trafficker to protect transportation of drugs or money; and

d. Assisting drug organizations in finding new locations for their drug trafficking.

Dowd's own testimony at the Mollen Commission hearings contradicted his plea allocution. Dowd testified to a multitude of ways in which he aided drug organizations, in particular the Diaz Organization, in exchange for weekly payments of $4000. Dowd said that he offered two types of assistance:

> [O]ne would be intangible things and then there would be the tangible things . . . Intangibles would be a drug dealer would be able to brag amongst other drug dealers that he's got a cop on his payroll and that would give him a lot of respect in the drug world. By getting respect, that would give him power amongst other drug dealers to leave him alone, not to compete with him, various things of that nature that would come with that. He'd have juice . . . tangible benefits, see, you're talking about being able to, if you come across information, to tip him off with it. Also you're able to put pressure on his other drug dealers that are giving him competition in the neighborhood . . . On one specific occasion I was able to save their day.

(Mollen Tr. 112–13).

Dowd also testified that the drug organizations wanted him to use his authority as a New York City police officer to protect them from rival drug dealers. He stated:

> They wanted us to keep pressure on them. So what we would do, there was times when we would . . . we'd camp out in front of their stores so that they couldn't do business . . . We would also sometimes have the guys that used to be on the job would come in, and they'd pressure them. They'd go in and make believe they were Brooklyn North narcotics, do a fake raid on the place, and we'd be outside in the radio car . . . I was able to maybe put paperwork in on other locations. In other words, intelligence reports.

(Mollen Tr. 118–20). Dowd also testified about following drug traffickers to protect them in case law enforcement or rival drug dealers tried to stop them, and about assisting drug traffickers in finding specific spots or locations from which they could sell their drugs. (Mollen Tr. 121–2).

In sum, in sharp contrast to his statements to this
Court and to this Office previously, Dowd agreed with
Mollen Commission counsel's characterization that he was
''a fairly central figure to these drug organizations''
because he told them ''when they could deal drugs,''
''where they could deal drugs,'' and ''how they could deal
drugs,'' and that ''they looked to [Dowd] to tell them how
they could survive, how they could make money.'' (Mollen
Tr. 123).

Second, at his plea, the Court asked Dowd if he
agreed to distribute, and to possess with intent to
distribute, drugs, and Dowd answered, ''I did aid and abet
them. I had no direct dealings in the narcotics.'' (Plea
Tr. 23).

To the contrary, the Government's investigation
revealed that in 1987 and 1988, Dowd repeatedly received
ounce quantities of cocaine from the Diaz Organization.
(PSR, at 9). That information is based on the statements of
Eurell, Diaz and the Diaz Organization Worker, each of
whom witnessed such transactions.

In addition, Dowd testified at the public hearings
about other ''direct dealings'' with narcotics. He stated
that he stole drugs from a murder scene, which he later
resold through Perez (Mollen Tr. 74–75), and that he rode
shotgun for drug dealers, meaning ''guarding somebody as
they transport drugs or money.'' (Mollen Tr. 121).

Thus, in his allocution to this Court, Dowd was
untruthful in two respects, both of which attempted to
minimize the seriousness of his crimes.

4. Dowd's Public Testimony Before the Mollen Commission

After Dowd's proffered cooperation was rejected by
this Office because of his lack of truthfulness and candor
(based on our numerous first-hand sources of information
who largely corroborated each other and contradicted
Dowd),[14] Dowd entered into a ''cooperation agreement''

---

[14]The Government's investigation included the
following sources of information, among others: (a) the
cooperation of almost all principal accomplice witnesses,
including former officers Kenneth Eurell and Thomas
Mascia, Borrent Perez, a/k/a ''Baron,'' Adam Diaz, and
workers of the ''Diaz Organization'' and the ''Company'';
(b) tape recordings of Dowd from his home telephone and
others' telephones based on court-authorized wiretaps
conducted in Suffolk County; (c) consensual tape
recordings of Dowd made by Eurell in July 1992; (d)
evidence seized during federal and state search warrants
of the residences of Dowd and his co-conspirators; and (e)

with the Mollen Commission dated March 24, 1993. On
September 27, 1993, Dowd testified at the Mollen
Commission's public hearing.

Although we do not quarrel with the Mollen
Commission's view that Dowd's testimony has been valuable
to the Commission, Dowd's testimony at the public hearings
frequently attempted to shift responsibility for his
crimes away from himself and toward the NYPD and was, at
times, incorrect and misleading. Examples of such
testimony include the following:

First, Dowd's public testimony is replete with
attempts to shift responsibility for his criminal conduct.
Over the course of his testimony, Dowd claimed that he
committed his crimes because of, among others, the other
corrupt officers, the non-corrupt officers who refused to
work with him, the officers who did work with him, his
supervisors, senior officers who took over a case that he
should have handled, the Internal Affairs Division and the
Police Department generally. Without addressing the
NYPD's anti-corruption efforts at the time Dowd was
committing crimes as a police officer, the Government
submits that Dowd's public shifting of blame away from
himself and toward the NYPD evidence his failure truly to
accept personal responsibility for the crimes that he
committed.

Passages of Dowd's public testimony in which he
attempted to shift responsibility for his crimes are:

- Counsel: ''During your first year in the 75th
                Precinct, did you feel compelled to show
                other cops in that precinct that you were a
                good cop in the way you described it
                (meaning a corrupt cop)?''

  Dowd: ''Yes.'' (Tr. 44).

- Dowd: ''I notice a table . . . filled with drugs
                . . . some other officers arrived at the
                scene . . . I was a young cop, so they took
                over the scene, and they were in the
                undercover units, and it wasn't really
                their job, but they took over. Out of
                frustration, I remember reaching into a box
                full of cocaine and taking out two big
                handfuls and putting them in my pocket and
                walking out.'' (Tr. 59).

- Dowd: ''I had gotten a new partner at the time. I

a thorough review of Police Department records to verify
the statements of the accomplice witnesses.

had to prove to him that I was good.'' (Tr. 79).

- Dowd: ''The original reasons a lot of things are done is not to be so corrupt. In the beginning you start out saying, you know, you're angry that the drug dealers basically run the street, and you're angry that you have no dent into what they're doing. So in the beginning you start, well, what the heck. If we arrest them, we get a complaint by our CO or our sergeant that what did you do. You took two crack vials off the street. You cost the City sixteen hours overtime. What's going on here? . . . This is how it begins, and this is how it began with us. And then the negative reinforcement constantly. You say what the heck, make them pay a tax. Make the drug dealers pay a tax. Don't get me wrong. I didn't go there intending to rob drug dealers. I made drug arrests when I first got there, but very, very quickly you're turned off to this by the Department itself. And if anybody tells you any different, they're lying.'' (Tr. 89).

- Counsel: ''When you returned to the 75th Precinct, did you go back expecting to continue business as usual?''

- Dowd: ''No. . . . I intended on doing the right thing. . . . I had, I thought, a new attitude, and I was hoping to be able to survive a career as a police officer at this point. I knew it would be difficult, but I didn't think that it would be as difficult as it turned out to be. . . . Because many of the police officers there wouldn't work with me for many reasons.'' (Tr. 95).

- Dowd: ''The day before we had missed $11,000 in another house, and he thought I was setting him up. So I had to—you know, I felt desperate to prove to him that I wasn't setting him up, and that's why I did that.'' (Tr. 98–99).

- Dowd: My supervisors ''were happy that I wasn't making arrests because it wasn't costing the City any money.'' (Tr. 138).

- Dowd: ''Senior officers . . . showed me how to give him a little beating, and then I felt compelled, I was embarrassed and scared,

but I felt compelled to hit the guy
myself.'' (Tr. 196).

On one occasion in his testimony, Dowd speculated
about other officers' knowledge of his crimes when in fact
he had no idea whether other officers knew what he was
doing.[15] Dowd testified that after tipping off the Diaz
Organization about an undercover raid, not one supervisor
ever questioned him. ''I was surprised. I was actually
waiting to be questioned. I thought I was maybe caught on
tape somewhere. I was surprised.'' (Mollen Tr. 117). When
asked what message that sent to him that not a single
supervisor in the Police Department ever asked about that
incident, Dowd said ''[i]t was obvious that they didn't do
anything. I don't, it was obvious they couldn't catch me or
they couldn't do anything.'' (Mollen Tr. 118).

Yet there is no evidence—from Dowd himself or any of
the Government's sources—that other officers saw or knew
what Dowd claimed to have done. In fact, Eurell has told
the Government that he does not believe there even was a
raid, but that Dowd merely saw some street-crime officers
doing a car stop in the area. Likewise, neither Diaz nor
the Diaz Worker had any knowledge of the raid that Dowd
described.

Second, Dowd's testimony unfairly suggested that
certain officers not only knew about his and Eurell's
criminal conduct but also participated in it. For example,
in describing his and Eurell's theft of drugs from a murder
scene, Dowd said, ''I had my partner watch the door while I
searched this room. Well, he got a little excited. He came
in the room with me, and we had another cop outside
watching the door.'' (Mollen Tr. 74).

To the contrary, Eurell has told the Government that
no other officer participated with them in the theft and
that no other officer ''watched the door'' for them.
Eurell said that he and Dowd were in a room looking for
drugs and that Eurell closed the door. One officer opened
the door and then withdrew after seeing Eurell and Dowd,
and Eurell said that that officer might have suspected
wrongdoing but did not discuss it—or participate in
it—with them. Moreover, in Dowd's proffers with this

---

[15]Dowd was instructed by Mollen Commission counsel at
the outset of his testimony that, ''in responding to my
questions, please do not speculate. Base your answers on
your first-hand knowledge and experiences.'' (Mollen Tr.
28).

Office, he never mentioned another officer assisting
Eurell and him in this theft.

Another example where Dowd exaggerated other
officers' involvement in his own crimes is his testimony
that at least ten to fifteen other officers in the 75th
Precinct provided him and Eurell with ''assistance'' in
their criminal activities, although Dowd's public
testimony on this subject is less than clear. (Mollen Tr.
123-27, 135-37, 142-45). Dowd first testified that ten to
fifteen officers in the 75th Precinct were direct
participants in his criminal activity.

> There were, many of the officers in the precinct knew
> we were doing things, and they would be willing to
> help us at any cost . . . about another ten or fifteen
> different cops . . . they knew that we needed
> information. If they had any information, they would
> give it to us. If they knew of a location that was
> doing some business, they would tell us.

(Mollen Tr. 124-25).

However, he later equivocated in the
characterization of these officers' assistance. In
response to the question, ''they weren't helping you with
your major drug organizations, is that what you're
saying,'' Dowd answered, ''No, no.'' (Mollen. Tr. 125).
Dowd added:

> There's a distinction of being actually involved
> with me and being supportive of me. Involved was just
> me and my partner in that one specific thing. But
> there was other officers that were basically
> frothing at the mouth to be involved, so they'd do
> anything to assist us.

(Mollen Tr. 136).[16]

There is no evidence in the Government's
investigation that ten to fifteen officers in the 75th
Precinct assisted Dowd and Eurell in their criminal
activities. Eurell has stated that the only active law
enforcement officer who participated with Dowd and Eurell

---

[16]Dowd was asked, ''They would assist you, they
wanted to be a part of your activities?,'' and he replied,
''Yes.'' He was then asked, ''And how many officers
indicated to you that they were interested in joining with
you and your activities?,'' and he answered ''Ten to
fifteen at least.'' Dowd was asked, ''But you didn't let
all of them in, did you, Mr. Dowd?'' and Dowd replied,
''No. I told them to go wear out some shoes first and we'll
talk.'' (Tr. 136).

in their work for the Diaz Organization was Dowd Brother #2. According to Eurell, there were approximately ten to fifteen young officers who socialized with Dowd and Eurell but they did so because they knew Dowd and Eurell had money, liked to socialize and would pay for drinks at the bar.[17]

Significantly, when Dowd and Eurell needed other persons to assist them in their crimes, such as raids on drug locations, they turned to two former officers who had worked with Dowd in the 75th Precinct, and one present officer, Dowd Brother #2.[18] They did not turn to other officers then assigned to the 75th Precinct.[19]

Third, Dowd mischaracterized his interaction with the NYPD in the proffers conducted with this Office following his arrest, in yet another attempt to publicly shift the blame away from himself and toward the NYPD. Dowd was asked, ''Was there no time that you were asked about any of your activities by anyone in the New York City Police Department,'' and Dowd replied, ''Not specifically, no.'' (Mollen Tr. 209). Dowd was asked again if the NYPD questioned him at any point prior to the Mollen Commission speaking to him, and Dowd said that ''at the request of my attorney, not at the request of Internal Affairs or at the request of the Southern District of New York, we sat down at a proffer session.'' (Mollen Tr. 210). Dowd was then asked if any arrests were made by the NYPD as

---

[17]Dowd also testified that other officers ''tried to cling to me. They chaperoned themselves around me. They wanted to know what I was doing. They wanted to be part of it.'' When asked, ''Who wanted to be part of it exactly?,'' Dowd replied: ''Whoever knew me.'' (Mollen Tr. 143). Dowd makes this claim, despite his earlier statement that ''many of the police officers there wouldn't work with me.'' (Mollen Tr. 95).

[18]The following are incidents in which persons other than Dowd and Eurell participated: (1) 4/16/87 theft of money by Dowd and two former officers; (2) 1987 raid of the drug location of a competitor of the Diaz Organization, conducted by Dowd, Eurell, the same two former officers, Dowd Brother #2 and their civilian friend; and (3) planned robbery of drug dealer's apartment by Dowd, Eurell, and the same two former officers.

[19]Moreover, Dowd did not tell this Office in the proffer sessions about any officers, let alone ten to fifteen, who were involved with him and Eurell. Rather, he stated only that one officer had been paid to provide assistance to the Company in July 1988, after Dowd had already left the 75th Precinct.

a result of what Dowd said during the sessions, and Dowd replied: ''It's fair to say that they were not quite interested in what I had to say, so they just took the information, walked away with it, and they proceeded to put it under the rug.'' (Mollen Tr. 211).

As Dowd knows, following Dowd's release on bail from Suffolk County, the NYPD was investigating Dowd's ongoing criminal activity, namely, the robbery and abduction scheme. Yet Dowd did not testify about any crimes following his Suffolk County arrest; instead he criticized the NYPD for putting things under the rug, when in fact the NYPD was exposing—and making Dowd accountable for—still other crimes, as well as saving the life of the intended victim of the robbery and abduction plan.

In addition, following Dowd's Suffolk County arrest, the NYPD did request to interview Dowd administratively, during which interview Dowd would have had to answer self-incriminating questions with ''use-immunity'' protection. Dowd refused, and was therefore fired from the NYPD in July 1992.

Moreover, the NYPD attended several proffer sessions with Dowd at this Office, listened to everything Dowd had to say, heard obvious contradictions with the information provided independently by other government sources and nonetheless conducted initial investigations into Dowd's information, looking for corroboration, and found little.

Fourth, Dowd offered testimony attempting—unfairly—to mitigate the seriousness of his crimes. A prime example of such testimony is when Dowd attempted to minimize the potential consequences of his tipping off the Diaz Organization to an impending law enforcement raid. As noted earlier, (see p. 26 supra), Dowd's claim to have tipped off the Diaz Organization may itself have been an exaggeration inasmuch as none of the Government's witnesses have any knowledge of the raid that Dowd described.

At the hearings, Dowd testified as follows:

> I hate to minimize things but I did make sure that they (the Diaz Organization) had no guns or anything like that in the location. I told them straight up, no guns in your location because I didn't want agents or anybody getting hurt because I still was a police officer. Even though it doesn't seem that way at times, I still had my heart there half the way.

(Mollen Tr. 116). There is no support based on the Government's investigation for the claim that Dowd instructed the Diaz Organization not to have guns in its locations.

No Government witness—not Eurell, Adam Diaz or the Diaz Worker—corroborates Dowd's claim that he told the Diaz Organization to remove its guns from its locations at any time. In fact, Diaz and the Diaz Organization Worker have stated that their drug trafficking locations were, by necessity, routinely armed, which is corroborated by arrest reports showing numerous firearms vouchered from Diaz Organization locations during the time of Dowd's conspiracy with them, and that Dowd knew that and personally gave them a gun on one occasion.

In addition, Dowd's self-serving testimony about guns conflicts with his earlier testimony before the Commission when he was asked what he did with the guns he stole on raids. Dowd said: ''I wasn't much for guns, but I'd give them out. Give them to people, sell them to people.'' When asked what kind of people he gave them to, he answered, ''I'd give them to store owners, one time to a drug dealer.'' (Mollen Tr. 54).

5. The Pre-Sentence Investigation Report

The Pre-Sentence Investigation Report (''PSR'') and Dowd's objections thereto further demonstrate Dowd's attempt to shift responsibility away from himself, and also reveal—by describing certain of Dowd's conduct before joining the Police Department—how Dowd's casting of blame to the Police Department for his own misdeeds is unavailing.

The PSR reveals that Dowd's criminal and other problems existed prior to his joining the NYPD. Dowd's wife said that Dowd has had a drinking problem since he was 15 years old. She said ''Michael is usually drinking twenty-three hours a day, and throwing up the other hour.'' She also said he was often involved in extramarital affairs and that he started using cocaine in December 1987. She said that for years:

> Dowd was on the run, drinking constantly, using cocaine, running around with his brother [ ], and treating her badly. . . . She described Dowd as a 'psycho' who has an infantile personality, and who never received the correct love and attention from his family. She feels that her husband's behavior is explained by his upbringing in that his parents did not give him love or friendship and always expected more from him.

(PSR at 19–20.) The PSR further states that Dowd:

has been drinking alcohol since he was 12 years old. He stated that at the age of 12, his friends had to carry him home because he was so drunk. He continued to drink on the weekends and 'whenever he wanted to.' He drank alcohol before he left for high school. He stated that he knew he had an alcohol problem when he was 23 years old. He stated that he gets into trouble when he drinks alcohol.

(PSR at 23.)

THE PSR also reports that Dowd:

tried marijuana for the first time in the 8th Grade. He smoke marijuana approximately three times a week for two years before he stopped using it. Approximately one year later, the defendant began to smoke marijuana again while in high school. He stated that he stopped smoking marijuana the day before he became a police officer in January 1982.

(PSR at 23.) Dowd also told the Probation Office that he ''took speed (black beauties) once a week while in high school and college. He stated he did it for fun with his friends.'' (PSR at 23.)

Two notable assessments are found in the PSR, one from the Probation Officer in 1993 and one from a Police Department psychologist in 1988. The Probation Officer concluded that ''[Dowd] appears to have an infantile and manipulative attitude and seems to blame his actions on others and on other events in his life.'' (PSR at 22.) The PSR also quotes the results of an interview with Dowd by an NYPD Senior Psychologist on March 10, 1988: ''He presented as glib and bitter, and he blamed others for his predicament. Clinical impressions were that he was a manipulative person whose self-report lacked credibility.'' (PSR at 21 (emphasis added).)

Dowd has submitted numerous objections to the PSR, which seek to minimize his own culpability and, in particular, distance himself from any involvement with firearms. Dowd remains, to this day, untruthful and evasive about his criminal conduct.

The most notable of his objections[20]—and the Government's responses—are described below:

a. Dowd objects to ¶ 35, which describes Dowd and Eurell responding to a robbery at one of the Diaz Organization's locations on February 6, 1988, and subsequently looking for—and finding—the robber in

---

[20]Dowd's other objections have been addressed in a separate letter to the Probation Department.

the days that followed. Dowd claims that ''[t]he Diaz Organization was closed 1/06/88 (not 2/06/88).''

Dowd is absolutely incorrect in his assertion. The Government's proof shows that the Diaz Organization was in full operation in January 1988, that on February 6, 1988, they were robbed, that several days later Dowd gave a summons to ''Franklin,'' the person that robbed them, that they continued in operation until March 23, 1988, when several key employees, including the Diaz Worker, were arrested at the organization's main location while they were working. The Government's proof also shows that subsequent to the March arrests, Adam Diaz reopened his business at other locations and that Dowd continued to be involved sporadically.

Notably, at his plea before this Court, Dowd also denied that the Diaz organization was in business when he issued the summons to Franklin in February 1988 and stated therefore that in issuing the summons, he ''could not have influenced them in any way at that point.'' (Plea Tr. 30). That claim is false.

b. Dowd objects to ¶ 36, which describes how the Diaz Organization was hurt by the February 6, 1988, robbery and the March 1988 arrests of the Diaz Organization Worker. Dowd states that the ''[p]ayments [from the Diaz Organization] stopped in late October or November.''

The Diaz Organization Worker, who did not begin working for the organization until approximately December 1987, stated that he made several payments to Dowd in 1988. Adam Diaz told the Government that he continued to make payments—on an inconsistent basis—even after the arrests in March 1988. In fact, Diaz remembers paying Dowd four days before Diaz's June 1989 arrest.

If Dowd's objection were true, it would mean that Dowd continued to do work for the Diaz Organization for several months without being paid. Work performed after late October or November 1987 included finding two new locations for the Diaz Organization, giving the gun to the Diaz Organization, receiving cocaine from the organization, responding to the robbery at the organization's location, and harassing the person believed to have committed the robbery. In addition, when Dowd traveled to the Dominican Republic in early 1989, he attempted to see Adam Diaz.

c. Dowd states that ¶ 47, which describes an offer from

Dowd's cocaine supplier Ray to earn $10,000 by
transporting cocaine from Texas to New York, is
''[s]ubstantially true, except Eurell and Mascia
came to Dowd with the proposition, and Dowd declined
it.''

That statement is preposterous. First, Mascia and
Eurell barely knew each other, having met only twice,
both times through Dowd. Neither had a relationship
with Ray; they knew him only through Dowd. Second,
according to both Mascia and Eurell, Dowd approached
them, separately, with the proposition from Ray that
they could earn $10,000 for driving a truckload of
cocaine from Texas to New York, and each declined the
offer.

Dowd states that ¶¶ 49 & 50, which describe the
kidnapping scheme, are ''substantially true except
that . . . Kenneth Eurell encouraged and importuned
Michael Dowd in the development and furtherance of
these acts.''

Eurell told the Government that it was Dowd's idea,
and that Dowd solicited Eurell's participation. The
tape recordings of telephone calls and in-person
conversations make clear that Dowd was not
encouraged or importuned but that he desperately
wanted to participate in that scheme and he wanted
Eurell's assistance.

Dowd states in an ''Addendum'' that ''during a
substantial portion of the time that Michael Dowd's
criminal activity was taking place, Michael Dowd was
suffering from alcohol and drug addiction. He
attempted to deal with these problems, with limited
resources available to 'police officers.' As a
police officer there are no programs, or treatments
available for drug addictions, without him losing
his job.''

For several reasons, this claim is overstated.
First, Dowd's use of drugs (other than cocaine) began
at age 15, and his abuse of alcohol at age 12. Second,
Dowd's criminal activity pre-existed his use of
cocaine. Dowd began his corruption shortly after he
became a police officer in 1982, and he apparently
began using cocaine in late 1987. By that time, based
on his testimony before the Mollen Commission, he had
already committed hundreds of crimes. Third, as for
Dowd's cocaine use from late 1987 on, he was faced
with a simple choice. He could either admit his drug
use and receive help for it (thereby losing his job)
or he could deny his drug use and not receive
Department help for it (thereby keeping his job).
Dowd chose to keep his job, and now seeks to blame the

Police Department for his choice. That the Police Department chooses to make drug use a basis for automatic dismissal is not surprising. Nor is Dowd's decision to deny drug use and keep his job.

6. Dowd's Appearance on ''60 Minutes''

On October 17, 1993, Dowd appeared on the nationally televised program ''60 Minutes'' and again shifted the blame away from himself and toward the NYPD, misled the public about the extent of other officers' knowledge of particular criminal activity, and unfairly criticized the NYPD for their conduct following his arrest. (A copy of the transcript of that program is attached as Exhibit B.)

Much as he falsely blames Eurell for causing him to participate in the robbery and abduction scheme, Dowd blamed his superior officers and the Police Department generally for his career of crimes. Dowd stated: ''I'm not a bum. I wasn't a bum before I became a police officer. But becoming a police officer led me in these directions. If your peers happen to be doing these things, then you do them too.'' (60 Minutes Tr. 8). Dowd ignores the fact that from 1983 through 1992, the common thread in these crimes is Michael Dowd, in conjunction with his first regular partner, his second regular partner, and then his third regular partner. Dowd cannot fairly claim that his peers got him involved in these crimes.

Dowd also misled the public about the extent to which other officers knew of particular criminal activity. In describing the theft of drugs from a murder scene, Dowd said:

Dowd: Well, I had to walk past 15 cops to get it outside into the police car.

Wallace: How'd you do it?

Dowd: I just put the bag over my shoulder and I walked out the door with it.

Wallace: A bag of cocaine?

Dowd: Well, it didn't say cocaine on the bag.

Wallace: And you walked past a line of cops, past the sergeant?

Dowd: Well, they knew what I was doing. . . . . I know they knew because they were smiling. 'Oh, there goes Mike.'

(60 Minutes Tr. 3).[21]
   To the contrary, Eurell has told the Government that,
at that particular crime scene, Dowd had the drugs
secreted in a brown paper bag, that Dowd, when going down
the staircase to leave the building, hid the bag by the
staircase until the sergeant passed by him, and that Dowd
then retrieved the bag and left the building.
   Finally, Dowd stressed once again that the Police
Department did not come to talk to him after the Suffolk
County arrest.

   Wallace: But after you were arrested by Suffolk County,
            did the New York police get involved again and
            question you?

   Dowd: They—they never—they never once came to
            question me.

   Wallace: Why?

   Dowd: They were embarrassed.

   Wallace: Dowd says New York City police officials still
            wanted to look the other way, still wanted to
            avoid a scandal but now it was too late.

(60 Minutes Tr. 8). Far from closing their eyes to Dowd's
wrongdoing, the NYPD was, at that time, attempting to
prevent (and eventually expose) still further crimes by
Dowd, namely, the robbery and abduction scheme. After
Dowd's next arrest and his federal detention, the NYPD did
question him, as discussed above.
7. Letters to Adam Diaz
   Still further evidence of Dowd's failure to divorce
himself from his career of crime and corruption is found in
two letters Dowd wrote in or about November 1993 to Adam
Diaz, which Diaz turned over to this Office. (Copies of
those letters are attached as Exhibit C.) In stark
contrast to the picture painted by Dowd in his public
testimony and television appearance as a vulnerable
individual victimized by a corrupt and inept Police
Department, these letters show Dowd, even at this late
date, reaching out to the leader of a major drug
organization seeking financial assistance.

---

   [21]Mike Wallace stated: ''Dowd says that most of the
cops in his precinct knew that he was a drug user and a drug
dealer,'' and Dowd added: ''Every cop knew what I was
doing, and what the whole crew of cops were doing in my
precinct and in every precinct in Brooklyn.'' (60 Minutes
Tr. 5).

In the letter, Dowd actually requests that Diaz—who has been incarcerated since his arrest and whose source of money was from the trafficking of narcotics—provide financial help to Dowd's wife and children, and Dowd gives Diaz the address of one of Dowd's brothers. Dowd tells Diaz that he does not hold any ''ill will toward any of you (apparently referring to those members of the Diaz Organization who cooperated against him), just Kenny (referring to Eurell).''

Dowd also tells Diaz that Dowd's sentencing is upcoming and that Dowd has ''an ace or two up my sleeve hopefully it all works out at my sentence.'' Dowd concludes the letter by writing: ''one day we'll have a beer together in Dominica like we were supposed to.'' Even on the eve of sentencing, Dowd is attempting to benefit from his criminal associations and seeks for his family still further illicit proceeds from narcotics trafficking.

8. The Inappropriateness of a Downward Departure

Based on all the facts and circumstances discussed herein, the Government respectfully submits that a downward departure for Michael Dowd would be inappropriate. Dowd should be sentenced at the high end—not below—the applicable Sentencing Guidelines range for the reasons stated in this Memorandum, including the heinous and repetitive nature of Dowd's criminal activity, his lack of truthfulness and candor to this Office at proffer sessions, to this Court at his plea and to the Probation Department, his incorrect and misleading public statements and shifting of responsibility, and his brazen and unrepentant letters to co-conspirator Adam Diaz.

To the extent Dowd claims that he should receive credit for his ''assistance'' to the Government absent a § 5K1.1 letter, that claim should be rejected summarily. The United States Supreme Court has held that ''a claim that a defendant merely provided substantial assistance will not entitle a defendant to a remedy or even to discovery or an evidentiary hearing.'' Wade v. United States, 112 S. Ct. 1840, 1844 (1992). A defendant would be entitled to a remedy only if the Government's refusal to file a substantial-assistance motion ''was based on an unconstitutional motive. . . . say, because of the defendant's race or religion.'' Id. (emphasis added). ''[G]eneralized allegations of improper motive'' are insufficient. Id.; see also United States v. Khan, 920 F.2d 1100, 1104 (2d Cir. 1990) (''Absent a specific agreement, the decision by a prosecutor to refuse to

recommend a downward departure is generally not subject to
judicial review.'').[22]

Nor is a downward departure based on § 5K2.0
available for Dowd based on his attempted cooperation with
this Office where the Government has decided not to sign a
cooperation agreement and not to submit a letter pursuant
to § 5K1.1[23] The Second Circuit has held that the ''very
existence of § 5K1.1 demonstrates that the sentencing
commission clearly considered the question of whether
assistance to the government should be taken into
account.'' Khan, 920 F.2d at 1107. Accordingly, ''§ 5K2.0
has no application at sentencing where the basis for
defendant's motion has been considered and rejected by the
government as a basis for a § 5K1.1 downward departure
motion.'' Id.; see also United States v. Gonzalez, 970
F.2d 1095, 1102–03 (2d. Cir. 1992) (reversing District
Court's decision to depart downward based on cooperation
with the government, which evidenced defendant's
contrition, in absence of Government motion); United
States v. Agu, 949 F.2d 63, 66–67 (2d. Cir. 1991) (§ 5K2.0
downward departure not authorized where defendant
conveyed helpful information to the prosecution that did
not result in § 5K1.1 motion by the government;
defendant's ''sole claim is that he supplied names and
other information that could assist the Government in the

---

[22]Even where the prosecution has signed a cooperation
agreement with a defendant (which was not done here),
''the prosecutor's discretion is generally the sole
determinant of whether the defendant's conduct warrants
making the motion.'' Khan, 920 F.2d at 1105. The
prosecution's decision that it is dissatisfied with the
defendant's performance under the cooperation agreement
is controlling, as long as the prosecution is ''honestly
dissatisfied.'' Id.
[23]Section 5K2.0 of the Sentencing Guidelines provides
that ''the court may depart from the guidelines, even
though the reason for departure is taken into
consideration in the guidelines (e.g., as a specific
offense characteristic or other adjustment), if the court
determines that, in light of unusual circumstances, the
guideline level attached to that factor is inadequate.''
See also 18 U.S.C. § 3553 (b) (Sentencing court can depart
from the applicable Sentencing Guidelines range if it
''finds that there exists an aggravating or mitigating
circumstance of a kind, or to a degree not adequately taken
into consideration by the Sentencing Commission in
formulating the guidelines that should result in a
sentence different from that described.'').

prosecution of other persons.''), <u>cert. denied,</u> 112 S. Ct. 2279 (1992).

Likewise, a downward departure pursuant to section 5K2.0 based on Dowd's cooperation with the Mollen Commission should not be granted. The Second Circuit has suggested in certain circumstances a downward departure pursuant to section 5K2.0 might be warranted for assistance provided to someone or some institution other than the prosecution. <u>See, e.g., United States</u> v. <u>Zackson,</u> No. 92-1525, slip op. at 6383, 6407 n.2 (2d Cir. Oct. 4, 1993) (''trial judge may have discretion'' where ''claimed assistance, helping to save [someone's] life, might place him within this narrow exception''); <u>United States</u> v. <u>Garcia,</u> 926 F.2d 125, 128 (2d Cir. 1991) (district court has ''sensible flexibility'' to depart where defendant facilitated the proper administration of justice in the District Courts); <u>United States</u> v. <u>Khan,</u> 920 F.2d 1100, 1107 (2d Cir. 1990) (helping to save the life of a DEA informant who had been kidnapped by Pakistani traffickers could be grounds for § 5K2.0 departure where information could not assist ''government in its prosecution of others'').

Those cases are not helpful to Dowd, however, because they involve defendants who, for the most part, signed cooperation agreements and did all they could for the prosecution, but whose assistance—through no fault of their own—resulted in a benefit other than the investigation or prosecution of another person. <u>See, e.g., Zackson,</u> slip op. at 6389 (unable to raise sufficient money to gain release of kidnapped informant, defendant contacted FBI, which secured informant's release); <u>Garcia,</u> 926 F.2d at 126, 128 (where defendant entered into cooperation agreement with the Government, admitted his criminal conduct, disclosed other facts and agreed to testify against co-defendants at trial, who subsequently pled guilty, defendant ''not only helped the government develop the case, his cooperation after the indictment resulted in the disposition of the charges against the remaining two defendants.''); <u>Khan,</u> 920 F.2d at 1106-07 (if true, the fact that the defendant, who had cooperation agreement with the Government, saved the life of confidential informant kidnapped by Pakistani heroin traffickers ''reflects well on defendant's character and could have provided a mitigating factor at his sentencing.'').

In this case, Dowd was not fully honest or candid in his attempted cooperation with this Office, and he was not

offered a cooperation agreement. He should not then
receive a downward departure pursuant to section 5K2.0—or
even credit within the stipulated Guidelines range—for
having cooperated with another office by taking center
stage and relating, in part, the litany of crimes he
committed while a police officer and taking the occasion
to also attempt to continue to blame others and
institutional failures for his own criminal conduct. His
''assistance'' thus included some incorrect and
misleading public testimony.[24]

We do not take issue with the Mollen Commission's
conclusion that Dowd's cooperation was of use to them. As
Judge Mollen stated in his letter to this Court, however,
what may make Dowd ''valuable'' to the Mollen Commission
does not mean he should receive a reduced sentence. Judge
Mollen stated: ''Ironically, it is the seriousness and
extent of Mr. Dowd's criminal conduct, and his notoriety
as a corrupt cop, that made his testimony and cooperation
so valuable to the Commission and the public. He was able
to seize public attention in ways that other witnesses
could not.'' That Dowd ''seized public attention'' based
on the ''seriousness and extent'' of his criminal conduct
should not result in a lesser sentence for Dowd.

Dowd's cooperation with the Commission, especially
when placed in the context of his other conduct both prior
to and subsequent to his 1992 arrests, does not ''reflect
well on his character'' such that he should receive a
reduced sentence. See Khan, 920 F.2d at 1106–07.[25] Dowd

---

[24]We do not in any way fault the Mollen Commission
with respect to Dowd's testimony. Because of ongoing
investigations and prosecutions, all of the sources of
information necessary to corroborate Dowd's testimony
could not be provided prior to Dowd's testimony. These
sources included Dowd's co-racketeers Kenneth Eurell,
Thomas Mascia, Borrent Perez, a/k/a ''Baron,'' Adam Diaz,
the Diaz Worker and members of the Company, who are
cooperating with this Office, the NYPD and the DEA.

[25]Nor can Dowd's public testimony be credited for
many of the significant institutional reforms instituted
by the NYPD. Two days after Dowd's May 6, 1992, arrest, the
NYPD announced that the arrest would lead them to re-
evaluate the department's methods to root out corruption.
On June 15, 1992, then-Commissioner Lee Brown appointed
then-First Deputy Commissioner Raymond Kelly to conduct a
full examination of the NYPD's investigation of previous
allegations against Dowd. In November 1992, Police
Commissioner Kelly completed ''An Investigation Into The
Police Department's Conduct of the Dowd Case and An
Assessment of the Police Department's Internal

took advantage of the situation he found himself in to recite his crimes publicly, and, in doing so, attempt to shift responsibility for them, without the adverse consequences that accompany cooperation with the Government.

Because Dowd's proffered cooperation with this Office was rejected as not fully truthful or candid, Dowd did not provide ''substantial assistance'' in investigations or prosecutions of other persons. The three men who participated with Dowd in the robbery and abduction scheme (two of them lived in one of Dowd's houses) were not apprehended. Unlike defendants who enter into cooperation agreements with the Government, Dowd did not have to reveal all his prior bad acts, plead guilty to all his prior criminal activity,[26] or reveal all crimes committed by other persons. Dowd did not testify at a criminal trial and was not subject to cross examination.

Dowd used the opportunity created by the crimes he committed as a police officer to appear at the locally televised Mollen Commission hearings and on the nationally televised ''60 Minutes'' to attempt to create a better image of himself and to create a worse image of the NYPD and other police officers. His public criticism of the NYPD following his Suffolk County arrest—both at the Mollen Commission hearings and on ''60 Minutes''—is particularly audacious. It was the NYPD that fired Dowd in July 1992 following his refusal to be interviewed administratively, that investigated Dowd's ongoing robbery and abduction crime, which he was committing while released on bail from Suffolk County, that removed the intended victim from her residence hours before the planned robbery and abduction by Dowd and his co-conspirators, that arrested Dowd on federal charges, which led to his pre-trial detention, and that attended several

Investigation Capabilities,'' which included various ''improvements to the Police Department's system of corruption investigation.'' On May 24, 1993, Walter Mack was appointed to the newly-created position of Deputy Commissioner of the Internal Affairs Bureau. Dowd did not testify publicly before the Mollen Commission until September 27, 1993.

[26]By the time Dowd testified publicly, he had already entered into a plea agreement that bound this Office, the Suffolk County District Attorney's Office and the Brooklyn District Attorney's Office to a specific Sentencing Guidelines range, and did not permit the Government to move for an upward departure from that range.

proffer sessions with Dowd, after which Dowd's proffered
cooperation was rejected for his lack of truthfulness and
candor.

Conclusion

Based on all of the above facts and circumstances,
the Government respectfully submits that Dowd should be
sentenced at the high end of his Guidelines range. Dowd's
crimes are serious and many. Dowd involved each of his
three long-term partners in his criminal activities, and
two of his own brothers. Dowd planned to flee Suffolk
County after his arrest in 1992 and sought to fund that
flight through the robbery and kidnapping of a woman, who
was going to be turned over to Colombian drug dealers for,
in all likelihood, her execution. Dowd also provided
misleading and incorrect information to the United States
Attorney's Office during proffer sessions, to the Court
during his plea, to the Probation Department, and to the
public, during his testimony at the Mollen Commission
hearings and his nationally televised appearance on ''60
Minutes.'' Now, just prior to his sentence, Dowd has asked
his former benefactor—Adam Diaz—to once again provide him
with drug proceeds.

Accordingly, for the reasons described herein, the
Government respectfully requests that Michael Dowd be
sentenced at the high end of the applicable Sentencing
Guidelines range.

Respectfully submitted,

MARY JO WHITE
United States Attorney

By: DAVID B. FEIN/ROBERT E. RICE
Assistant United States
Attorney
Tel.: (212) 791-9009/9253

cc: Marvin Hirsch (counsel for Michael Dowd)
Deborah Fortgang (U.S. Probation Officer)

On the eve of Michael Dowd's sentencing I called Joe
Trimboli at home. The publicity hounds from the
Mollen Commission were going to be in court, no doubt
desperately hoping for a speaking part. But they didn't
invite Trimboli, so I did. We came into this together, we
would go out together. It ended on the fourth floor of the
Manhattan Federal Courthouse. Joe Trimboli deserved to
see the final act.

They were all there that morning, the heroes and the
pretenders. James Catterson, the Suffolk County DA,
was there with his narcotics chief, Robert Ewald, and his
former assistant, Tracy Hoffman. If it wasn't for their
work, Michael Dowd would still be a cop, and Milt Mollen's name wouldn't be in the headlines. They made a
drug case against Suffolk County residents who just happened to be New York City cops.

In a highly unusual move, Catterson even wrote a letter to the judge, Kimba Wood, saying he wouldn't back
down on the maximum fifteen-year sentence because of
Dowd's testimony before a political commission. As
District Attorney, Catterson had only addressed a judge
on one prior occasion, which involved a friend's murdered daughter. Michael Dowd had murdered the image
of police everywhere. It was time to speak out. Catterson

273

patiently took his seat next to the brilliant federal prosecutor, David Fein, and waited his turn.

Trimboli walked into the courtroom and took a seat in a row beside the Dowd family, which greeted him with angry stares. The television people saw Trimboli and began maneuvering for interviews. But Trimboli wasn't there for his own glory. He was there to see, not to be seen.

Michael Dowd was the last person to enter the room, looking pale and haggard. The federal marshals did allow him to wear a suit. It was gray. The infamous cop finally had the sense to abandon blue. He turned and faced his family and friends, smiling all the while. His lawyer gave him a playful slap on the face. The handcuffs were removed. After his appearances before the Mollen Commission and "60 Minutes," Dowd had glorified corruption and become a celebrity along the way. This was his final performance.

Kimba Wood was actually quite kind. She looked to the cop's family first and thanked them for their letters.

"No one feels the pain of sentencing like the family," the judge said. Then she heard from Dowd's preposterous lawyer. He wanted the minimum and wondered if Dowd shouldn't be awarded with freedom for helping the Mollen Commission. If you send Dowd to jail, who else will come forward to help? he asked. He forgot to mention that Dowd didn't help prosecutors. His cooperation was a joke, yet another outlandish distortion.

Trimboli began writing notes on a pad of paper. Occasionally he wrote. Occasionally he stared. He was calmer than anyone might have imagined. And angrier.

"A lot of people might feel that I didn't do enough, or criticize what I managed to do," Trimboli wrote. "All I can say is that I tried and that when people ran for cover, I stood alone. All the cowards who want to criticize me stood in the shadows and thought of nothing but protecting their own careers."

Michael Dowd's father rose in the front row. It was

terrible to see him humbled. He spoke and cried for his son. He tried to argue that Dowd's problem was drug addiction. He spoke of his son as "a bright star on the horizon of life," before joining the NYPD. He blamed a lost son on drug addiction, or as he said, "the devil's curse." The father's tears were real, but they came too late. As he walked away from the podium, Jack Dowd turned to his corrupt son and said, "I love you, Michael." It was poignant, even heart-rending. But a father's love could not overcome, or even diminish, a son's shame. Remembering his own dad, Trimboli felt like crying. The sight of Dowd rising to speak erased any feeling of compassion.

The disgraced officer would try one last desperate move. He would cry on command.

"Thank you, Your Honor," the defendant said. "I think the first thing I'd like to do is apologize to each and every police officer that's had to work under the guise I left them two years ago. It's a very difficult job, and I made it more difficult, and for that I apologize. I also want to apologize to my family. As you can see, they are destroyed.

"My two sons are not present in court today because I didn't think it would be proper to have them here for this. My wife, she is busy with her own life right now. I think I have probably lost her. We will see in a couple of years from now. I apologize to her for this.

"I want to thank Mr. Catterson and the Suffolk County Police Department. While it may appear that my life was ruined, it wasn't. They saved my life, and I thank them for that. Having a drug addiction and being a police officer is one of the most difficult things to deal with. As a police officer, your heart is ripped in half when you are addicted to drugs. There were times I wished I was dead because I couldn't stop what I was doing.

"One day I was driving to work and I was having a heart attack, I thought. Rather than go for help, I pulled off to the side of the road so I wouldn't crash and waited for the pains to subside. That night I did cocaine again.

"I lost my job, which I didn't take seriously enough, my family, my freedom. I don't know, Your Honor, what ten or fifteen more years in jail is going to do for me. I know today I am a different person than I was two years ago, and I am not angry at anybody, and I would just like to be able to live a normal life."

By then, Dowd was sobbing. Trimboli watched, and sighed.

"What a phony," he said. Then Joe started writing notes again. "Dowd spoke," he wrote. "Con artist to the end. Not sincere. Would laugh all the way down the street if the court let him go right now."

Judge Kimba Wood wasn't falling for crocodile tears. She had studied the government sentencing report and knew the truth. She would not let Michael Dowd escape again. When you talk about heroes, you talk about Kimba Wood. Once she was supposed to be Attorney General of the United States. Bill Clinton backed down in the face of a "nanny scandal." Wood stayed on the bench in New York. The city got lucky there.

They weren't as lucky in other areas. The same city had a police commissioner, Lee Brown. Michael Dowd never had to worry about Internal Affairs under Brown. When Brown quit and went to work in Washington for the man who would not hire Kimba Wood, she wound up, quite literally, cleaning up Brown's mess—Michael Dowd. The irony was delicious.

"Mike doesn't look like the same guy," Trimboli wrote. "In fact, I wonder if all this really happened. Yeah, I guess it really did happen and I was there. I remember eating Sunday dinner in a car parked outside Dowd's house. I neglected my own family to catch him, and here I am surrounded by Michael Dowd's family."

The prosecutors who made this happen sat directly in front of the judge. None of these people were thanked in public by Mollen, but Wood wanted them all in the room.

There was no seat, or speaking part, in the final Michael Dowd proceeding for anyone in the Mollen Commission. Here justice was being served; they didn't belong. When the chief counsel, Joe Armao, rose to speak in defense of Michael Dowd, the judge looked right through him. "Anything else?" she asked. She heard from Jim Catterson, who spoke eloquently against Dowd, and then Assistant U.S. Attorney David Fein revealed the information contained in the sentencing report. The charade was over. Then Judge Kimba Wood began to read her sentence. As soon as you heard the tone in her voice you knew it was over.

"Your crimes betray an immorality that is rarely encountered." She stated, "You did not just fall prey to temptation and steal what was in front of you, or take kickbacks, or sell confidential law enforcement information. You also continually searched for new ways to abuse your position and at times you recruited fellow officers to join in your crimes."

At the defense table, Dowd gasped and muttered, "Oh, my God. Oh, my God." He actually believed this whole testimony scheme would work. The Mollen people told him it would help. But the judge said no. She gave him fourteen years, which included one year off for Mollen, which was probably too much. She couldn't tell the truth, which was that Dowd's testimony was a worthless exercise in self-promotion.

The Watcher wrote his observation of Michael Dowd.

"He slumped when she gave him the sentence, the spine went out of him."

Joe did not feel happy, or even vindicated. He refused to gloat, but felt oddly complete. Dowd was placed in handcuffs and led from the room. Trimboli watched him disappear behind the door and made one last entry.

"I wonder, in the future, what cop will be sitting here in my place," Trimboli wrote. "There will be more corruption, just as there will be another Joe Trimboli. In twenty years, I wonder what will be going through that

cop's head as he waits to hear a judge administer justice
that the NYPD refused to.''

And then he quietly left the courthouse, slipping out a
side exit to avoid the television cameras. That night
Frank Serpico called him.

CPSIA information can be obtained at www.ICGtesting.com
Printed in the USA
LVOW10s1338160815

450310LV00001B/40/P